D0206285

Jules Verne Rediscovered

Jules Verne, age 50 (engraving c. 1880)

JULES VERNE REDISCOVERED

Didacticism and the Scientific Novel

ARTHUR B. EVANS

Contributions to the Study of World Literature, Number 27

Greenwood Press

NEW YORK • WESTPORT, CONNECTICUT • LONDON

PQ
2469
.Z5
E88
1988

Library of Congress Cataloging-in-Publication Data

Evans, Arthur B.
  Jules Verne rediscovered : didacticism and the scientific novel
Arthur B. Evans.
      p.   cm. — (Contributions to the study of world literature,
ISSN 0738-9345 ; no. 27)
    Bibliography: p.
    Includes index.
    ISBN 0-313-26076-1 (lib. bdg. : alk. paper)
    1. Verne, Jules, 1828–1905–Criticism and interpretation.
2. Didactic fiction, French–History and criticism.   3. Science
fiction, French–History and criticism.   4. Voyages, Imaginary.
5. Science in literature.   I. Title.   II. Series.
PQ2469.Z5E88   1988
843'.8–dc 19   87-36096

British Library Cataloguing in Publication Data is available.

Library of Congress Catalog Card Number: 87-36096
ISBN: 0-313-26076-1
ISSN: 0738-9345

First published in 1988

Greenwood Press, Inc.
88 Post Road West, Westport, Connecticut 06881

Printed in the United States of America

The paper used in this book complies with the
Permanent Paper Standard issued by the National
Information Standards Organization (Z39.48-1984).

10 9 8 7 6 5 4 3 2 1

For my daughter, Kelly

Contents

Illustrations ix

Acknowledgments xi

Prologue xiii

Introduction: Jules Verne? Which One? 1

PART ONE: The Educational Project of the *Voyages Extraordinaires* 7

Chapter 1: "The best of times . . . the worst of times" 9

Chapter 2: The Birth of the Scientific Novel 16

Chapter 3: The Hand of Hetzel 23

PART TWO: Ideological Subtexts in the *Voyages Extraordinaires* 33

Chapter 4: The Positivist Perspective 37

Chapter 5: The Romantic Vision 58

PART THREE: Didactic Discourse in the *Voyages Extraordinaires* 103

Chapter 6: Narrative Exposition and Pedagogy 109

Chapter 7: Ancillary Didactic Devices 138

Conclusion: Jules Verne and SF: The "Adaptivity Effect" 159

Bibliography 165

I. Primary Sources 165

II. Secondary Sources 173

III. Other Cited Works 187

Index 191

Illustrations

Jules Verne, age 50   Frontispiece

1   Verne's publisher and *père spirituel*, Pierre-Jules Hetzel   22

2   Professor Aronnax tours the engine room
of Captain Nemo's *Nautilus*   36

3   Professor Lidenbrock and Axel discover runes pointing
their way toward the center of the earth   46

4   The sunken continent of Atlantis   60

5   Professor Lidenbrock, Axel, and Hans aboard a
storm-tossed raft on a subterranean sea   72

6   Jules Verne, age 76   80

7   An illustration of fish species   120

8   Attack of the giant squid   130

9   The interior of Barbicane's "space bullet"   154

Acknowledgments

I wish to extend my sincere gratitude to the following persons for their suggestions, insights, and encouragement. Without their kind assistance, this book would not have been possible: Professors Léon S. Roudiez and Gita May, Columbia University, New York; Dr. Olivier Dumas, President of the Société Jules Verne, Paris; Professor Christian Robin, Centre de Recherches Verniennes, Nantes; Professor and dear friend Jean Dermy, Université de Nantes; Mme. Luce Courville, Bibliothèque Municipale de Nantes; Mme. Cécile Compère, Archives Jules Verne, Amiens; Professor Marc Angenot, McGill University, Montréal; and William Butcher, Vernian scholar.

I also wish to thank my loving wife, Jan, who by her unflagging moral support and infinite patience deserves the most credit of all for seeing this project through to its completion.

Prologue

Throughout this study, the collective title *Voyages Extraordinaires* has been retained when speaking of Jules Verne's series as a whole. However, the titles of Verne's individual novels have been translated. Similarly, the title abbreviations of Verne's works appearing in the parenthetical data are in English, but the page numbers cited are from the original French sources.

To facilitate quick referencing for both the primary and the secondary works cited, a roman numeral and a letter are included in each parenthetical citation. They are keyed to the bibliography in the following manner:

    I. PRIMARY SOURCES
        A. Original Verne Publications and Reprints
        B. Modern English Translations of Verne Works
        C. Correspondence
   II. SECONDARY SOURCES
        A. Bibliographies and References
        B. Biographies
        C. Critical Studies—Books
        D. Critical Studies—Articles
        E. Critical Studies—Dissertations and Theses
  III. OTHER CITED WORKS
        A. Books
        B. Articles

Due to the extremely poor quality of most previous English translations of Jules Verne's *Voyages Extraordinaires*, all quotations have been done by the author with the assistance of Professor Jean Dermy, Maître de Conférences at the Université de Nantes. Except as noted, all other French quotations have been translated by the author.

To illustrate the extent to which Verne's texts have been poorly translated— most date from the nineteenth century—the following paragraphs from the beginning of *Journey to the Center of the Earth* are offered. First, a reasonably accurate translation of the original French text:

On Sunday May 24, 1863, my uncle, Professor Lidenbrock, came rushing back home to his little house at 19 Königstrasse, one of the oldest streets in the old quarter of Hamburg.

Our maid Martha must have thought that she was behind schedule because the dinner was only just beginning to sizzle on the kitchen stove.

"Well," I said to myself, "if my uncle is hungry, he's going to rant and rave. He's the most impatient of men."

"M. Lidenbrock? Here already?" exclaimed Martha in astonishment, cracking open the kitchen door.

"Yes, Martha. But don't worry if the dinner isn't cooked, because it isn't even two o'clock yet. Saint Michael's clock has only just struck half past one."

"Then why is Professor Lidenbrock coming home?"

"He'll probably tell us himself."

"Here he is! I'm off, Monsieur Axel. You'll get him to see reason, won't you?"

And our good Martha went back into her culinary laboratory.

I was left alone. But as for getting this most irascible of professors to see reason, that was something quite beyond my rather timid nature. So I was getting ready to beat a prudent retreat to my little room upstairs, when the front door creaked on its hinges, heavy footsteps shook the wooden staircase, and the master of the house, passing through the dining room, rushed straight for his study.

On his way, he flung his nutcracker-head cane into a corner, his broad-brimmed hat onto the table, and these few thunderous words at his nephew:

"Axel, follow me!"

Following is the standard English translation of this same passage—the one most commonly used by American publishers (from *The Works of Jules Verne*, ed. Claire Boss, p. 219).

Looking back to all that has occurred to me since that eventful day, I am scarcely able to believe in the reality of my adventures. They were truly so wonderful that even now I am bewildered when I think of them.

My uncle was a German, having married my mother's sister, an English-woman. Being very much attached to his fatherless nephew, he invited me to study under him in his home in the fatherland. This home was in a large town, and my uncle was a professor of philosophy, chemistry, mineralogy, and many other ologies.

One day, after passing some hours in the laboratory—my uncle being absent at the time—I suddenly felt the necessity of renovating the tissues—i.e., I was hungry, and was about to rouse up our old French cook, when my uncle, Professor Von Hardwigg, suddenly opened the street door and came rushing upstairs.

Now Professor Hardwigg, my worthy uncle, is by no means a bad sort of man; he is, however, choleric and original. To bear with him means to obey; and scarcely had his heavy feet resounded within our joint domicile than he shouted for me to attend upon him.

"Harry! Harry! Harry!"

Beyond the initial shock of wondering if these two passages were indeed drawn from the same novel at all, it is interesting to analyze some of the alterations made and to speculate as to what might have inspired them. Unfortunately (understandably?) the translator is not named but was undoubtedly British; note the anglicizing of not only the names of the principal characters (as Lidenbrock—Hardwigg, Axel—Harry) but also the ancestry of Axel/Harry, who now comes from English parents and whose mother is still alive and presumably living in England. This fact seems further substantiated by the veiled chauvinism in such phrases as "My uncle was a German" and "the fatherland" and "our old French cook." Aside from these rather nationalistic additions (none of which figure in the original novel, which simply identifies Axel as Lidenbrock's nephew and an orphan), there are a number of other oddities in the text as well. The use of such archaic expressions as "to attend upon him" and the speaker's circumlocutory speech patterns are intended, one supposes, to add depth to the portrayal of Axel/Harry. And consider the important differences in the syntagmatic flow of these two passages. For example, Verne first posits two identifier statements—indicating time, place, and characters—and immediately follows them up with a brisk interchange of dialogue, which provides an *in medias res* introduction to the narrator, certain information about the maid and Lidenbrock, and a tinge of drama and mystery to this opening scene. The translator, on the other hand, connects together a long series of descriptive statements, leaning heavily on denotative background-building, paraphrases, and pseudostylistic humor for his effects.

Reading such translations, one can easily understand the recurring complaints of Anglo-American critics who have always contended that Verne's narratives have no "style" and that his prose is as wooden as his characters. And, sadly, it is precisely these English translations of the *Voyages Extraordinaires* that are the most widely read in America even today.

Jules Verne
Rediscovered

Introduction: Jules Verne? Which One?

Despite the recent efforts of a small number of university scholars, the current literary reputation of Jules Verne in America continues to be a patchwork of myth and error. Few people have read his actual texts, yet almost everyone has heard of him. And opinions rarely vary. He is known as the nineteenth-century inventor of the popular literary genre called "Science Fiction," or SF for short. He is believed to be a writer whose novels deal almost exclusively with forecasting the future: an exotic world of submarines, space travel to distant planets, and complex technological devices undreamed of during Verne's own time. As such, he is generally hailed as a scientific visionary, a prophet of things to come. Yet, ironically, his works themselves are most often dismissed as adolescent adventure stories: action-packed yarns about intrepid heroes exploring far-flung regions of Earth and Space. Verne's books are said to reflect their author's unreserved enthusiasm for technological progress and the many benefits such scientific advances would someday bestow on humanity. But they are also thought of as not really being literary in the true sense of the word—first, because he wrote primarily for children, and second because his novels are intellectually shallow, stylistically poor, and somewhat comparable to westerns or mysteries, in other words, good reading for escapism but not at all appropriate for formal academic study.

But do we *really* know Jules Verne? For example, each and every one of the preceding statements is false. They are part of a continuing misunderstanding of this author that, in America at least, has effectively precluded any serious study of his works. Through bad translations, Hollywood cinema, university snobbism, and the familiar pigeonholing effect of literary histories, Verne's reputation has not evolved here since the early years of the twentieth century when he was first dubbed the "father of SF."

Here are the facts. Jules Verne was *not* the inventor of SF as we know it today. There were many writers of this brand of narrative who preceded him (in France: Bodin, Souvestre, Defontenay et al.) but who never had the popular success of Verne and remain all but forgotten today.[1] A more likely candidate for this particular honor would be H. G. Wells, if one were to examine the thematic and structural character of the two writers' works. On the other hand, Jules Verne might quite justifiably be termed the "father of scien*tific* fiction." The distinction is paramount. Popularizing science *through* fiction, Verne's novels contain little of what the general reading public sees as standard SF fare. One finds, for example, no E.T.s or BEMs (bug-eyed monsters) in Verne's narratives. There are no *Star Wars*-like space cruisers or *2001*-like time warps. There is very little real extrapolation—in fact, over 90 percent of his fictional plots take place in the recent past. Verne's celebrated technological devices and "extraordinary" vehicles were almost always technically feasible at the time of his writing; Verne merely transposed the theoretical discussions of scientists contemporary to him or was inspired by experimental prototypes in existence at that time. And only about 20 of Verne's total literary output of 63 novels and 21 short stories (not to mention his many plays and nonfictional writings) could even be termed scientific in the technological sense. The bulk of his work resembles, rather, a gigantic travelogue—filled with visits to hundreds of foreign locales and offering lengthy and detailed descriptions of the geography, the indigenous flora and fauna, and the customs of the people living there. Hardly the stuff of true SF.[2]

Further, Jules Verne was not unreservedly pro-science. He evolved during his lifetime from being an early St.-Simonian optimist and firm believer in scientific and industrial growth, to later becoming deeply skeptical as to the benefits that science could bring to an imperfect world. Such proud claims as "When Science has spoken, it behooves one to remain silent!" (*Voyage* 126, IA) soon metamorphosed into more guarded statements such as "nothing should be rushed, not even Progress. Science must not get ahead of social customs" (*Robur* 246, IA). Almost half of Verne's literary output reflects this change of attitude.

Although his publisher required that his texts be geared to teaching scientific principles to French youth, Verne immediately conquered the adult reading public of his time as well. Critics celebrated him as one of the most popular authors of the latter half of the nineteenth century.[3] And they did so with good reason: sales of his novels, skillfully managed by his publisher Hetzel, rapidly grew to over a million volumes. Plays based on his works earned him rave reviews in the theatres of *la Belle Epoque*. Even today Verne continues to rank among the top five most translated authors of all time. Over 25 million copies have been printed in 40 different languages, three times greater than Shakespeare, nine times greater than the next-ranking French author, Saint-Exupéry.[4] In fact, there are many efforts today in France to adapt Verne's works to young readers,[5] a revealing commentary on an author who throughout his lifetime (and still in America) was constantly rebuffed by the literary establishment because he was "merely" a writer of children's stories. And this reputation seems all the more puzzling, given the many accolades he received during his own lifetime by such nineteenth-century literary figures as Alexandre Dumas fils, Stéphane Mallarmé, Théophile Gautier, and George Sand, as well as during the twentieth century by such well-known writers as Alfred Jarry, Guillaume Apollinaire, Raymond Roussel, Blaise Cendrars, Jean Cocteau, Michel Butor, and Roland Barthes.

Finally, consider the fact that in France since the 1960s there has been a major revival of Jules Verne, both in the publishing industry and in university and non-university literary circles. As a result, the status of Verne and his *Voyages Extraordinaires* has accordingly undergone a complete reappraisal—to such an extent, in fact, that one critic now places him "in a first-rank position in the history of French literature" (Angenot, "Jules Verne . . . Literary Criticism I" 37, IID) and another bemoans the lack of decent English-language criticism on him and the resulting dilemma of the "Two Jules Vernes" in literary studies—one French and one Anglo-American (Miller, *20,000* xv, IIC). The very dimensions of this recent scholarship are quite remarkable. For example, of the 1,336 critical studies devoted to Verne from 1866 to 1979, listed in the most recent Vernian bibliography,[6] a total of 922 of them or nearly *75 percent* were written after 1960. Paralleling this astonishing numerical increase, the critical orientations of these studies have multiplied as well: biographical (Marc Soriano, Jean Jules-Verne), structural (Roland Barthes, Michel Serres), psychoanalytical (Marcel Moré, Michel Carrouges), sociological and political (Pierre Macherey, Jean Chesneaux), archetypal and mythic (Michel Butor, Simone Vierne), and others. Further, in 1978, Verne's *Journey to the Center of the Earth* was placed on the French university Agrégation reading list; several professors in France have recently completed their Doctorat d'Etat theses on Verne;[7] and such respected French academic journals as *Critique, Poétique, La Revue des sciences humaines, Littérature,* and *La Revue des Lettres Modernes* have begun to publish scholarly articles on his works.

Do we really know Jules Verne? Evidently not. But how did this myth about him—so obviously brimming with error and misjudgment—come to be? And why has there been so little academic interest to date in Jules Verne in America? Exactly what have French readers and scholars discovered in the *Voyages Extraordinaires* that could possibly justify so much sustained study for so long among writers, among readers, and within universities? Undoubtedly, there must be more to this author than we have heretofore believed.

The purpose of this study is to address, either directly or tangentially, most of these questions. It is first and foremost a comprehensive analysis, making use of the tools of modern literary criticism, of one central aspect of Jules Verne's massive oeuvre that has never been investigated: the omnipresent theme of Verne's pedagogy, the nature of his "didactic discourse."

Viewed as *écriture*, Jules Verne's scientific novels represent a unique narrative (and social) configuration in the history of nineteenth-century literary prose. Verne's insertion of scientific pedagogy into the traditional thematic and stylistic format of the French novel created a radically new reading experience. And because of the popular success of his works, they offer certain insights into the literary conventions, the social preoccupations, and the semiological dynamics of the society of that time. Of course, the word *success* is a very relative term—amply demonstrated by the categorical rejection, until quite recently, of Verne's *Voyages Extraordinaires* from the ranks of officially recognized literature. But this circumstance in itself adds yet another very suggestive dimension to the study of these works—highlighting such concerns as their place within nineteenth- and early twentieth-century critical practices and the role played by Academe in the social consecration of certain authors and works.[8]

As Vernian scholar François Raymond has often recommended, the *Voyages Extraordinaires* need be viewed through a "plurality" of critical perspectives (*Le Développement des études sur Jules Verne* 30, IIC). Further, when proposing to analyze an aspect of Verne's writing such as his scientific didacticism—an element that is central to the very identity of his *roman scientifique* as a genre—such an approach seems essential. In no other way can the many literary and social ramifications of this particular brand of narrative discourse be understood. A multidirectional critical stance necessarily implies, in addition to a thematic and stylistic reading of the texts themselves, an investigation into the relationship of the author and his works to their specific historical milieu, that is, into the various ideological underpinnings upon which such texts rest and through which they communicate.

Accordingly, I have adopted in this book a threefold methodological orientation, with each of the next three parts roughly corresponding to a different critical approach offered by modern literary criticism. Part One is rather traditional in its scope, intending to give some basic historical and biographical background to such questions as the impact of the Industrial Revolution on nineteenth-century French society, courses of scientific instruction in the curricula of the public schools during this period, how Verne came to create his first *Roman de la Science*, and to what extent his publisher, Pierre-Jules Hetzel, had a hand in shaping the *Voyages Extraordinaires*. Part Two presents Verne's scientific pedagogy in a more ideological light, focusing on the complex relationship of Verne's texts to the intellectual fabric of his times, to the then-prevalent (and until Verne antithetical) ideologies of Positivism and Romanticism. Part Three analyzes the poetics of Verne's narrative practice and concentrates on the textual mechanics of his didactic discourse; in other words, his unique handling of rhetorical tropes and narrative voice, the function of the illustrations in his texts, his reliance on footnotes, prefaces, semantic repetition, and various kinds of "alienating-dealienating" semiotic structures, and so forth. And finally, as a conclusion, the question of Verne's place in the context of SF as a whole is reassessed in the light of the preceding investigations and the implicit pedagogical nature of these two brands of fiction.

But this study also has a second goal. It seeks to be a kind of academic stepping-stone, a bridge bringing together two separate worlds of Vernian scholarship: those badly outdated and rather shallow studies heretofore available

America, and the vast and infinitely richer resources of recent efforts in Europe. As one team of Vernian bibliographers has observed:

> English language criticism on Verne has not passed beyond a sterile and superficial level. There are few provocative overviews, few close analyses of individual works, and the pessimistic dimension to his works is virtually unknown. . . . There is a clear need . . . for a translated volume of selected French criticism to help spread the sociological, psychoanalytic, mythic, structuralist, and psychohistorical insights into Verne. (Gallagher et al. xiv–xviii, IIA)

Admittedly, I cannot hope to entirely satisfy that need with the study that follows. But I can nevertheless begin to chart the course toward a more accurate appreciation of what Jules Verne and his *Voyages Extraordinaires* truly represent, both in the context of contemporary literary studies and in the history of world literature. And, in America at least, the myth-worn reputation of Jules Verne can only benefit from such a revamping.

NOTES

1. V. Marc Angenot's study entitled "Science-Fiction in France before Verne," *Science-Fiction Studies* 5:1 (1978), 58–66.

2. V. My recently published article entitled "Science Fiction vs. Scientific Fiction in France: From Jules Verne to J. H. Rosny Aîné," *Science Fiction Studies* XV: 1–11.

3. V. Marius Topin, *Romanciers contemporains* (Paris: Charpentier, 1876), pp. 395–96.

4. V. Marc Soriano, *Jules Verne* (Paris: Julliard, 1978), pp. 306–7.

5. For example, Hachette's collection "Lectures pour collège," Bordas's collection "Classiques Junior," and others. See also Marc Soriano's article entitled "Adapter Jules Verne," *L'Arc* 29 (1966), 86–91.

6. Edward J. Gallagher et al., *Jules Verne: A Primary and Secondary Bibliography* (Boston: G. K. Hall, 1980), pp. 45–333.

7. Jean Delabroy, "Jules Verne et l'imaginaire" (Université de Paris III, Sorbonne, 1980) and Charles-Noël Martin, "Recherches sur la nature, les origines, et le traitement de la science dans l'oeuvre de Jules Verne" (Université de Paris VII, Jussieu, 1980). To date, there are a total of four English-language Ph.D. dissertations devoted in whole or in part to Jules Verne: in England, William Butcher, "A Study of Time in Jules Verne's *Voyages Extraordinaires*" (Queen Mary College, 1981) and Andrew Martin, "The Knowledge of Ignorance: Science, Nescience, and Omniscience in Some French Writers of the Eighteenth and Nineteenth Centuries" (University of Cambridge, 1982); in the United States, Stanford L. Luce, "Jules Verne: Moralist, Writer, Scientist" (Yale University, 1953) and Arthur B. Evans, "Jules Verne and the Scientific Novel" (Columbia University, 1985).

8. V. Renée Balibar's *Les Français fictifs* (Paris: Hachette, 1974) as an example of one scholar's inquiry into this latter phenomenon.

Part One
The Educational Project of the
Voyages Extraordinaires

CHAPTER 1

"The best of times . . . the worst of times"

The eruption of what Mumford called "technics" (*Technics and Civilization* 3, IIIA) into the social structures of nineteenth-century France drastically altered the bases upon which this society had functioned for hundreds of years. This traditionally agrarian culture, at a pace equal to the ever-growing presence of machines in its newly constructed factories and mills, was suddenly thrust into the industrial age. Some of the immediate effects of this phenomenon were undeniably positive. Material goods became abundant and reasonable in cost, raising the overall standard of living. New and rapid means of transport put people into closer contact than ever before. And advances in agricultural techniques and medical research finally eliminated the threat of famine and plague. As a result, the utopian dreams of the eighteenth-century French *philosophes* seemed on the verge of materializing.

But this dream of prosperity soon became a living nightmare for large sectors of the population as the unforeseen costs of (what was later to be called) this Industrial Revolution became evident. Increasing urbanization began to displace normal demographic patterns, spawning industrial slums, broken families, and child labor abuse. Automated mechanical production supplanted the individual craftsman and artist, blurring the distinctions between an object's value and its cost, between the artificial and the real.[1] A growing proliferation of newsprint and cheap reading material redefined the social function of the printed word itself, reducing it to a vehicle for simple information dissemination or for escapism.[2] Human activities became regulated, accelerated, and quantified as workers conformed their lives to factory shifts, to production quotas, and to the monotonous repetition of the machines they tended. Personal identity and self-concept dissolved into the anonymous collectivity of the "labor force." Even the notion of time metamorphosed into a linear and wholly abstract continuum: itself an objectively measured commodity of exchange. And among the other experiential prices paid for such industrial growth were social ennui, ever-widening class schisms, and, above all, a fundamental sense of alienation.

The recurring phenomenon of alienation (if not its precise definition) is probably as old as modern Western civilization. From Rousseau to Hegel and Marx, from Freud to the existentialists, the same notion (if not always the same word) has been used to describe the uprootedness, the lack of unity, and the loss of meaning inherent in the relationship of human beings to their society. Whether formulated epistemologically as estrangement and objectification, historically as social reification, poetically as *le mal du siècle*, or in psychoanalytic terms as the necessary sublimation of the instincts, the phenomenon of alienation seems a constantly recurring corollary to the human condition. Some have viewed aliena-tion in a more positive light, as a necessary step toward the discovery of the true self or toward a more exteriorized awareness (Hegel, Freud). Some have used its principle to create unique distancing effects in drama (Brecht). But most under-stand the term in its more sociological sense, indicating the loss of a meaningful rapport with one's environment: a kind of *dépaysement* or "future shock" pro-voked by rapid social change—usually characterized by the symptoms of disori-entation, a growing sense of insecurity, and feelings of dehumanization.

During the nineteenth century, Karl Marx described in *Das Kapital* the pro-foundly alienating effects of capitalism and the social (as well as psychological) impact of commodity fetishism. But an even deeper source for the alienation of this period can be seen in the substructure upon which such an economic system was based and depended, that is to say, the advent of modern *science* and its many technological applications. Alienation to social change brought on by science was not new. In Western culture, the progressive rationalization of life, the relentless elimination of magic, myth, and metaphysics from the explanation of Nature, and the ongoing quantification of all human experience date well back to the early Renaissance. But during the early nineteenth century, the social impact of scientific discovery began to intensify at an exponential rate, affecting every sector of society and influencing every sphere of its activities. Traditional anthropomorphic visions of the universe were shattered. Mechanical and chemical principles of life replaced the organic. Parameters of mass and energy became the standards by which reality was defined and given value. And Pascal's vertigo at the infinite emptiness of space became an almost daily experi-ence—a product of the apparent absence of permanency in life and the triumph of "progress."

Response to this growing social alienation to science was typically expressed throughout this period via two opposing (and successive) ideological modes: the outright rejection (or occultation) of the basic principles of scientific thought by *Romanticism*, and the corresponding glorification and popularization of them by *Positivism*.

In its exaltation of emotion and instinct, its gothic medievalism, its Rousseau-ist view of Nature, its religiosity, and its consistent valorization of the organic over the inorganic and of the qualitative over the quantitative, Romanticism might reasonably be viewed as a kind of cultural counterattack against the pervasive rationalism of Cartesian science and its capitalistic applications. One critic has gone so far as to describe this movement wholly in terms of such reactionism:

> Romanticism was only new unintentionally: it may indeed be thought of as the way a whole generation attempted to shelter itself, as an organism wards off shock, against that stupendous, total, and unprecedented transformation of the world. . . . All the feudal postures and political daydreams, all the atmosphere of religious and medieval objects, the return as for renewal to older . . . primitive societies are therefore to be understood first and foremost as defense mechanisms. (Jameson, *Marxism and Form* 94, IIIA)

Such a view is suggestive of the extent to which Romantic writers consciously "cult-ivated" various forms of escapism—both physical and emotional—to cope with what they saw as the alienation of modern life: by evoking the pristine exoticism of foreign locales, by praising the unexplored freedom of the New World, by nostalgically eulogizing the virtues of preindustrial cultures, and by valorizing the affectivity of Nature. For the Romantics, Nature was not to be objectively analyzed; it was to be subjectively penetrated. The individual was seen as neither its product nor its rival but its privileged communicant and supreme celebrant. And the entire world view and moral stance of Romanticism was an outgrowth of these basic premises. Instead of physics, the Romantic saw biology at the heart of science; instead of atomism, the Romantic saw evolution and metamorphosis; instead of observed facts to be learned and applied, the Romantic saw intrinsic moral lessons to be assimilated intuitively as well as a host of profound metaphors for the human condition.[3]

Very different was the attitude of the Positivists. For them, Nature was an objective phenomenon, quantifiable and subject to mathematical laws. All truth was seen as "positive" (a term first used by Bacon) in that it was totally nonanthropomorphic and could be apprehended only by the patient accumulation of empirical facts. It was only through Man's progress toward this end that he could discover true meaning in the universe, and it was only through the use of experimental science that he could make such progress. Bacon's nineteenth-century French descendants—Henri de Saint-Simon, Auguste Comte, Ernest Renan, and Hippolyte Taine—raised this philosophy to the status of a religion, naming science itself as Man's greatest hope for the future and his only real means for moral transcendence.

Witness, in this regard, Saint-Simon's call for a multinational state, to be directed by scientists, artists, and industrialists, and to be founded on a new "religion" of scientific knowledge and work:

> this renewed religion is called on to bring everlasting peace to all the peoples of the world . . . it is called on to bring together the scientists, the artists, and the industrialists and to make them the general directors

of the human species . . . it is called on to make knowledge of the arts, the sciences, and industry the most sacred of endeavors . . . and, finally, it is called on to condemn as anathema all theology and to treat as sacrilege any doctrine whose goal is to teach Man that eternal life can be gained by any means other than hard work. . . . ("Le Nouveau Christianisme," *Oeuvres complètes* 163–64, IIIA)

The Positivists were tireless proselytizers of science and devoted themselves to educating the French populace as to its mechanics, its history, its discoveries, and its moral implications. Comte's *Cours de Philosophie Positive*, the many texts of scientific "vulgarization" by popular writers like Louis Figuier, and the efforts of individuals like Jules Simon, Victor Duruy, and Jean Macé to include more scientific subject matter in the Second Empire's public schools are but a few examples of the Positivists' awareness of the need for science to be understood if it was not to be feared.

Since it was, in particular, this nationwide lack of natural science instruction in the French schools that was largely responsible for the original publication of Jules Verne's *Voyages Extraordinaires* and their subsequent popularity in "de-alienating" science for the country's youth, a brief examination of French educational practices during this period seems warranted. Upon investigating this sociohistorical context, two facts quickly become evident: first, the study of natural sciences in the predominantly Catholic-controlled primary schools of nineteenth-century France was most often deemed to be counterproductive and even at times dangerous; second, its presence in the secondary French curriculum was almost always a reflection of the political regime in power at that moment. More often than not, from the French Revolution to the Third Republic, the question of the scientific instruction of the young provoked bitter confrontation between two interest groups: the clergy and political conservatives on the one hand, and the Positivists, progressives, and anticlericals on the other. As described by Emile Durkheim:

> The representatives of traditionalism, in religious matters as well as in social and political, saw the old literary education as the best support structure to what they considered as sound doctrine while the study of science, on the other hand, was suspect. From then on, liberals of every kind and degree were inclined to support the opposite cause.
>
> It quite naturally resulted that, according to the political party that was in power and whether it was oriented towards the future or towards the past, education oscillated back and forth between these two extremes. (*L'Evolution pédagogique en France* 353–54, IIIA)

Given this social scenario, it is not surprising to discover that throughout the century the sciences found themselves in what Durkheim calls "a perpetual state of nomadism" (354, IIIA) in the schools. From their central position in the curriculum during the years immediately following the Revolution and throughout the Napoleonic era, to their total deletion during the Restoration, to their minimal inclusion during the July Monarchy and the Second Empire, to their cautious reinsertion during the Third Republic, science instruction was consistently viewed as a religious and ethical matter as much as an intellectual one. For the Romantic De Laprade, proponents of more science in the schools were "materialists, atheists, and subversives" (355, IIIA); for the archbishop Kopp, "any retreat from classical studies has the effect of shaking the very foundations of Christianity" (355, IIIA). In response, their opponents charged that a predominantly literary education was essentially aristocratic—a vestige of the past— and was purposefully maintained by the bourgeoisie as a mark of class exclusiveness and of social status (Anderson 132, IIIA).

In the wake of the aborted educational reforms of 1848 and in the early days of the authoritarian regime that would soon become the Second Empire, proponents of secular and science-oriented education were handed a major setback in the form of the Falloux law. Acting out of political expediency and the need for Catholic support, Armand de Falloux, minister of education for the newly elected Louis-Napoléon, drafted a piece of legislation stating that all matters relating to primary education would be controlled by the Catholic Church and that all restrictions would be lifted concerning the establishment of religious secondary schools and colleges. The law was passed in 1850 and had a dominant influence on the ensuing 30 years of French educational practices.

For some, the law was a godsend, and they promptly set about to consolidate their religious authority in the nation's schools. Flaubert's portrayal in *Bouvard et Pécuchet* of the encounter between a schoolmaster and the local curé following passage of this law illustrates one dimension of its social impact. For others, it was seen as extremely retrogressive, harking back to the Guizot mandates of 1833, which put moral and religious instruction at the head of the academic subjects to be taught in public schools. The latter also saw in this law a further solidification of traditional class apartheid policies—nontechnical, moralistic, and paternalistic education for the lower classes, intending to form "good" (meaning unquestioning and obedient) citizens, versus the much broader preparatory education for the middle and upper classes, leading to the universities or technical schools.

Throughout the 1860s it became increasingly evident that serious problems were developing in the French educational system under the policies of the Second Empire. In 1863 a government report showed 25 percent of the nation's students left school knowing only how to read and write, 13 percent had not learned even these basic skills, and an estimated 600,000 children in over 1,000 French communities had no schools at all.[4] In spite of the continuing efforts of Jean Macé and the Ligue de l'Enseignement to encourage free, secular secondary schools for both boys and girls and Victor Duruy's attempts to increase the scientific content of the nation's curricula via special programs, preuniversity education in France was rapidly falling behind the technological advances of the times.

It was at this moment that an innovative Positivist publisher named Pierre-Jules Hetzel had a twofold inspiration. First, he created a unique bimonthly journal-magazine, which he called the *Magasin d'Education et de Récréation*—a "family" publication intended both for the enjoyment and the education of his readers—and a companion series of individual works in the same vein called the *Bibliothèque d'Education et de Récréation*.[5] Second, he chose to include in these publications (in *feuilleton* format in the former, then as complete novels in the latter) a new and very different brand of fictional narrative, one that mixed scientific didacticism with fast-moving dramas of travel and adventure, authored by a young unknown writer named Jules Verne.

Hetzel assigned Verne and his *Voyages Extraordinaires* an explicit task: to be a kind of literary home remedy, a recreational antidote to this serious lacuna in the educational exposure of French youth, that is, to teach science through family readings. As Hetzel stated in his preface to the second volume of the *Magasin*: "We will therefore continue to give a great amount of emphasis to instruction, to this portion of instruction not contained in the programs of public education. . . . Our role is to complement the education offered in the schools and not to replace it" ("A Nos Abonnés" II:2, 375, IIIA). Tailored as they were to this society's rapidly changing view of itself and to its vision of a better future, these publications took root and soon sold by the millions. And the rest is history.

As a postscript, it must be noted that during those final years of the nineteenth century as the Third Republic succeeded in passing legislation to overhaul and fully modernize the French public educational system, the popularity of Hetzel's didactic publications continued to flourish for a while, but they progressively began to lose their appeal as science instruction in the schools improved. But Hetzel's battle had already been won. He had not only succeeded in making a lasting imprint on the social reality of his times, but had also helped to create an "extraordinary" literary legacy that would continue to fascinate readers of all ages and nationalities for more than 100 years after his death—Jules Verne's *Voyages Extraordinaires*.

Such, then, is a brief sociohistorical look at the factors surrounding the birth of Verne's new literary genre called the *roman scientifique*. It would be unwarranted and unreasonable to attribute to them the label of "social origins" for the very notion of a mechanical cause-effect relationship between a literary work and its historical milieu is misleading and dangerous. But insofar as the purely pedagogical aspect of Verne's texts corresponded to a recognized social need during this period—and the texts themselves were deliberately shaped to address that need—such an overview seems intrinsically relevant.

It was not, of course, the simple presence of scientific pedagogy in the *Voyages Extraordinaires* that originally made them so popular and has kept them alive through so many generations of young readers. It was, rather, the way in which Verne *used* science and technology to evoke an entirely new perspective on the world and the individual's place in it—a "de-alienated" perspective where Man and Machine could function as one and together expand the frontiers of their universe. If the overt didacticism of these novels was necessary, as a kind of "pre-text" insuring their ostensible social utility, it was always less an end in itself than a springboard to an adventurous journey into the realms of the unknown. What gave Verne's novels their "literary" merit was not his pedagogy per se, but rather his epic portrayal of modern Man as a kind of Industrial-Age Jason or Aeneus, conquering the elements with the aid of his technological devices, piercing the mysteries of Nature with his science, and triumphantly returning home from his journey beyond the horizon to share with his countrymen the talisman of his victory: Knowledge.

NOTES

1. V. Walter Benjamin, "The Work of Art in the Age of Mechanical Reproduction." *Illuminations*, ed. Hannah Arendt, trans. H. Zohn (New York: Harcourt, Brace, Jovanovich, 1968), 217–51 for an interesting discussion of the ramifications of this particular phenomenon.

2. For firsthand observations and commentary, v. C.-A. Sainte-Beuve, "De la littérature industrielle." *La Revue des Deux Mondes* (Sept. 1, 1839), 675–91.

3. V. Charles C. Gillispie, *The Edge of Objectivity* (Princeton, N.J.: Princeton University Press, 1960), 198–200.

4. Figures cited in Antoine Prost, *Histoire de l'enseignement en France 1800–1967* (Paris: Armand Colin, 1968), 123.

5. For a more detailed discussion of these publications in the context of their times v. Isabelle Jan, "Children's literature and bourgeois society in France since 1860." *Yale French Studies* 43 (1969), 60–71. Also Esther Kanipe, "Hetzel and the *Bibliothèque d'Education et de Récréation.*" *Yale French Studies* 43 (1969), 72–83.

CHAPTER **2**

The Birth of the Scientific Novel

Legend has it—and most biographers unfortunately agree[1]—that Jules Verne was a student whose intellectual promise was always much greater than his application. It was said that he cared little for bookish pursuits, that he was an unusually boisterous young man who preferred practical jokes, the rowdy company of his *copains*, and being a kind of Cocteau-esque Dargelos—*le coq du collège*. As a Parisian bachelor in his twenties, he supposedly pursued a somewhat bohemian life-style, refusing to take his studies of law seriously, borrowing large sums of money from his father, and spending most of his time frequenting the backstages of theatres in the company of his frolicsome bachelor friends who had dubbed themselves the *Onze-Sans-Femme*. His feelings toward education, even as an adult, were believed to be best illustrated by the following comment to his father in the 1850s (long before his association with Hetzel's publishing house): "Ah yes! these children who never studied during their youth! But it has always been that way; fortunately, studious children usually grow up to be stupid adolescents and imbeciles as adults" ("63 Letters," *BSJV* 82, IC). And one wonders, in the light of such evidence, how Jules Verne could possibly have become the dedicated pedagogue of science that his *Voyages Extraordinaires* shows him to be.

But these myths, like those surrounding his literary reputation, conceal a very different story, which, although less colorful, is infinitely more faithful to the facts of Verne's life.[2]

As a child and young man, Jules Verne was actually quite a good student. He repeatedly won awards for meritorious performance in geography, in music, and in Greek and Latin during his years in primary and secondary schools. But he also loved machines.

> while I was quite a lad I used to adore watching machines at work. My father had a country-house at Chantenay, at the mouth of the Loire, and

near there is the government machine factory of Indret. I never went to Chantenay without entering the factory, and standing for hours watching the machines. . . . This penchant has remained with me all my life, and to-day I have still as much pleasure in watching a steam-engine or a fine loco-motive at work as I have in contemplating a picture by Raphael or Corregio. (Sherard, "Jules Verne at Home" 118, IID)

Intending that his son follow in his footsteps as an attorney, Pierre Verne sent Jules to Paris in 1848 to continue his study of law begun the year before in Nantes. The correspondence during the ensuing years between father and son indicates that, contrary to rumor, Jules not only took his studies very seriously but also found time to write a number of plays and short stories. And he even became the secretary of the Théâtre Lyrique through the intervention of Alexandre Dumas père, to whom he had been introduced in 1849 as an aspiring young dramatist by their mutual friend the chevalier d'Arpentigny. Although plagued by poverty, Jules continued his literary activities while preparing for his law exams, and in January 1851, he finally earned his degree. It was then that he informed his father that he was not returning to Nantes to join the family law firm as expected. Not only had he decided to remain in Paris to pursue another degree in French literature, but he was also having severe reservations about his very future as an attorney. It should not have come as a complete surprise, for a close examination of certain portions of Verne's correspondence with his father during these four years clearly reveals this evolution in the young man's priori-ties: "If, as a result of my literary studies (which, as you well know, are useful in any position), I find that I have a few ideas to try out in this field, rest assured that they will always remain secondary and won't affect my overall goals" (Martin 51, IIC). "It's really a pleasure all too misunderstood in Nantes to be on the leading edge of the literary world. . . . There are serious studies to be done on the present genre of literature and especially on that of the future" ("63 Let-ters" 57, IC). "Don't think for a minute that I'm just playing around; my des-tiny keeps me here. I can be a good writer, whereas I would always be a bad lawyer . . ." ("63 Letters" 62, IC). "Literature above all . . . my mind is focused uniquely on this goal! What's the use repeating all my ideas on this subject . . . my dear father, whether I do law for a couple of years or not, if both careers are pursued simultaneously, sooner or later one of them will destroy the other. . . . And in my opinion, the bar would not survive" ("63 Letters" 65–66, IC).

Through a perusal of such documents, one witnesses the earliest stirrings of Jules Verne's subsequent writing career. As he continued to compose plays and an occasional short story or essay in the requisite poverty of his cramped one-room apartment, the young Romantic was steadily becoming obsessed with the idea of becoming a recognized Parisian dramatist—a dream that would never materialize. But such passing comments as "the genre . . . of the future" are richly suggestive of the very different literary path that would eventually lead him to fame and fortune.

Many years were to pass before Verne would reluctantly decide to abandon his theatre aspirations and redirect his energies toward writing scientifically didactic adventure stories. During those difficult years prior to his fateful meeting with Hetzel, Verne began to earn some extra income by penning short articles on scientific and historical topics for journals such as the *Musée des Familles*. This activity, though relatively lucrative, required long days of research in the Bibliothèque Nationale to gather the necessary documentation, poring over reference works of geography and world history and carefully examining new studies in the then-prevalent scientific journals. And although this continual research might appear to some as laborious and the epitome of tedium, Verne seemed to revel in it, saying: "I'm working a lot now . . . I'm very often at the library, which offers me endless resources" (Martin 74, IIC) and "I work from morning till night . . . all this labor amuses me to an extraordinary degree" (Martin 95, IIC).

Marius Topin was later to characterize these formative years in Verne's literary life as follows: "It was proof of a rare sense of discipline and energy, to quit the literary scene where he had already settled in, and to condemn himself for ten long years to a dry and esoteric apprenticeship. By this voluntary withdrawal, by this unceasing preparatory travail, he provides an example that the impatient artists of our own time would do well to follow" (Topin 385–86, IIC). The facts of the matter, although somewhat less heroic than Topin's portrayal of them, are nevertheless quite fascinating in that they enable one to discern the origins of certain work habits, intellectual interests, and fictional formats that would later congeal into Verne's first "scientific novel."

This period actually contains two quite distinct phases. The first, extending from 1851 to 1856, is characterized by Verne's continuing work at the Théâtre Lyrique with Alexandre Dumas, the beginnings of his research efforts in the Bibliothèque Nationale to accumulate the necessary data for his articles, a number of plays (for he still persisted in believing in his future as a dramatist during this time), and his association with Pitre-Chevalier who was then director of the *Musée des Familles*. Pitre-Chevalier was a publisher who had an uncanny sense of what would interest his Second Empire reading public. And he correctly guessed the one topic among others that would generate broad-based popular enthusiasm would be educational articles dealing with geography and the history of exotic foreign lands, with exploration and discovery, and with the many contemporary advances in science and technology. But they always had to be explained in lay terminology and/or integrated into easy-reading fictional narratives. Verne's earliest articles conformed to these dictates perfectly: *The First Ships of the Mexican Navy* (1851), *A Balloon Trip* (1851), *Martin Paz* (1852), *Master Zacharius* (1853), and *Wintering in the Ice* (1853), as well as a few other unsigned scientific articles generally attributed to him.

It was during the preparation of these short stories that Verne first conceived of the possibility of writing a new type of novel, what he called a *Roman de la Science*, a kind of narrative that would fully incorporate the large amounts of factual material he was accumulating through his continuing library research as well as that gleaned from other articles in the *Musée des Familles* and similar journals. Although no record exists of their discussions, Verne is said to have often talked with Dumas about such a project. The older Dumas, having attempted a similar undertaking in the historical realm with his unfinished *Isaac Laquedem* (a work that may well have had a great deal of influence on Verne's proposal), heartily encouraged his young friend's plan. But at this juncture the particulars of such a unique novel remained only a vague idea in Verne's mind and were not immediately acted upon. He continued to write plays and musical comedies (the vast majority unperformed) and an occasional short story for Pitre-Chevalier to supplement his meager income.

The second phase of this period, from 1856 to 1862, is very different. Verne, newly married, finally left his post at the Théâtre Lyrique to assume a full-time job as *agent de change* at the Paris stock market with the firm of Eggly & Cie. He spent his early mornings at home writing (at a desk with two drawers—one for his plays, the other for his scientific works) and most of his days at the stock market. The remainder of his time was spent either with his theatre friends of the *Onze-Sans-Femme* (all of whom were married by this time) or patiently gathering scientific and historical facts that he copied onto notecards for future reference (a particular work habit he was to continue throughout his life). As at least one biographer has noted, however, the long sessions he spent in the reading rooms of the library throughout this period might well have been as much motivated by a desire for peace and quiet (his son Michel was born during this period and greatly annoyed his father with his incessant crying) as by any extreme devotion to his research (Soriano 97, IIB). But whatever the case may have been, his long-contemplated ideas for a *Roman de la Science* soon crystallized into a rough draft of what was later to be called *Five Weeks in a Balloon— A Journey of Discovery Across Africa*. Many years later, when interviewed, Verne spoke in retrospect about the birth of this first novel, saying: "It struck me one day that perhaps I might utilize my scientific education to blend together science and romance into a work ... that might appeal to the public taste. The idea took such a hold upon me that I sat down at once to carry it into effect, the result being *Five Weeks in a Balloon*" (Jones 64, IID). "I really think that my love for maps and the great explorers of the world led to my composing the first of my long series of geographical stories" (Belloc 212, IID).

The inspiration for this story of Dr. Fergusson's balloon flight across the then largely unexplored continent of Africa was the culmination of a variety of different circumstances, both in Verne's own life and in the events taking place during this period in France.

On the one hand, due to a violent dispute with Pitre-Chevalier in 1856, Verne no longer contributed articles and short stories to the *Musée des Familles*, and he would refuse to do so until 1863, when Pitre-Chevalier died and a new director took command of the journal. Increasingly determined, however, to expand his short narratives into a full-length scientific novel, Verne discussed his ideas with his colleagues, his friends, and with three individuals in particular:

Jacques Arago (famous traveler, author of *Voyage around the World*, and brother to the respected physicist and astronomer François Arago), Henri Garcet (Verne's cousin, mathematician at the lycée Henri IV, and author of *Elemental Mechanics*), and especially Félix Tournachon, known as Nadar.

The influence of Nadar during this period was decisive. Known mostly as a photographer, daredevil, and cofounder of the Society for the Encouragement of Air Travel via Heavier-Than-Air Vehicles (of which Verne eventually became secretary and later incorporated many of the Society's precepts into his novel *Robur the Conqueror*), Nadar quickly initiated Verne into the mysteries of air travel and soon brought him into his own circle of friends, which included such noted engineers and experimenters as Jacques Babinet[3] and Ponton d'Amécourt.[4] The friendship between Nadar and Verne, based in part on their common scientific interests, would last throughout their lives: in Nadar's honor, Verne would later even use an anagram of his friend's name for one of the heroes of *From the Earth to the Moon* (Michel Ardan). The many theoretical discussions with Nadar and his acquaintances helped to provide Verne with the technical knowledge that eventually enabled him to compose his first "scientific novel," complementing as it did Verne's own rapidly growing geographical and historical erudition.

On the other hand, the subject matter itself was timely. The accounts of several African explorers—Barth, Burton and Speke, Grant, and others—were being published in France during this period (1857-62), creating widespread public interest in their continuing exploits. There is no doubt that Verne, conscientious as he was about staying abreast of such developments, saw in these explorations not only the ideal ingredients for his first *Roman de la Science*, but also the strong likelihood of its immediate commercial success.

In September of 1862, Verne was introduced to Pierre-Jules Hetzel through a common friend of the publisher and Dumas. Verne promptly asked Hetzel if he would consider reviewing for publication his newly completed manuscript tentatively entitled *Voyage through the Air* (a manuscript that, according to his wife, a despairing Verne had very nearly destroyed a few weeks earlier after rejection by another publishing house). Hetzel, already well known for having published the works of such writers as Lamartine, Balzac, Hugo, de Vigny, Sainte-Beuve, and George Sand, nevertheless had a reputation for taking a keen interest in aspiring young novelists, and he agreed to the request. A few days later Verne signed his first contract—starting what would prove to be a highly successful collaboration, lasting for more than 40 years and resulting in over 60 novels in an educational series called the *Voyages Extraordinaires*.

Shortly following Hetzel's publication and the immediate commercial success of *Five Weeks in a Balloon*, Verne bid his final farewells to his colleagues at the Parisian stock market, saying (according to interviews supposedly collected by his great niece):

> My friends, I bid you adieu. I've had an idea—the kind that every man, according to Girardin, should have once every day but that I have had just

once in my life—an idea which should make me rich. I've just written a novel in a new style, truly my own. If it succeeds, it will be a gold mine. So, I'll continue to write and write without rest while you buy stocks low one day and sell them high the next. I'm leaving the Stock Market. Good bye, my friends. (Allote de la Fuÿe 94, IIB)

NOTES

1. For examples, v. Kenneth Allott's *Jules Verne* (London: Crescent Press, 1940) as well as Mark Soriano's *Jules Verne* (Paris: Julliard, 1978).

2. The first "authoritative" biography on Jules Verne was published in 1928 by his great niece Marguerite Allotte de la Fuÿe entitled *Jules Verne, sa vie, son oeuvre* (Paris: Simon Kra); English translation: *Jules Verne*, trans. Erik de Mauny (London: Staples Press, 1954). Although serving for nearly half a century as the canonical history of Verne's life—based as it was believed to be on authentic documents jealously guarded by the Verne family since the author's death—modern scholarship has proven it to be riddled with well-meaning exaggeration and error. Many of the common myths associated with Verne, faithfully repeated by literary historians, such as his youthful flight from home on a freighter named the *Coralie* or his ability to read and write English, originated in this text. A much more reliable biography of the author was completed in 1973 by Verne's great grandson Jean Jules-Verne, entitled *Jules Verne* (Paris: Hachette); English translation: *Jules Verne: A Biography*, trans. Roger Greaves (New York: Taplinger, 1976). For a detailed analysis of this and other aspects of literary criticism's treatment of the life and works of Jules Verne (as well as a lengthy discussion of Verne's sources and intertexts both literary and scientific), v. my Ph.D. dissertation entitled "Jules Verne and the Scientific Novel" (Columbia University, 1985), pp. 9–100, 114–20.

3. French physicist and astronomer, inventor of the hygrometer, among other scientific instruments.

4. Designer of one of the earliest scale model helicopters, with Gabriel de la Landelle, in the early 1860s, and undoubtedly a source for the airship *Albatros* in *Robur the Conqueror*.

Verne's publisher and *père spirituel*, Pierre-Jules Hetzel (photo c. 1875)

CHAPTER 3

The Hand of Hetzel

When discussing the "educational project" of Verne's narratives, it is essential to give some attention to the large role played by his publisher, Pierre-Jules Hetzel, in the initial creation and subsequent shaping of the *Voyages Extraordinaires*, especially as regards the pedagogical intent of these works.

In 1862, when he accepted for publication Verne's first *roman scientifique* called *Five Weeks in a Balloon*, Hetzel had long ago decided to move his publishing efforts in an entirely new direction. Having begun his career in the 1830s during the height of the Romantic movement (publishing the works of such noted authors as Balzac, Hugo, Lamartine, de Vigny, George Sand, et al.), Hetzel began, during the ensuing years, to devote more and more of his time and energies toward developing a high-quality literature for children that could be shared by adults as well. Writing under the pseudonym of P.-J. Stahl (a pen name he would retain throughout the rest of his life) and already popular for such satiric novels as *Scenes from the Public and Private Life of Animals* (1842), Hetzel published one of his first collections of children's stories in 1844. It included, in addition to his own *New Adventures of Tom Thumb* (inspired from its English version), various short stories in this genre by such authors as Alfred de Musset, Charles Nodier, Alexandre Dumas père, and other well-known literary figures of the time.

A political activist and firm believer in the Republican ideals of 1848 (he was a cabinet minister under Lamartine during the short-lived Second Republic), Hetzel was exiled by Napoléon III in 1851 and fled to Brussels. However, although not permitted entry into his homeland, he still continued his publishing efforts in absentia, bringing to press Hugo's *Les Châtiments* and his own journal of children's literature called the *Nouveau Magasin des enfants* (continued through 1857), among other works.

But it was especially following his return from exile during the amnesty of 1859 that Hetzel gave himself over entirely to his dream of creating a radically new kind of family publication in France, one that would combine fiction with nonfiction, scientific pedagogy with moral didacticism, and high literary merit with an equally high-quality format in terms of bindings, typography, and illustrations. Soon after, the *Magasin d'Education et de Récréation* was born.

Reading the publisher's preface to the first volume of this encyclopedic bimonthly publication, one can easily discern the public to whom the *Magasin* was addressed, the goals it sought to achieve, and, more importantly, those ideological parameters within which Verne was expected to write the majority of his *Voyages Extraordinaires*:

> We are attempting to create a journal for the entire family that is educational in the true sense of the word; one that is both serious and entertaining, one that would be of interest to parents and of profit to children. Education and recreation—these two terms, in our opinion, should complement one another. Instruction should be presented in a manner so as to incite real interest; otherwise, it tends to be too off-putting and disheartening. Entertainment should contain a moral lesson; otherwise, it tends to be pointless and empties heads instead of filling them. . . .
>
> Our ambition is to supplement the necessarily arduous lessons of the classroom with a lesson that is both more personal and more trenchant, to round out public education with family readings . . . to fulfill the learning needs of the home, from the cradle to old age. . . .
>
> We have created a *Magasin* wherein everything is tailored to different age groups and nothing is displeasing to anyone. ("A nos lecteurs," I:1, 1–3, IIIA)

The overtly didactic intent of the *Magasin d'Education et de Récréation* (and its companion series, the *Bibliothèque d'Education et de Récréation*) is clear indeed. The *récréation* aspect of their contents, if entertaining, is nevertheless always geared toward a more effective implantation of useful knowledge and healthy moral growth in its readers—be they young or old (as Hetzel continually points out, hoping to appeal to adults as much as to children and adolescents). And this concern for didacticism is echoed again and again in Hetzel's subsequent prefaces as well as in his correspondence with authors like Octave Feuillet who were potential contributors to the two publications:

> We would immediately stop publishing if we ever found it necessary to sacrifice utility in order to be superficially entertaining. . . .
>
> We will therefore continue to give a great amount of emphasis to instruction, to this portion of instruction not contained in the programs of public education and which belongs in the home. ("A nos abonnés," II:2, 375, IIIA)

I thought that, after having written for adults, it would be possible for you as a father to come up with a nice book for young people, and that it would not be at all demeaning to create a masterpiece which would become a classic for the youth. Don't you think that a law should be passed requiring the death penalty (or worse!) for all writers of great talent who refuse to use this talent, at least once, toward educating those at the threshold of adult life? (Parménie et al. 611, IIC)

Hetzel's determination to have a moral and pedagogical impact on the youth of France, understandable given his disgust with the Second Empire, grew into an obsession after the catastrophic Franco-Prussian War of 1870. To provide his nation's young people with the cultural and educational means to reassert their collective identity, regain their pride, and match the technological advances of their conquerors became a top priority, not only to Hetzel but to the entire country. As the legislative history of the Third Republic shows, during this time France entered into a series of divisive internal political struggles over the nation's educational system and how it could best be improved. Hetzel summarized his feelings on the subject to his son in 1871, saying:

Our poor France! Well, the greater her misfortunes, the more we will love her, and more! It's our generation that has allowed her to fall into the abyss; it's yours, my child, that will pull her out of it. And military strength is not the first weapon to be used. No. It is first through the combination of education and learning that we can put this defeated country back on track. Have we lacked guns or personnel? No. It's Science . . . and, above all, discipline . . . We have to bring back a respect for good and for beauty, a respect for the law and what's right. . . . (Parménie et al. 536, IIC)

Hence, the central position of science pedagogy in the thematic makeup of Hetzel's post-1850 publications and the persistent moralizing tone of these texts are the direct result of his personal views concerning the society of his time—what he saw as the crippling political and educational policies of the Second Empire, the ensuing disaster of the Franco-Prussian War, and the hopes for change inherent in the Third Republic. And in this regard the overall ideological orientation of Verne's *Voyages Extraordinaires* is a palpable testament to these views.

The *Magasin* was not the first periodical of this sort to be successful in France. The tradition for this type of family-oriented publication dates from the *Magasin des Evénements de tous genres* (1741) and includes: the *Journal d'Education* (1768), which intended to "make young people . . . virtuous and knowledgeable citizens"; Edouard Charton's historic *Magasin Pittoresque* (1833), the first to incorporate illustrations, labeling them as "a complement to instruction"; Girardin and then Pitre-Chevalier's *Le Musée des Familles* (1833); and Charton's very popular *Le Tour du Monde* (1860).

But Hetzel's *Magasin d'Education et de Récréation* was by far the most varied, the most attractive, and the most illustrated among these various publications. Hetzel himself, using his pen name of P.-J. Stahl, was responsible for the *récréation* portion of the journal, whereas his old friend Jean Macé (professor at the Lycée Henri IV, later founder of the Ligue d'Enseignement, and outspoken supporter of public secular education) organized the *education* sections. Between them, they succeeded in obtaining contributions from a vast number of their professional and literary peers: popular writers such as Hector Malot, André Laurie, and Jules Sandeau (not to mention the texts of Stahl and Macé themselves or their translations of such writers as Vergil, Locke, Andersen, Wyss, H. Rider Haggard, et al.); scientists such as Camille Flammarion, Vivien de Saint-Martin, and Sainte-Claire Deville (as well as translated articles by Faraday, Ben Franklin, et al.); architects like Viollet-le-Duc; poets such as Victor de Laprade and Louis Ratisbonne; artists like Gustave Doré and Gavarni; and many others.

But it was Jules Verne who was to play an increasingly central role in unifying the twofold educational/recreational character of the *Magasin*. And from the publication of the sixth volume onward, it is significant that Verne's name begins to appear between those of Stahl and Macé on the title page of the publication. This was undoubtedly the result of his own widening popularity—a marketing strategy on the part of Hetzel—but nevertheless revealing.

Given this increasingly closer collaboration between Hetzel and Verne, one question becomes proportionately more important: to what extent, aside from simply providing Verne with a publishing outlet for his novels, did Hetzel actively participate in the actual composition of the *Voyages Extraordinaires*? For example, it is a well-known fact, and repeatedly pointed out by a number of Vernian critics,[1] that Hetzel was not only Verne's literary mentor but also a kind of spiritual father. It was common for Verne to ask for Hetzel's aid in improving his style and in making his fiction more literary in nature. It was always Hetzel who acted as a critical first reader of Verne's manuscripts prior to their publication. And it is certain that Hetzel was an inexhaustible source of encouragement and advice for Verne during the many years of their professional association.

But the matter does not end there. Hetzel was also Verne's prime censor, requiring him to conform his narratives to "house rules" in all matters of pedagogy, morality, and ideology—a dictate that caused Verne at one point to complain about the "rather narrow confines that I'm condemned to move around in" (Parménie et al. 107, IIC). And the consequences of this continual and uncompromising censorship on Hetzel's part is visible throughout the *Voyages Extraordinaires*, particularly if one compares those novels *not* first published in the *Magasin d'Education et de Récréation* (or published there after Hetzel's death in 1886) with those of Verne's works (the majority) that were. In the former texts, the long pedagogical passages are diminished in length and intrusiveness, science and technology are less central to the plot itself,[2] Verne's (sometimes risqué) humor and wordplay are more apparent,[3] and the political and/or religious elements are more explicit and less carefully neutral.[4]

And Hetzel's censorship of Verne's narratives is even more visible if one examines the voluminous correspondence between them. Here the documentational evidence is irrefutable: Hetzel not only had a tangible effect on Verne's style and treatment of certain topics, he had a fundamental impact on the overall character of those works in which he collaborated. Examples of Hetzel's often dictatorial influence on Verne are too numerous to quote in their entirety, but a selected number of excerpts will give an idea of its proportions.

From the very beginning, Verne was amenable to Hetzel's comments, and unless he saw them as directly contradictory to the basic integrity of his narrative, he invariably incorporated such advice into his texts. Note, for example, his reaction to the sizable list of corrections proposed for his *Adventures of Captain Hatteras*:

> I promise you that I will take them into account, for all your observations are correct. I myself felt while writing that their antagonism was pushed too far, but I have not yet achieved total mastery over myself. . . .
> I feel as you do. We'll strike out the duel with a wave of the pen; as for the reconciliation between the two men, we'll make it occur earlier. . . .
> We'll chat about all this upon your return, and we'll discuss it at length. Have you ever found me to be recalcitrant when it came to making cuts or rearrangements? Didn't I follow your advice in the *Five Weeks in a Balloon* by eliminating Joe's long narrative, and without pain? (Martin 138, IIC)

Here is Verne's response to those "suggestions" offered for *The Black Indies*:

> I have received your proofs and I thank you for the great amount of time you spent on them. My original idea, of an underground England with steamers and railways, having evaporated (the times having changed), I couldn't see clearly.
> And when one can't see clearly, one must proceed blindly, as I am doing by following your lead. . . . (Martin 205–6, IIC)

Among Hetzel's strongest remarks are those in reaction to a manuscript that Verne sent to him in 1871 entitled *Uncle Robinson*:

> Where is the science? . . . They [the characters] are too dumb! . . . 82 pages of text and not a single invention that a cretin wouldn't have figured out! . . . It's a collection of totally listless beings; not a one of them is alert, lively, witty . . . Drop all these guys and start over again, from scratch. (Martin 199, IIC)

Needless to say, Verne completely overhauled this particular text. But when later receiving from Hetzel yet another list of massive changes to be made in the new version, it was Verne who then reacted strongly:

> It would take pages to answer you, and these discussions by mail don't lead anywhere. I will be in Paris next week and we will chat as long as you wish.
>
> . . . All that you say about Ayrton's savageness is of little importance. All the mental illness experts of the world can't change the fact. I need a savage. . . .
>
> Several times now you've raised doubts in my mind about this work. But I'm convinced—and I'll say it to you as I would to any other—that it is no worse than the others and, if promoted like them, it will succeed . . . I repeat, it's like cold water that you're throwing on my brain. . . .
>
> Questions of form, agreed. I've told you a hundred times that I can't visualize it clearly except on the galleys. The differences in language between the various characters, also agreed. But all that can be done without difficulty. We'll talk. . . . (Martin 200–1, IIC)

The manuscript in question here would, after another series of give-and-take battles over editorial revisions, become the highly successful *Mysterious Island*.

And, finally, Verne's most uncompromising response to Hetzel's demands for textual changes (the former having grown progressively less willing to "blindly follow" the latter, it seems) occurred in 1882 and concerned another *robinsonnade* called *The School for Crusoes*:

> it seems to me that the philosophical consequences that you mention are irrelevant to my subject matter and will weigh it down. . . .
>
> In your comments, there are some things that I will take into account, but others are totally inadmissible. . . .
>
> Believe me, my dear Hetzel, and rest assured that I wouldn't ignore a correct observation, but there are some here that are in complete conflict with the topic as I understand it and as I wanted to treat it. (Parménie, "Huit lettres," 106, IC)

In spite of Verne's sometimes energetic defense of the rough drafts as exhibited in these letters, Hetzel's direct impact on the *Voyages Extraordinaires* was nevertheless substantial. Another indication of the magnitude and nature of his requested changes can be seen when actually comparing these many earlier texts with the final published versions. For example, the original ending for *The Adventures of Captain Hatteras* would have had him plunge to his death into a volcano, followed by his faithful dog Duk, whereas the final version has him rescued, but forever after insane. Or, an obvious politically motivated alteration, all reference to the then-current czar of Russia or his father was stricken from the final version of *The Courier of the Czar*, and the title itself was changed to a more neutral *Michel Strogoff*. A number of violent passages in *Twenty Thousand*

Leagues under the Sea were axed by Hetzel; Verne was even obliged to fight his editor in order to keep the memorable Captain Nemo as he had portrayed him. Also deleted were certain risqué paintings in Nemo's study, like the portrait of a "half-clothed woman," which subsequently became a virgin by Leonardo da Vinci, and a "courtisan," which became a biblical personage by Titian. Other "religious" cuts occurred in such works as the short story *Frritt-Flacc* where sentences such as "'God! God's money! Has anybody ever seen the color of it?' The Doctor whistled for Hurzof" were changed to read "Without answering, the Doctor whistled for Hurzof." And when portraying an Islamic protagonist, Verne's original description of "He cursed like a christian, got up, and looked around" was chopped to "Cursing, he got up and looked around." And so it continues throughout most of Verne's novels.[5]

Finally, one must recognize not only the extent to which Hetzel affected the actual textual content of the *Voyages Extraordinaires*, but also that the very idea for such a collection was Hetzel's. If it was Verne who had initially conceived of a *Roman de la Science*, a novel where the discoveries and innovations of modern science would act as the mainspring to the plot, it was Hetzel who transformed this notion into an ambitious educational project that would significantly broaden the thematic scope of such a series, take as its implied reader the French youth of that era, and make it a vehicle for scientific and moral pedagogy. No better expression can be found of Hetzel's intent in this regard than in his publisher's Preface to the *Voyages Extraordinaires* series. In it, Hetzel reintroduces Jules Verne (already known by the success of his three novels, *Five Weeks in a Balloon, Journey to the Center of the Earth,* and *From the Earth to the Moon*) and succinctly outlines the author's supposedly now-formulated fictional goals. Although somewhat lengthy, the Preface bears repeating here, for it not only aptly summarizes Hetzel's own ideological beliefs (as discussed above), but it also clearly states the didactic purpose assigned by the publisher to the *Voyages Extraordinaires* as a whole, charting the narrative course that Verne would follow throughout most of his writing career.

> The excellent books of M. Jules Verne are part of a very small number of those that one can give to the new generation with absolute confidence. In the contemporary market, there exist none better to answer society's needs for learning about the marvels of the universe. There exist none which have been more justifiably greeted with instant success from their very first appearance.
>
> If the public's fancy sometimes wanders toward works that are flashy and unwholesome, its basic good taste never permanently settles on any work that is not fundamentally wholesome and good. The two-fold merit of the works of M. Jules Verne is that the reading of these charming books has all the flavor of a spicy dish while providing the substance of a nourishing meal.
>
> The most respected critics have acclaimed M. Jules Verne as a writer of exceptional talent who, from his earliest works, has made a place for him-

self in French letters. An imaginative and exciting storyteller, a pure and original writer with a lively sharp wit . . . and, in addition, a profoundly learned author, M. Jules Verne has succeeded in creating a new genre. What is promised so often and what is delivered so rarely, instruction that is entertaining and entertainment that instructs, M. Verne gives both unsparingly in each one of his exciting narratives.

The Novels of M. Jules Verne have moreover arrived at the perfect time. When one sees the general public hastening to scientific lectures given all over France and that, in the newspapers, art and theatre columns are making way for articles on the proceedings of the Academy of Science, one must conclude that Art for Art's Sake is no longer enough for our era. The time has come for Science to take its place in the realm of Literature.

The merit of M. Jules Verne is to have, boldly and masterfully, taken the first steps into this uncharted land and to have had the unique honor of a well-known scientist say of his works: "These novels will not only entertain you like the best of Alexandre Dumas but will also educate you like the books of François Arago."

Young or old, rich or poor, learned or uneducated, all will find both pleasure and profit from these excellent books of M. Jules Verne. They are sure to become friends to the entire family and will occupy a front shelf in the home's library.

The illustrated editions of the works of M. Jules Verne that we are offering at an unusually low price and in a luxurious format show the utmost confidence that we have in their value and in the ever-growing popularity that they will achieve.

New works of M. Jules Verne will be added to this series, which we shall always keep up-to-date. All together, they will fulfill the intent of the author when he chose as their sub-title: "Voyages in Known and Unknown Worlds." The goal of the series is, in fact, to outline all the geographical, geological, physical, and astronomical knowledge amassed by modern science and to recount, in an entertaining and picturesque format that is his own, the history of the universe. ("Avertissement de l'Editeur," *Hatteras* 7–8, IA)

In the 1890s, Verne humorously underscored the truly gargantuan proportions of this undertaking in his incomplete and unpublished memoirs, saying: "This task is to depict in novel format the enter Earth, the whole world, by imagining adventures unique to each country and by inventing characters indigenous to the habitats in which they live. Yes! But the Earth is very large, and life is very short! In order to leave a completed work behind, one would need to live to be at least 100 years old!" ("Souvenir d'Enfance" 62, IC)

NOTES

1. In particular Marcel Moré, *Le Très Curieux Jules Verne* (pp. 21–53) and Marc Soriano's *Jules Verne* (pp. 118–20).

2. To verify this observation, one need but to compare the "straight" science in *Twenty Thousand Leagues under the Sea* or *Mysterious Island* with its more fanciful novelistic treatment in *Journey to the Center of the Earth* and *Mathias Sandorf*, or even its comparative absence in novels such as *Around the World in 80 Days* or *The Tribulations of a Chinaman* (all these first published in the journal *Le Temps* instead of the *Magasin*).

3. An example of this difference can be seen in the Victorian decorum of *The Children of Captain Grant* versus the occasionally bawdy puns of *Clovis Dardentor* (published in 1896).

4. This fact is immediately evident when comparing most of Verne's early works with his more socially critical later ones such as *Family Without a Name*, *Little-Fellow*, and especially *The Survivors of the "Jonathan."*

5. A great deal of fine scholarship has recently been done in disclosing the particulars of Hetzel's censorship of Verne's texts and from which I have borrowed certain of my examples. Of special mention is the ongoing work of Olivier Dumas, president of the Société Jules Verne, in such articles as "Les versions de 'Frritt-Flacc' ou la liberté retrouvée," *Bulletin de la Société Jules Verne* 59 (1981), 98–100 and *"Les Aventures de Trois Russes et de Trois Anglais*, revues et corrigées," *BSJV* 67 (1983), 104–5. Also of note is Marcel Destombes's "Le Manuscrit *Vingt mille lieues sous les mers* de la Société de Géographie de Paris," *BSJV* 35:6 (1975), 56–69, and the work of other Vernian scholars such as Daniel Compère, Piero Gondolo della Riva, and Simone Vierne (see the bibliography).

Part Two
Ideological Subtexts in the
Voyages Extraordinaires

INTRODUCTION

As discussed in Part One, the 63 *romans scientifiques* that constitute the *Voyages Extraordinaires* are a fictional by-product of Verne's desire to create a viable scientific novel and Hetzel's ambition to better educate French youth. The publisher's preface to the series clearly identifies the pedagogical intent of these works and the vast "educational project" that Verne's novels were supposed to implement. Such an explicit declaration of purpose, when viewed from a critical standpoint, offers a relatively solid point of departure for an analysis of the ideological relationship of these literary texts to their times.

Verne's works are, in this context, particularly enlightening. Because of their pedagogical character, they functioned not merely as a passive reflection of their historical milieu but rather as part of a dynamic mediation with it, in other words, as having *affected* their society as much as having been an effect of it. They were not simply the manifestation of their author's socially derived conception of the world, or *Weltanschauung* (as Lukács once called it), but rather the fictional medium whereby this society's view of the world was substantially reshaped and redefined. The social impact of the *Voyages Extraordinaires* went well beyond being simple popularizations. Verne's texts provided the children and parents of the latter half of the nineteenth century more than just that up-to-date scientific knowledge deemed necessary to live productively in their new industrialized world. They offered an entire new social mythology as well, a mythology of the future, a mythology of the Machine.

But equally significant is the manner in which they did so, by portraying an untroubled status quo continuity in all matters relating to family life, economic systems, class distinctions, and the social institutions upon which that society was built. This very characteristic feature of Verne's *Voyages Extraordinaires*—combining, in a fictional format, technological change with social stasis—was an extremely effective pedagogical strategy in two ways. First, the reader assimilated the various scientific lessons directly into his or her own frame of reference. Second, the text itself acted as a kind of representational model for enlightened social adaptation to the complex technology and/or alien environments that it described. The reader's identification with the known and the familiar thus served as a stepping-stone to an access to and eventual acceptance of the unknown and the strange.

As pointed out, within the *Voyages Extraordinaires* there also existed a second, more implicit educational project. In the words of Verne's publisher, this series was meant to be "fundamentally wholesome and good." And Hetzel's stringent censorship of Verne's texts prior to their publication in the *Magasin d'Education et de Récréation* assured their conformity to the intended moral didacticism of this journal. As Hetzel had formulated this goal: "entertainment should contain a moral lesson. . . . Therein will be the unity of our journal which will, if successful, augment both the knowledge and the wholesome ideas, the logic and the taste, the compassion and the wit which constitute the moral and intellectual fabric of French youth" ("A nos lecteurs," I:1, 2, IIIA). As an intended model for reader emulation, the *Voyages Extraordinaires* contain rich material for an ideological analysis of this society's value system—how it defined for itself (or, more importantly, for its youth) fundamental questions of morality such as good versus evil, Man's relationship to Nature, matters of religion, love, honor, duty, and the like. Such continual moralizing sought to instill a specific code of ethics in the many readers of these family publications, a set of beliefs that would insure the *constructive* use of scientific knowledge and would minimize the social threat of its technical applications. Further, such moral didacticism served to reinforce the very identity of this bourgeois society as it faced an uncertain future, guaranteeing (through its youth) the survival of its own traditions and way of life—a need felt most acutely following the disaster of the Franco-Prussian War of 1870.

This "wholesome and good" dimension of the *Voyages Extraordinaires* constituted yet another means whereby Verne adapted his technological visions to the social fabric of his time. Like his static portrayal of basic societal structures, Verne's moral proselytism had the effect of both enhancing the mimetic and phatic dimensions of his fictions and counterbalancing the distancing effects of those textual elements that were considered to be *extraordinaires*. Thus, by consistently embedding his science and technological extrapolations in easily recognizable social institutions and mores, Verne succeeded in creating a unique "narrative recipe" that was perfectly tailored to his own fictional needs and to the perceived educational needs of his society. And partly thanks to Hetzel's efforts, the commercial success of his *romans scientifiques* was proportionate.

For modern readers, distant as we are from the Industrial Revolution and the French bourgeoisie of the Second Empire and Third Republic, it is principally via these two so-called educational projects (explicit and implicit) that we experience the "historicity" of the *Voyages Extraordinaires* and feel them as anchored to a specific time and place. For us, as well as for the nineteenth-century reader, the latter dimension of these works (moral didacticism) provides the hermeneutic framework within which the former (scientific didacticism) is actualized and given meaning—in much the same way as the fictional structure of the text provides a narrative format within which the nonfictional elements of the text are presented.

In the following chapters, the dual modes of scientific and moral didacticism are examined in more detail. There is no attempt to show how these texts faithfully reflect the dominant political ideology of their time or contain certain homologies with their social milieu. Rather, restricting all analyses to the texts themselves, I indicate the extent to which the scientific orientation of these works affected the portrayal of the moral didacticism therein, and vice-versa. In other words, how, between these two pedagogical dimensions of Verne's oeuvre, there existed a constantly changing ideological rapport ranging from perfect complementarity to mutual exclusivity; how the configuration of this intratextual relationship metamorphosed from Verne's earlier works to his later ones; and, finally, how the interaction of these two forms of discourse is highly representative of the oxymoronic nature of the scientific novel itself as a fictional genre.

Professor Aronnax tours the engine room of Captain Nemo's *Nautilus*
(*20,000*, engraving by E. Riou, 1870)

CHAPTER **4**

The Positivist Perspective

One of the most fundamental features of Verne's works is their profound heterogeneity. Each novel of the *Voyages Extraordinaires* is a fictional composite of many juxtaposed elements: fiction and nonfiction, scientific theory and pure melodrama, mathematics and poetry, and so on. And the persistent didacticism (explicit or implicit) of these texts reflects that same multiplicity. The thematic diversity of the subject matter recalls Hetzel's hyperbolic comments concerning the purpose of this series: to "outline all the geographical, geological, physical, and astronomical knowledge amassed by modern science and to recount . . . the history of the universe." The stylistic diversity of its textual articulation (discussed in a later chapter) spans the full gamut of rhetorical devices, registers, and representational strategies typical of a variety of literary and nonliterary narrative practices. And its ideological diversity is a source of continual surprise and puzzlement, as the lessons of geography, history, and science are alternately valorized or subverted by their own philosophical and moral underpinnings—often resulting, as Pierre Macherey has pointed out,[1] in texts that seem strangely at odds with their own focus.

The subject of the following pages is this Januslike ideological dimension in Verne's didactic fictions. To facilitate such an exegesis (although at the risk of excessive simplification), I label the two major opposing ideological tendencies in the *Voyages Extraordinaires*, as they specifically relate to science, as Positivist versus Romantic—as discussed at the outset of this book. The presence of Positivism in Verne's works derives from what one might call a "positively pedagogical" approach to the treatment of his subject matter, an approach that predetermines to a large degree certain thematic and stylistic tendencies in his prose. But only partially so. Acting as a kind of ideological counterweight to this purely empirical viewpoint, other fictional elements expand and/or dramatically alter its message—even at times directly contradicting it—through repeated expressions of morality and/or concern for social issues, "nonpositive" anthropomorphisms of various sorts, and periodic effusions of pure emotionalism. As noted, Verne's twofold scientific and ethical educational project required a constant narrative oscillation between these two general poles, both in order to initially create his *romans scientifiques* and to maximize their social effectiveness as a dealienating teaching tool. But I would stress that the resulting textual configuration was usually *not* neatly bipolar (Positivistic in its scientific pedagogy, Romantic in his moralizing). It was, rather, a complex intermingling of ideology and didacticism that itself evolved from novel to novel. The following discussions may provide some insight into these dynamic subtexts of the *Voyages Extraordinaires*.

TAXONOMIES

One particular fictional motif occurs again and again throughout Verne's works. Appearing at times almost obsessional in its repetition, it punctuates each "voyage" with clocklike regularity and seems to continually preoccupy every Vernian hero. This simple theme—central to the ideological composition of these texts and to their pedagogical functioning—is the following: the verifying of one's present location, the determination of one's exact place, the precise calculation of one's coordinates. Whether measured in geographical space (like Cyrus Smith and the castaways of *Mysterious Island*), in time (like Phileas Fogg of *Around the World in 80 Days*), in investment capital (like the industrious hero of *Little-Fellow*), or in social standing (like Robert Morgand of *The Thompson Travel Agency*), the basic ingredients of this leitmotif are invariably the same. The yardstick used is a universal, fixed, abstract, and highly ordered superstructure (latitude and longitude, time, economics, and so on), a kind of pre-existent grid or "meta-standard" that is always exterior to the protagonists and viewed by them as inherently determinative.

It is through this narrative "tic" of constant self-localization, for example, that one can understand the role of the many maps, sextants, timepieces, calendars, travel guides, diary journals, and almanacs that are so prevalent in Verne's oeuvre. They function as anchoring instruments linking the "voyage" to a stable macrocosmic context. Further, they underscore the difference between subjective experience and objectively verifiable fact and highlight the essential antithesis between them.

It is through this same mechanism that one can understand the efforts of many Vernian heroes to elevate themselves above their physical surroundings in order better to "get their bearings"—whether by scaling a mountain (a favorite theme of Verne's, and richly symbolic) as in *Mysterious Island*, by climbing a tree as in *The Children of Captain Grant*, or by fastening oneself to a kite as in *The Two Year Vacation*. Only from an exterior bird's-eye view can the parts be seen in relation to the whole and the hero's real "place" in the world be revealed.

In terms of its ideological significance, this particular narrative trait might be interpreted in a variety of ways. For example, one might be tempted to discern in this continual fixation (in both senses of the term) certain social and narrative functions. In the social context it could be seen as an effort by this society to define itself, to locate its origins and chart its evolution, to valorize its accomplishments and its image of itself in the midst of a rapidly changing world, to more fully anchor its own identity. Or it might be viewed as a fictional response to the social alienation produced by such change (as noted earlier), providing a metaphysical model of order, stability, and structure against which the nineteenth-century reader might reaffirm his or her place in the scheme of things. Or as a purely narrative device, it might be seen as a break in the syntagmatic flow of the text, a moment of textual self-reflection, where the protagonists take stock of how far they've come, the reader measures his own progress through the story, and the narrator reconfirms his role as a fixed, external observer to the events presented.

But, assuming a more pedagogical perspective, I prefer to see in this motif a recurring metaphor for the *Voyages Extraordinaires* themselves as a novelistic location of science. That is to say, the movement (thematic/ideological) of these fictions takes place within the framework of a specific set of presuppositions derived from their own scientific nature. Primary among such presuppositions, and acting as an overall ideological matrix for these works, is the notion that the natural universe is a complex but ordered assemblage of laws and forces, that is, a vast and intricate cryptogram (significantly one of Verne's favorite narrative devices, both thematically and structurally). It is unchanging in its principles, ultimately understandable to the individual, and wholly reducible into a circumscribed body of human knowledge. Modern science is its privileged decoding tool—the patient accumulation and classification of disparate data, which permit both this deciphering and an eventual application of its results. As Professor Lidenbrock repeatedly explains to young Axel in *Journey to the Center of the Earth*: "however great are the marvels of nature, they can always be explained by physical laws" (302, IA), "Science is eminently perfectible" (48, IA), "Science, my boy, is made from mistakes, but such mistakes are good to make because they lead little by little to the truth" (249, IA).

All Vernian "progress" is a function of its location within this twofold macro-context. Scientific progress is portrayed as movement toward totalizing humanity's acquisition of this knowledge. Social progress is portrayed as movement toward totalizing its eventual dissemination and constructive use. And moral progress is portrayed as movement toward totalizing ethical identification with it. Each is measured against the hypothetical total. Each is linear motion within a fixed field—each a kind of epistemological "voyage." And each is fundamental to an understanding of Verne's Positivistic treatment of the value of learning as the prime motor propelling such motion. Thus, in much the same way as the various maps, sextants, and clocks are intermediary devices helping Verne's heroes better to define their geographical and chronological locations, experimental science is the intermediary to knowledge, helping the individual better to understand his overall place in the universe, just as the scientific pedagogy in Verne's novels is the textual intermediary helping the reader to locate himself in this world of progressing science and industrialization. All are essentially metonymic structures relating the part to the whole. All are ideological extensions of the continual Vernian practice of "mapping."

The taxonomic nature of such scientifically derived knowledge is exemplified throughout the *Voyages Extraordinaires* by the omnipresence and prestige of the museum. Always the object of pride and admiration in Verne's works, the museum is an organized showcase of human knowledge exhibiting a variety of artifacts, each labeled and assigned a specific niche in a neatly preestablished and ordered system. There exist many variants of this structure in Verne's oeuvre (in addition to simple textual references to the national museums of Paris, London, New York, and the like), and each is used as a vehicle for scientific pedagogy. Some museums are quite explicit, for example, Captain Nemo's various collections aboard the *Nautilus* (itself a kind of underwater museum of applied scientific knowledge), Professor Lidenbrock's study (also used predictably as Axel's "school"), or Cousin Bénédict's portable insect collection in *The Boy Captain*. Some are more implicit: such repositories as the many books, maps, and atlases mentioned in the *Voyages Extraordinaires*, continually updated and expanded with new geographical discoveries (and name tags) by scientists like Paganel in *The Children of Captain Grant* or Doctor Clawbonny in *The Adventures of Captain Hatteras*. And some museums (the most significant sort) are not localized in a physical milieu at all, but are purely mental: Conseil's taxonomic identification of fish in *Twenty Thousand Leagues under the Sea*, Paganel's classification of South American bird species, and Axel's paleontological enumeration of dinosaur types, to name but a few.

Adjacent to the motif of the museum, and utilizing the same ideological presuppositions, is that of the encyclopedia: an ordered and systematized compilation of facts (rather than artifacts), a textual (rather than institutional) representation of the totality of human knowledge. This also is a preferred theme in the *Voyages Extraordinaires*—themselves a sort of encyclopedia—for the transmission of scientific pedagogy. But the encyclopedia that appears most often in Verne's novels is a human one: the ubiquitous hero-scientist-pedagogue, a living reference book capable of reeling off from memory page after page of detailed information on any subject desired (and modestly so). For example, note Doctor Clawbonny's appraisal of his own abilities in this regard as he chooses to participate in *The Adventures of Captain Hatteras*: "I know nothing at all if I don't realize that I am insufficiently educated. You're offering me a chance to round out—or, to be more precise, to refurbish—my knowledge of medicine, surgery, history, geography, botany, mineralogy, conchology, geodesy, chemistry, physics, mechanics, hydrography ... well, I accept!" (*Hatteras* 26, IA). Or consider, in this context, the narrator's metaphorical portrayal of the engineer Cyrus Smith: "Cyrus Smith instructed his companions in all things, and he especially explained to them the practical applications of science. The colonists had no library at their disposition; but the engineer himself was like a book—always ready, always open to the exact page they needed, a book that solved all their problems for them and that they leafed through regularly" (*Mysterious* 292, IA). Or even the geographer Paganel's description of himself: "'You speak like a book, Paganel,' answered Glenarvan. 'And that's exactly what I am,' replied Paganel. 'You are all invited to leaf through me as much as you like'" (*Grant* 159, IA). In Verne's fictional world, scientific knowledge is always encyclopedic in nature—learned through accumulation and then transmitted through regurgitation.

Thus, the first phase of Verne's Positivistic thought is the conviction that the natural universe is a complex but stable whole, taxonomically reducible to its constituent parts, and understandable via science. The second phase of his Positivistic thought is the conviction that scientific knowledge is a cohesive and growing whole, taxonomically accumulative in museumlike or encyclopedia-like fashion, and accessible via reason. And the third phase of his Positivistic thought is the conviction that one can (and must) "localize" and then persistently advance one's respective place in this double movement via learning. The enigmas of Nature are seen as finite in number, and the task of science their continuous reduction (in both senses of the word). Scientific knowledge is seen as infinite in its perfectibility, and the task of humankind is seen as its constant expansion. Verne's *Voyages Extraordinaires* are, in this light, not only a textual dramatization of this particular society's efforts to conquer Nature with science—and thereby more fully "possess" the world—but also stand as a fictional monument to one of the more dominant *epistemes* of this historical period: its belief in the very possibility of creating complete and unified models of physical reality and human knowledge through the collection, representation, and collation of diverse facts. Verne's scientific pedagogy is largely based on this *Bouvard et Pécuchet* type of assumption.[2] And its structural dynamics (later examined in more detail) are a faithful reflection of the same.

HIERARCHIES

The representation of Nature as a fixed and taxonomically reducible entity has its social counterpart in the *Voyages Extraordinaires*. Society is depicted in these novels as an extremely hierarchical one, with each person permanently assigned a place in it according to his or her "merit" (a very Saint-Simonian concept). And one's merit is invariably measured by the same quantitative standards of scientific knowledge. Accordingly, the traditional literary ruling caste of aristocracy-clergy-military is entirely replaced in Verne's fictions. Education in the sciences is substituted for birth as a class determinant. And the resulting social model, although still essentially fixed and pyramidal in structure, now features scientists and engineers occupying the highest echelons.

This new social order is perhaps nowhere more clearly portrayed than in Verne's many *robinsonnade* narratives, most particularly in *Mysterious Island*. This Crusoe-like novel presents a true microcosm of civilization à la Verne, where the engineer Cyrus Smith is described alternately as "their natural leader" (25, IA) or "their indisputable leader" (61, IA). In the words of one of his castaway companions, the sailor Pencroff believes him to be almost superhuman: "In his eyes, if Cyrus Smith wasn't a god, he was surely much more than a man" (118, IA). Pencroff himself represents the common man in this novel, in the same way as Smith's servant Nab represents the "lower" orders—described, rather predictably, as "Negro . . . vigorous, agile, adroit . . . gentle and quiet, sometimes naïve, always smiling, obliging and good natured" (16, IA). The professional of the group is Gédéon Spilett, a reporter for the *New York Herald* (Verne's most-quoted American newspaper) and the keeper of the castaways' daily journal. The younger generation is portrayed by Harbert, a *brave enfant* who is a child prodigy of natural history and, ostensibly, the someday successor to Cyrus Smith. And the order of "socialized" animals is symbolized by the engineer's super-intelligent dog named Top; to be contrasted with the "wild beasts" of the island who are unsocializable, dangerous, and worthy only of total extermination (a frequent theme of the *Voyages Extraordinaires*—whether it be the jaguars, or pirates, of *Mysterious Island*, the tigers of India in *The Steam House*, or the giant squids of the oceans in *Twenty Thousand Leagues under the Sea*). To complete this social microcosm, there are even two "missing link" characters. The first is an orangutan named Jup who is adopted by the group and progressively "civilized" by them—helping Nab in the kitchen chores and even (considered the height of socialization) learning to smoke tobacco. And the second is the savage beast-turned-hero Ayrton who, rescued from his island isolation, not only re-evolves into a man but also compensates "society" for his criminal past. It is quite characteristic that there are no women in this mini-civilization nor any members of the proletariat class. Also characteristic are the diminutive names attached to the "lower" classes—their graphic textual identity reflecting their comparatively limited store of scientific knowledge.

These social stereotypes are repeated over and over again throughout the *Voyages Extraordinaires*, to such an extent that, proceeding from one novel to the next, one comes to anticipate them (an expectation rarely left unfulfilled, generating a certain amount of reader reassurance and gratification). They are most often portrayed in fictional triads of scientist/common man/servant as in *Twenty Thousand Leagues under the Sea* (Pierre Aronnax, Ned Land, Conseil), of scientist/professional/servant as in *Hector Servadac* (Palmyrin Rosette, Hector Servadac, Ben-Zouf), of scientist/acolyte/servant as in *Journey to the Center of the Earth* (Otto Lidenbrock, nephew Axel, Hans), or in somewhat larger groupings. But the scientist is never depicted as a completely solitary figure; he is always an integral part of an overall social structure, one that is clearly demarcated and hierarchical, one that exists primarily to valorize him.

Within this stratified society, the Vernian scientist also personifies mobility. His scientific accomplishments (themselves the result of a "voyage") are depicted as progressive motion toward the total codification of Nature. His technological accomplishments permit greater freedom of movement in Nature (Nemo's motto, engraved on the *Nautilus*, is "Mobilis in mobile"). And his social status symbolizes the nineteenth-century ideal of the "self-made man," an individual who, through intelligence and work, has risen through the ranks to become a natural leader of others. In spite of their lofty social position, however, Verne's scientists are almost always portrayed as members of the bourgeois middle class. And the majority of their attitudes, their tastes, and their prejudices are a recognizable extension of that class (facilitating nineteenth-century reader identification with them); for example, knowledge is to be possessed, comfort to be increased, art to be collected, profit to be had, and so forth. All such traits consistently proselytize à la Saint-Simon the virtues of ownership and property. All are measured in terms of how far one has come, or one has yet to go. All are epistemological variants of the bourgeois will-to-accumulate.

If the scientist epitomizes the peak of the positive social pyramid, aborigines represent its lowest human level. Cannibals, in particular, are a constant thematic presence in Verne's texts, from the animalistic and bloodthirsty Nyam-Nyam tribes of central Africa in *Five Weeks in a Balloon*, to the more cultivated but equally vicious Maoris of New Zealand in *The Children of Captain Grant* and *Twenty Thousand Leagues under the Sea*, to the primitive and perpetually starved Australian tribes in *Mistress Branican*. They are most often characterized as human "beasts" and responsible for the slaughter of numerous scientific explorers (whom Verne dutifully enumerates, eulogizing them as martyrs of science). Even their orgiastic flesh feasts are depicted in the pages of the *Voyages Extraordinaires*, and sometimes in surprising detail—given the fact that these texts were destined for young readers and closely monitored by Hetzel. The following scene, for example, is representative:

Six poor wretches were brought before the dead bodies of their masters. They were the servants, now made slaves by the merciless rules of war. . . . They appeared to be resigned to their fate. . . .

Sudden knife thrusts by six robust warriors, and the victims dropped to the ground amid a widening pool of blood.

A horrible scene of cannibalism followed . . . The sacrifice now complete, a large mass of natives—chiefs, warriors, old men, women, children, of all ages and both sexes—went into a bestial frenzy and pounced on the lifeless remains of the victims. In less time than it takes to describe it, these bodies, though still warm, were torn apart, chopped up, and reduced to bits and pieces. Each of the two hundred Maoris at the sacrifice had his share of this human flesh. They fought over it, struggled, and argued over the smallest morsel. Warm drops of blood splattered over this repulsive horde, producing a red mist within which they swarmed. . . . (*Grant* II, 751, IA)

As Hetzel undoubtedly realized, the pedagogical function of such a scene is in its shock value as a comparative social model. It dramatically underscores "how far" modern civilization has progressed, much like the maps, sextants, and clocks discussed earlier. But it also valorizes the social standing of the scientist. He is seen as the heroic representative of the civilized world who intrepidly goes among such savages in the pursuit of knowledge. The living symbol of humanity's intellectual progress, it is the scientist who is also in touch with Man's anthropological origins. It is thus "natural" and quite proper that the scientist occupy the highest echelon in any unified social concept: his vision of the human species is an all-embracing one.

Built into this social hierarchy, of course, is a certain amount of elitism. As Michel Ardan phrases it, for example, in *Around the Moon*: "A few seconds from the life of a Pascal or a Newton are more precious than the entire lives of a crowd of imbeciles" (13, IA). But such elitism is usually tempered in Verne's texts by the scientists' paternal (occasionally paternalizing) concern for others, their personal modesty and sincerity, and their unshakeable "common sense" ethics.

In this respect, the scientists and engineers—of Verne's early works, at least— are natural leaders not only because of their great knowledge, but also because of their moral integrity and their devotion to human life. This basic altruism is evident, for example, in such fictional personages as Doctor Clawbonny who, in addition to his encyclopedic scientific wisdom, has the good-humored strength of character to be an unfailing source of moral support to his companions during their arduous trek to the North Pole: "This noble man was the soul of the group, a soul that glowed with honesty and justice. His companions trusted him totally; even Captain Hatteras liked and respected him. His kind words and his cheerful demeanor made living 6 degrees from the North Pole seem almost normal" (*Hatteras* 320, IA). Throughout the *Voyages Extraordinaires*, the scientists are often portrayed as a moral, as well as intellectual, emulative standard. And they are always "naturally" so. But one must understand that Verne's very conception of what is natural is itself an extension of his scientific Positivism. The scientist occupies the highest echelon in the social order for the same reason that homo sapiens are seen to be at the top of the animal kingdom—rational knowledge and awareness of "place." Such knowledge "naturally" breeds solidarity with one's own species. And the scientist incarnates human beings at their quantitative best in both regards.

These heroes, by their actions and their words, are emulative role models of the positive values of objectivity, courage, honor, prudence, optimism, virtue, honesty, and a commitment to hard work. Such moral traits are frequently depicted by Verne in terms of their usefulness, to one's own self as well as to others. For instance, they are shown to be the prerequisites for many types of success in life: financial, physical, intellectual, and spiritual. They allow one to overcome fear, or as Doctor Clawbonny put it: "Believe me, be good when it's possible to do so! Goodness is strength! . . . fear comes easily to those who try to be fearsome" (*Hatteras* 378, IA). And they provide one with the moral strength to act, rather than giving in to despair, in situations that seem hopeless. This latter quality could easily serve as an overall axiom for the moral didacticism of the *Voyages Extraordinaires*, so frequently is it evoked in these texts. Its most common expression is "It was not the moment to despair, but to act" (*Grant 593, IA*). The lesson is clear: one must not be passive, complacent, and "philosophical" in one's acceptance of the world, but rather seek to change it through disciplined and intelligent action. Needless to say, such a moral stance dovetails rather neatly with the ideological imperatives of conquest in Verne's "progressive" view of science and Nature, as noted above.

Hence, scientific knowledge imposes certain moral obligations. And foremost among them is the need to educate others. Scientific knowledge is not viewed as a private possession reserved exclusively for the "chosen few" in the upper registers of the social hierarchy, but rather as a huge and growing legacy willed to all humanity by its heroic explorers, experimenters, and scientific experts. As the chemist Cyprien Méré expressed it in *The Southern Star* when he became convinced that he had discovered a method to artificially synthesize diamonds:

> "Mister Watkins," he said solemnly, "if I kept the secret of my discovery to myself, I wouldn't be any better than a forger! I would be cheating the public on the quality of the merchandise that I sold them! The results of a scientist's experiments don't belong to him alone, but rather to society as a whole! In keeping the smallest part of it for himself, for personal gain, he would be committing one of the worst crimes that a man could commit! I won't do it!" (118, IA)

If true equality among people is contradictory to Nature's laws (because of their differing talents), all have nonetheless a common right of access to the benefits of science. If scientists and engineers are a privileged lot due to their understanding of the secrets of the physical universe, they have a moral duty to "enlighten" those beneath them. This ideological mandate is satisfied in a variety of ways by the Vernian scientist: by becoming a personal mentor and spiritual guide to some aspiring young lad and initiating him into the higher mysteries of science (like Lidenbrock and Axel in *Journey to the Center of the Earth*); by motivating, teaching, or coordinating members of a small community (like Cyrus Smith in *Mysterious Island*); or by becoming an object of national pride and an inspiration to its citizenry (like Barbicane in *From the Earth to the Moon*). But Verne's preferred means for assuring that the scientists' pedagogical message reaches the widest possible audience is (significantly) by having them write books.

Two successive motifs are very frequent in almost all of the early novels of the *Voyages Extraordinaires*: the scientist-hero triumphantly returns to his original point of departure, and he then promptly publishes his scientific findings. The return effectively closes the text (on the model of Ulysses returning to Ithaca) and re-establishes the status quo of the real world—a narrative trait

Professor Lidenbrock and Axel discover runes pointing their way toward the center of the earth (*Journey*, engraving by E. Riou, 1864)

quite common in the conclusions of many nineteenth-century fictional texts. The book motif extends the pedagogical element of the text into a fictional universality of global proportions, both in the geographical and in the ideological sense. That is to say, the scientist's publication is immediately greeted by the entire world as yet another "small step for man, but a giant leap for mankind," and the scientist receives glory and praise from all nations. But implicit in the scientist's fame are those same Positivistic presuppositions of science as the privileged decoder of the universe and the key to unlocking the mysteries of life, a presupposition now evidently shared by all the populations of the earth (the ultimate Saint-Simonian dream, the ultimate social conquest). As depicted in the conclusion of *Journey to the Center of the Earth*:

> To conclude, I must add that his *Journey to the Center of the Earth* created a sensation throughout the world. It was printed and translated into every language; the most eminent newspapers wrote up its principal episodes which were then discussed, commented on, and attacked or defended with equal conviction among opposing camps of believers and disbelievers. A rare thing: my uncle became a legend in his own lifetime, revelling in the glory he had acquired. (371, IA)

Verne thus neatly ties off the fictional, pedagogical, and ideological strands of his text with one richly polyvalent narrative device. And in so doing he accomplishes three additional narratological tasks.

First, he enhances the overall verisimilitude of his tale, the text of which is now seen to be the scientist's written account of his "voyage," produced from accumulated daily entries in his journal. In this respect, Verne's narrators are always careful to point out the details of this intratextual production. Time and again, the scientist (or one of his companions, designated as recorder) is shown jotting down the day's events in a log. For example, in *The Adventures of Captain Hatteras*, the narrator observes that "During his free time, the Doctor put his notes of the voyage in order—of which this narrative is the faithful reproduction" (371, IA). Entire chapters in novels such as *Journey to the Center of the Earth, The Chancellor, Mistress Branican,* or *The Amazing Adventure of the Barsac Mission* are composed uniquely of such daily entries. Certainly, this sort of activity is at the heart of taxonomic scientific methodology. But in biographical terms it also recalls Verne's own note-taking in the Bibliothèque Nationale, of which the novels of the *Voyages Extraordinaires* themselves are a kind of "faithful reproduction."

Second, in this conclusion Verne creates a realistic intertext for use in his own subsequent works. Throughout the *Voyages Extraordinaires*, one finds repeated reference to the characters, the plots, and the actual titles of novels belonging to this series. The most obvious manifestation of this phenomenon are the many "plugs" of his own novels that Verne manages to incorporate into his texts via footnotes, parenthetical anecdotes, prefaces, and even in the dialogue of his characters.[3] Another variant occurs in the three groups of serial novels consisting of the two trilogies of *The Children of Captain Grant/Twenty Thousand Leagues under the Sea/Mysterious Island* and *From the Earth to the Moon/Around the Moon/Topsy Turvy* and of the two-novel series of *Robur the Conqueror/Master of the World*.[4] In the first series, for instance, the castaways of *Mysterious Island*, having supposedly read Professor Aronnax's earlier publication called *Twenty Thousand Leagues under the Sea*, were then able immediately to "localize" the identity of the *Nautilus* and of Captain Nemo. Book knowledge is thus shown to be an eminently practical possession. But this practice of narrative self-reflection performs many other functions as well. Narratologically, it acts as a kind of fictional binder, adding a measure of unity to the series. Pedagogically, it points to Verne's own works as equal to those real scientific and literary works that he constantly cites (enhancing the didactic "author-ity" of the *Voyages Extraordinaires*). Semiotically, such self-referencing serves further to blur the boundaries between the real and the unreal, between fiction and nonfiction, between imagination and reality. The works cited enter into the signifying realm of the referent, thereby strengthening their own verisimilitude as real objects of mimesis.

Third, in this conclusion Verne draws attention to the value of his own works—both by emphasizing their useful character (rather than their literary merit!) and by dramatizing their huge public success. Such success, moreover, is described in commercial terms in addition to those of scientific accomplishment and personal celebrity. Do these "projections" constitute a kind of wishful thinking on Verne's part? Or can they be viewed as a self-fulfilling prophecy in the author's own lifetime? Or are they yet another instance of the text's (and author's) continuous practice of localization and self-reflection? All three interpretations seem reasonable, both biographically and textually.

Verne's linear and hierarchical vision of human progress is also expressed in these works via the many "constructive social applications" of scientific knowledge. Most of his early works are very optimistic in the regard, seeing in the industrial and technological uses of science an unending improvement of the human condition. Note, for example, the confident optimism in the following dialogue, taken from *The Steam House*, where the total conquest of the earth is envisioned:

> "Man, simple inhabitant of the Earth . . . even nailed to its crust, he can nevertheless discover all of its innermost secrets."
>
> "He can, and he must!" replied Banks. "All that's within the limits of the possible must and will be accomplished. Then, when Man has nothing more to learn of the globe that he inhabits. . . ."
>
> "He will disappear along with the sphere that has no more secrets for him," answered Captain Hod.
>
> "On the contrary!" replied Banks. "He will then reign as master over it, and bring out its very best." (274, IA)

The rapidity of such a conquest is most often evoked in Verne's works through the depiction of speed, such as the speed that modern technology generates in travel, communication, and industry. As described by Verne's fictional characters, such speed is awe inspiring, exhilarating, and, what's more, infinitely productive. Speed produces leisure, as in the case of the travelers of *The Steam House* who, comfortably ensconced in their luxurious coach, are able to visit all of India as their mechanical steam-driven elephant quickly transports them from one locale to another. Speed produces money, as the director of *The Thompson Travel Agency* well understands, as do the many game-players of *The Last Will of an Eccentric* who must scramble from state to state hoping to win millions in prize money. Speed even seems to produce time itself, as Phileas Fogg discovered (almost belatedly) at the conclusion of his rapid circumnavigation of the globe in *Around the World in 80 Days*.

A great many other constructive uses of scientific knowledge are touted in the novels of the *Voyages Extraordinaires*. Some of these ingenious technological applications serve to facilitate exploration of uncharted regions: the *Nautilus* roams the oceans and sea beds; Barbicane's space bullet circles the moon; Fergusson's balloon traverses central Africa, and so on. Some extend human life functions: the Galibert apparatus in *The Begum's Fortune*, which permits breathing in carbon dioxide; the similar Rouquayrol-Denayrouze apparatus for breathing underwater in *Twenty Thousand Leagues under the Sea*; the various telecommunication devices in *The Carpathian Castle* and in *The Day of an American Journalist in 2889*, which dramatically expand the field of normal vision and audition; or the helicopter airship that materializes the age-old dream of flight in *Robur the Conqueror* (the very title of which symbolizes science's conquest of Nature). And most such technology is shown to be very benevolent by nature and able to enhance (often even to save) human life: Davy's innovative mining lamp of *The Black Indies*, which lessens the risk of underground explosions; the electric power plant of *Propeller Island*, which provides the necessary energy for its population's lighting, heating, and transportational needs; or the Boynton wetsuits described in *The Tribulations of a Chinaman*, which allow Kin-Fo and his companions to survive the bitter coldness of the seas and to effectively navigate them.

Intrinsic to this socially constructive use of scientific knowledge—both for the invention of advanced technological devices and for simple daily problem solving—are a certain number of methodological presuppositions concerning human capacity to comprehend and control natural phenomena.

That is to say, Verne's confidence in Baconian classification as the pathway to knowledge (for an understanding of Nature) is also paralleled by his Cartesian faith in reason as the greatest tool humans have (for the conquest of Nature). And if the former leans heavily on the processes of naming and localizing within an ordered system—typical of Linnaean natural history or chemistry à la Lavoisier—the latter uses the principles of experimental logic, physical mechanics, and dynamics of force as its preferred instruments in the manner of Newton or Helmholtz. These are the two complementary modes of scientific thought that are the major ideological pillars upon which are constructed most of Verne's early *Voyages Extraordinaires*. Now we turn in more detail to the latter of these two modes of Positivism in Verne's texts, one I call "object-ive rationalism."

OBJECT-IVE RATIONALISM

If Nature is a wondrous but finite cryptogram to be deciphered via science, nonsubjective rational thought offers the individual the key not only to unlocking its mysteries but also to using them for his or her own purposes. It is revealing that the two *most* repeated thematic motifs throughout Verne's early works— and wholly pedagogical in their intent—are the following: the scientific explana- tion of what initially appears to be an enigma (natural or otherwise), and the resolution of a serious (and sometimes life-threatening) dilemma through deduc- tive reasoning. The first might be viewed as a textual manifestation of the nam- ing and localizing scientific approach described above, and the second a drama- tization of the productive use of empirical logic (object-ive rationalism)—the essence of scientific method.

For both, the narrative recipe is very often the same. The seemingly impene- trable nature of the enigma/problem is first vocalized by the vox populi person- age, and then the scientist of the group resolves the enigma/problem while carefully explaining his methodology and scientific references to his attentive "students." Consider, for example, the red snow encountered during the Hat- teras expedition:

> Imagine the group's surprise, their gasps, and even their first stirrings of fear as they confronted this crimson snowbank. The Doctor hastened to reassure and instruct his companions; he had heard of this strange red snow, and of the chemical analyses done upon it by Wollaston, de Candolle and Bauer. He explained that this snow was found not only in the Arctic, but also in Switzerland in the middle of the Alps. De Saussure collected a sizeable quantity of it on Le Breven in 1760, and, since that time, Captains Ross, Sabine, and other navigators have reported it during their northern expeditions.
> Altamont asked the Doctor about the nature of this extraordinary sub- stance, and the latter explained that the coloration was due to the pres- ence of microorganisms. For a long time, scientists wondered if these microorganisms were animal or vegetable; but they finally decided that they belonged to a species of microscopic mushrooms of the genus "Uredo" which Bauer proposed to call "Uredo nivalis." (*Hatteras* 400, IA)

Doctor Clawbonny's explanation of the strange red snow is typical of the use of taxonomic scientific methodology for the identification of a puzzling natural phenomenon and its place in the order of things. Other examples might include Aronnax's explanation of phosphorescent seawater (*20,000* 263-64, IA), Lidenbrock's giant subterranean mushrooms (*Journey* 240, IA), Cyrus Smith's mineral-bearing rocks (*Mysterious* 220-24, IA), Harbert's medicinal plants (*Mysterious* 253, IA), and Paganel's many species of birds (*Grant* 152, 212, 429, IA).

Similarly, consider the somewhat lengthy but quite typical demonstration of applied mathematical logic by Cyrus Smith:

Harbert, wishing to learn, followed the engineer to the base of the granite cliff. . . .

Cyrus Smith had brought along a straight stick 12 feet long which he had measured as closely as possible, comparing it to his own height . . . Harbert carried a plumb bob—a stone attached to a stringy piece of plant fiber—that Cyrus Smith had given him.

Twenty feet from the edge of the shore and about 500 feet from the granite cliff that rose perpendicularly from the sand, Cyrus Smith planted the stick and, wedging it carefully while using the plumb bob, he succeeded in making it stand perfectly perpendicular to the horizon.

That done, he moved back a distance needed so that, while lying down on the sand, his line of sight crossed both the tip of the stick and the top of the cliff. Next he marked that spot in the sand with a stake.

Then he turned to ask Harbert: "Are you familiar with the principles of geometry?" "A little, monsieur Cyrus," answered Harbert somewhat hesitantly. "Do you remember the properties of two similar triangles?" "Yes," replied Harbert. "Their corresponding sides are proportionate." "Well, my child, I've just constructed two similar triangles, one within the other: the first, the smaller of the two, has for its sides the perpendicular stick, the distance separating the stake from the bottom of the stick, and my line of sight as the hypoteneuse; the second has as its sides the perpendicular cliff—the height of which we wish to measure—the distance separating the stake from the base of this cliff, and my line of sight again as its hypoteneuse which extends that of the first triangle." "Ah! monsieur Cyrus, I understand!" exclaimed Harbert.

The horizontal distances were recorded. . . .

These measurements taken, Cyrus Smith and the young lad returned to the Chimneys. There, the engineer took a flat piece of stone that he had brought back from earlier excursions—a kind of slate schist—on which he wrote some numbers with the help of a sharp shell. He first set up the following equations:

$$15 : 500 : : 10 : X \qquad \frac{5000}{15} = 333.33$$

$$500 \times 10 = 5000$$

From which it was learned that the cliff measured three hundred and thirty-three feet high. (*Mysterious* 179–80, IA)

This latter thematic mode—the use of rational deductive logic for the solving of concrete problems—is the more commonly practiced of these two brands of scientific methodology in Verne's texts. And its fictional variants are many, both in number and in kind. They range in nature from one complex theoretical problem constituting the raison d'être of an entire novel (as in *From the Earth to the Moon*) to a seemingly unending series of practical engineering tasks (as in *Mysterious Island*). Such problems are not always totally resolved. If not, it is usually due to some recognizable error in the scientist's methodology (like the misplaced decimal in *Topsy Turvy*). Or if successful, the resulting solution sometimes causes more harm than good—usually due to basic human frailty (like the blind vengefulness of the scientist in *For the Flag*). The first two problem-solving variants are typical of Verne's earlier, more positivistic texts. The latter two occur more often in his later, more pessimistic and/or satirical works. But the procedure itself, regardless of its outcome, is almost always the same: the application of the magic wand of scientific method to the issue at hand. As the scientists of Verne's texts repeatedly say when faced with an enigma to be decoded or a project to be undertaken: "Let's reason this out" (*Mysterious* 702, IA), "That must be it, because there is a logic to everything here on Earth" (*Hatteras* 106, IA), and "When Science has spoken, it behooves one to remain silent!" (*Journey* 126, IA). Or, as the "common men" often exclaim when admiring the scientists' reasoning powers: "Ah! you practical men! . . . Positivistic souls! I admire you" (*Moon* 18-19, IA). Or, even as the invisible Vernian narrators affirm when valorizing such rationality: "In speaking thus, lieutenant Procope had to be speaking truth because he was speaking logically" (*Servadac* 430, IA). The lesson to be inferred by the reader is clear: more than simply a means for attaining truth, logic *is* truth.

As demonstrated earlier in this chapter, Verne's belief in Nature and science as structured totalities (and in all human progress as definable within that context) generated a number of spin-off narrative structures throughout his *romans scientifiques*. Likewise, the analytical procedures used in Verne's portrayal of scientific method are also pregnant with presuppositions and implications that spill over into many other areas of his fiction. And as such they constitute another important (scientifically derived) ideological subtext influencing the character of these novels.

For example, consider the intellectual mechanism most basic to such analytical reasoning: the initial object-ification of the problem. This procedure involves the conceptualization of all physical phenomena as objects, with each reducible to its constituent parts (seen to be its causes), and each ultimately explainable via the measurement of such parts (the whole seen to be no more or no less than the sum of the parts). This particular attitude is central to Verne's view of the essence of scientific methodology. And, predictably, its fictional articulation in the *Voyages Extraordinaires* is correspondingly ubiquitous. Note the analytical procedures used, for example, in Cyrus Smith's successful fabrication of nitroglycerine, in Robur's mechanical conquest of gravity, in Cyprien Méré's attempts to artificially create diamonds, or in Dr. Sarrasin's establishment of that utopia of hygiene called Franceville in *The Begum's Fortune*, to cite but a few examples.

But it is the use of this same modus operandi in Verne's treatment of a wide variety of human and social phenomena that constitutes an even more effective illustration of its status as a determinative ideological matrix. For example, in addition to his portrayal of society as a structured and hierarchical object, witness Verne's repeated use of the beehive as a metaphor for the social organization required to accomplish great scientific tasks in such novels as *The Black Indies* and *For the Flag*, among others. Similar to the industrial magnates of his era, Verne visualizes human effort as the constituent parts of an abstract labor force—a mass of objects, the correct manipulation of which (following their measurement according to merit) always yields the desired results and/or the solution to the problem. Or in addition to Verne's portrayal of scientists and engineers as walking encyclopedias, consider the overall mechanical quality of his characterizations. Fictional characters are continually described as assemblages of their respective physiognomical traits, each trait, in true Balzacian fashion, having its psychological and/or moral counterpart. Each character is treated as an object, defined by the sum of his or her parts and each part measurable according to such quantitative standards as muscular force (Cap Manifou in *Mathias Sandorf*), keenness of vision (Paganel's *nyctalopie*), precision of movement (Phileas Fogg), glibness of speech (Michel Ardan), and so on. Rare are the Vernian villains who do not exhibit cunning eyes or a sneering laugh. Rare are the Vernian heroines who are not blond and lithesome. And rare are the Vernian heroes who do not combine the features of early middle age (35–50), robust health, a high forehead, and thick curly hair.

Verne's (often criticized) mechanical characterizations are perhaps best exemplified by his frequent use of the principles of phrenology when initially describing his protagonists. The configuration of their cranial "bumps" is repeatedly cited as one way to objectively ascertain their intellectual capabilities, their psychic makeup in general, and their hidden moral inclinations. A typical example of this (once again quite reductive) use of "scientific" methodology is the following description of Michel Ardan in *From the Earth to the Moon*.

He was 42 years old, tall but already somewhat stooped like those caryatids that support balconies on their shoulders. His head was strong and covered with thick hair like a lion's mane. His face was short with a broad forehead and adorned with a moustache as bristly as a cat's; patches of yellowish whiskers grew on his full cheeks; round, wildish eyes that were a little myopic completed his very feline physiognomy. But his nose was firmly shaped, his mouth particularly expressive, his forehead high, intelligent, and furrowed with wrinkles like a newly-plowed field. His body was powerfully developed and stood firmly upon long legs. Strong, muscular arms and a decisive walk gave this European an appearance of solidity— "forged rather than smelted," to borrow a metallurgical expression.

From his cranium and his physiognomy, disciples of Lavater or Gratiolet would have easily deciphered tendencies of combativeness, courage, a willingness to overcome obstacles, benevolence, and a passion for impossible undertakings. On the other hand, they would have noticed that bumps indicating possessiveness and a need for material acquisitions were totally lacking. (221-22, IA)

In reading this portrayal of an archetypal Vernian hero, it is important to understand that this particular approach to fictional characterization—consistently condemned by critics as "superficial," "wooden," and "nonliterary"—is but an extension of those ideological parameters intrinsic to his chosen subject matter. That is to say, it is an object-ive fictional exposition of scientific methodology, where observable "facts" are seen to be rationally tied to overall "laws" (even if such laws, as in this case, are ultimately proven wrong). Each such characterization is a kind of scientific (and moral) *object* lesson, pedagogical in its intent and representative of a higher ordering system. In such a system human beings are seen as taxonomically analyzable objects. And a logical scientific account of their exterior physiognomy (like Conseil's fish, Paganel's birds, or Bénédict's insects) enables one to accurately define them. The implicit assumption, of course, in this reductive analytical procedure is that there exists a linear and one-dimensional causality linking the personage's moral character to physical appearance, and vice versa—a basic presupposition that is never questioned in Verne's wholly empirical treatment of the human species.

The practices of rational object-ivity and quantification have their moral counterparts in the *Voyages Extraordinaires* as well. Personal discipline and respect for authority and order are constantly proselytized, as is the necessary repression of one's emotions. The former is clearly discernible in Verne's texts in the authoritarian relationship of a captain (*Seul maître après Dieu*) to his crew, as depicted, for example, in *The Adventures of Captain Hatteras, Twenty Thousand Leagues under the Sea, Robur the Conqueror,* or *The Boy Captain.* This rapport also extends to the relationship between the Vernian scientists and their apprentices or coworkers (*Journey to the Center of the Earth* and *Mysterious Island*) as well as in the Vernian engineers' relationship to their laborers as in *From the Earth to the Moon,* where "Daily life was structured with discipline ... with perfect order" (177, IA). In human relations as in machines, efficiency of operation is a necessary prerequisite to achieving optimum productivity. And the most efficient organizational structure—in scientific research and technological invention, as in the military, as in manufacturing—is shown to be the ordered division of labor, the necessity of uniform discipline, and the concentration of decision making in the hands of a "natural" leader.

The latter moral ramification of object-ive rationalism in Verne's texts (the repression of emotions) is a standard personality trait of the great majority of his heroes. Masters of knowledge and masters of men, they are also "masters" of themselves. Accordingly, they are viewed by their peers as being sufficiently unshakeable and *maître de soi* to warrant their leadership roles (for example, Gordon of *The Two Year Vacation,* 28, IA). Such emotional control—along with their capacity to *agir*—is usually demonstrated in moments of crisis as well as at times of high narrative pathos. For example, note the following portrayal of Captain Hatteras as his vessel was running low on fuel in the Arctic: "If Hatteras didn't let his worries show on the outside, he felt them violently on the inside" (*Hatteras* 113, IA). Or the aplomb of Colonel Monro in a similar situation aboard the *Géant d'Acier* in India: "Colonel Monro considered the situation calmly. He felt no despair. Not the kind of man to give in to adversity, he pre-ferred looking at things realistically rather than clinging to some illusion which was unbecoming of one whom nothing could perturb" (*Steam* 481, IA).

Such rigorous self-control—rendered even more impressive by the violence of the emotions felt—attempts to neutralize the potentially negative impact of the hero's personal feelings on this rational objectivity and ability to reason logically. Such self-control, for example, requires the dissimulation of shock, as in the case of Mathias Sandorf where he learns of the existence of a daughter whom he had supposed lost at infancy: "Therefore, when the name of his daughter was sud-denly blurted out by Mme Bathory, he had enough control over himself to dominate his emotions. But his heart had stopped beating for a second and, had he been less master of himself, he would've dropped to the floor of the chapel as if struck by lightning" (*Mathias* II, 271, IA). It also requires the dissimulation of exclamations of joy, as in the case of Cyrus Smith following the success of one of his many engineering feats: "Cyrus Smith's plan had succeeded. But, as was his nature, he demonstrated no satisfaction. With no smile on his lips and his gaze steady, he remained unmoved and unmoving. Harbert was enthusiastic; Nab jumped with joy; Pencroff bobbed his head, muttering, 'He's all right, our engineer!'" (*Mysterious* 231, IA). And such self-control even requires the mask-ing of any expression of sentimentality, as in the case of the company of *The Amazing Adventure of the Barsac Mission* following Jane Buxton's tearful exhor-tation to continue their search for her lost brother: "She wasn't the only one to have tears in her eyes. Everyone was emotionally touched. But the men of the group struggled to hide it" (*Barsac* 204, IA).

The lesson is clear. The conquest of Nature by reason begins with the con-quest of one's self—the domination of one's own sentiments and the constant suppression of one's own subjectivity. In other words, it begins with one's deliberate and self-directed object-ification.

Another ideological spin-off of Verne's scientific perspective is the view of human relations as essentially conflictual, itself an extension of the Positivist view of the human being's overall relationship to Nature. This attitude is rein-forced in Verne's plot structures by the recurring presence of the "good guys versus bad guys" theme and the "us versus them" approach to problem solving, where one scientist's theories are pitted against another's, for instance. Para-digms of competition and contest are frequent throughout Verne's *Voyages Extraordinaires*, and the repeated depiction of one-upmanship (another sort of linear measurement) assumes a variety of forms in these texts. They are evi-dent not only in the many scientific endeavors described (the race to the North Pole, the rivalry of geographers in naming new sites, the lighter-than-air versus the heavier-than-air aeronauts, and the like), but also in the human and social sides of Verne's fictions. For example, various nationalities—seen as races—are often ranked in terms of their comparative force and stamina, their moral development, their riches, or their propensity for technical achievement.[5] Interpersonal disputes are settled by duels, by wagers, or by a demonstration of physical, intellectual, or moral strength.[6] Further, a protagonist's "competitive" worth is most often assessed not only by the amount of scientific knowledge he possesses but also by the level of his *énergie.*[7]

The measurement of one's energy—consistently used as a physical and moral determinant—is yet another very important locus for illustrating the impact of the basic principles of science on the ideology of Verne's narrative practice. The calculation of a phenomenon's energy—potential or kinetic—is fundamental to the laws of thermodynamics. More energy begets more power, both internally and externally, that is, both in the intrinsic strength of the object and in its capacity to affect other objects. And so it is with Verne's fictional protagonists. The typical Vernian hero is invariably described as having, in addition to a firm control over his emotions and a strong sense of competitiveness, a large amount of physical and moral *énergie.*

Witness, for example, the following cases: Captain Hatteras is described as "a man of great energy" who has an "energetic face," much "patriotic energy," and an "energetic constitution" (*Hatteras* 89–92, 186, IA). Cyrus Smith exhibits "superhuman energy: always active in body and spirit, impetuous, with incredible willpower" (*Mysterious* 14, IA). And Dick Sand's "intelligent physiognomy glows with energy" and his personality exudes a "moral energy anchored in his sense of duty"—a trait that causes one of his passengers to say that "because of your physical and spiritual energy, you have shown yourself to be a man, a man worthy of leadership" (*Boy* 20, 135, IA). Conversely, one of the principal features of nonheroic protagonists in Verne's texts is their relative lack of energy. Consider, for example, the weak-willed captain of the doomed ship in *Le Chancellor*, of whom the narrator explains, "It grew impossible to believe that this man had any character or sufficient physical and spiritual energy . . ." and "he has neither sangfroid nor energy" (4, 36, IA); or the banker's wife Madame Toronthal in *Mathias Sandorf* who, completely dominated by her husband, is described as "a woman lacking any moral energy" (310, IA). Once again, Verne turns to the basic elements and nomenclature of science for the metaphors to "flesh out" his fictional characterizations. His portrayal of human nature—like his view of the physical universe—is, once again, a direct derivative of his overall scientific empiricism. The narratological building blocks chosen are those that exemplify the physics of force and power.

Such then are a few of the ideological parameters of Verne's Positivism as evident in his scientific novels. Essentially taxonomic and hierarchical in their definition of the universe and object-ively rationalistic in their definition of Man (a composite of both Baconian and Cartesian thought), they serve as a comprehensive support structure to Verne's pedagogy, reinforcing the many lessons embedded in these fictions. Such pervasive ideology highlights the social function of the *Voyages Extraordinaires* as an educative instrument, one that seeks to provide its readers with both a unified and ordered vision of reality as well as a means to more effectively cope with it; one that attempts to dealienate science, both as a philosophy and as a practical tool, and to proselytize its value for a deeper understanding of (and one's survival in) the modern world.

NOTES

1. V. Pierre Macherey, "Jules Verne ou le récit en défaut," *Pour une théorie de la production littéraire* (Paris: Maspero, 1966), pp. 183–266.

2. V. Eugenio Donato, "The Museum's Furnace: Notes toward a Contextual Reading of *Bouvard et Pécuchet*." In Josué Harari, ed., *Textual Strategies* (Ithaca, NY: Cornell University Press, 1979), pp. 213–38.

3. Note, for example, the "theatre" conversations between M. and Mme. Caterna in *Claudius Bombarnac* (115) where casual mention is made of *Michel Strogoff* playing at Châtelet (it was during this period, of course, that the play was actually being shown there) or the many footnotes in *Topsy Turvy*—perhaps added by Hetzel?—that refer to previously published Vernian novels such as *The School for Crusoes* (31), *From the Earth to the Moon* and *Around the Moon* (43), *The Adventures of Captain Hatteras* (978), or *Hector Servadac* (160). One quite feasible hypothesis for the inclusion of such references could be the sluggish sales of Verne's later novels; these repeated "advertisements"—often quite gratuitously inserted into the text—occur only in those novels written after 1889. And it was precisely during this period that the booming sales of the *Voyages Extraordinaires* began to taper off, due in part to the changed educational environment of the Third Republic and the influx of similar texts of didactic fiction into the French publishing marketplace.

4. In these texts, the same characters reappear and continue the saga in a new setting, or one character provides the link between an earlier novel and a subsequent one: Robur is the hero and antihero successively, Barbicane and the Gun Club continue their (literally) world-shaking projects, Ayrton is discovered on the South Sea island where he was marooned, and so on.

5. For example, the competition among cash-raising nations to fund the space project of *From the Earth to the Moon* (145–58), the stamina of the French versus Americans in *Around the Moon* (24), German versus Italian opera in *Hector Servadac* (1, 4), Northerners versus Southerners in *Propeller Island* (120, 139), the race for technology among nations in *Master of the World* (344), various nations' reactions to a UFO sighting in *Robur the Conqueror* (10–18), and so on.

6. V., for example, *Robur the Conqueror* (1), *Around the World in 80 Days* (22–24), *Twenty Thousand Leagues under the Sea* (366), *Journey to the Center of the Earth* (46–51).

7. For an interesting look at Verne in the context of the nineteenth century's epistemological fixations on energy, v. Mireille Coutrix-Gouaux, "A Propos de matière et énergie chez Jules Verne," *Europe* 595–96 (1978), 3–9; also Alain Buisine, "Machines et énergetique" in François Raymond, ed., *Jules Verne III: Machines et imaginaire* (Paris: Minard, 1980), pp. 25–52.

CHAPTER 5

The Romantic Vision

A second major ideological subtext exists within Verne's oeuvre—one that serves to broaden and enhance the scientific didacticism of this series. And it does so by anchoring such pedagogy to certain nineteenth-century literary conventions and recognizable cultural archetypes. Acting as a counterweight to the empirical and rationalistic discourse in these texts, certain Romantic narrative elements add an esthetic and emotive dimension to these works, significantly increasing their overall phatic content and artistic appeal. Their function in the *Voyages Extraordinaires* is curiously double: rendering science more palatable and easier to assimilate on the one hand; questioning (particularly in Verne's later works) the social and moral implications of such science on the other.

Accordingly, to examine the nature and function of this second ideological aspect of Verne's *Voyages Extraordinaires*, let us proceed in two phases: first, to identify those Romantic components that complement (but do not contradict) the Positivistic proselytism in these texts, and second, to point out those that appear to consciously subvert it. The former are standard fare of those novels, written from 1862 to the mid-1880s during the first half of Verne's literary production, for which he is most known. The latter are found in progressively growing numbers from the mid-1880s to the end of his life, a period of increasing pessimism and—significantly—lack of Hetzelian censorship (the publisher having died in 1886).

CONTEMPLATION AND EXOTICISM

Within Verne's fictional universe, Nature is portrayed as an object not only of scientific conquest but also of esthetic contemplation. Its methodical "decoding" by science does not destroy its intrinsic grandeur or its power to captivate the affective imagination of those who grapple with its mysteries. In true Romantic fashion, Nature represents an ever-changing *état d'âme* for the protagonists of these novels—triggering numerous *rêveries* and often generating long passages of poetic description. Such passages act as a narratological counterpoint to the repeated (and wholly empirical) exposés of scientific pedagogy in these works, varying the discursive register and the overall tone of the narration while allowing it to "touch" the reader emotionally as well as intellectually. Science is thus enhanced in two ways: it is shown to be a tool for knowledge (an intermediary to truth) as well as a medium for esthetic appreciation (an intermediary to beauty).

Emphasizing the sensorial and analogical dimensions of human perception, such descriptions are most often metaphorical in nature and lean heavily on the connotative (as opposed to the scientifically denotative) aspects of language. They repeatedly utilize the favored Romantic tropes of antithesis and oxymoronic justaposition when depicting the dynamism and power of Nature's elements. For example, consider Dr. Clawbonny's pensive contemplation of what Verne suggestively called The Ice Desert near the North Pole:

> The moon, almost full once again, shone with incredible brightness in the pure sky. The light from the stars shimmered with intensity. From the summit of the iceberg, one could look across the vast frozen plain, bristling with strangely shaped mounds. To see them scattered there—glistening in the lunar light and criss-crossed against their own shadows like so many upright columns or fallen masts, like tombstones—made one think of a gigantic cemetery without trees, sad and still, infinite, as if twenty generations had taken their eternal rest there.
>
> Despite the cold and his fatigue, the Doctor became so pensive that his companions had difficulty in bringing him out of it. (*Hatteras* 208, IA)

One recognizes in this passage the typical Romantic theme (à la Byron, Lamartine) of the thoughtful poet-hero perched atop a mountain peak, gazing across a wide expanse of almost limitless space, and musing things eternal. The symbolism of the poet's "elevation" and "vision" is too obvious to warrant extensive commentary. But it is significant that, in Verne's world, the poet's role is now played by the scientist. And the localization motif discussed earlier is evoked once again—this time in spiritual terms rather than geographical, where the finding of one's place in the universe is less a function of one's physical coordinates than of one's metaphysical meditations (both shown to be equally "fixating").

Another even richer example of this particular theme (one of Verne's favorites) is the following, drawn from *Twenty Thousand Leagues under the Sea.* It relates the thoughts of Professor Aronnax as Captain Nemo escorts him on an underwater promenade somewhere in the mid-Atlantic:

> I looked out and saw an immense clearing lit by violent flashes of light. This underwater mountain was a volcano! Fifty feet below its peak, beneath

The sunken continent of Atlantis
(*20,000*, engraving by A. de Neuville, 1870)

a veritable rain of rocks and slag, a wide crater was spewing forth torrents of lava that streamed like a fiery cascade through the seawater. Like a huge torch, this volcano illuminated the plain below as far as the horizon. . . .

Suddenly, before my eyes were the ruins of a demolished city—its roofs caved in, its temples collapsed, its arches broken, its columns lying on the ground . . . Over there, the remains of a gigantic aqueduct. Here, the foundations of an Acropolis and the floating piers of an ancient port which must have harbored merchant vessels and war triremes . . . Further over, long lines of crumbled walls, wide empty streets, an entire Pompeii buried beneath the waves . . . Captain Nemo had brought it all back to life before my eyes.

Where was I? What was this place? . . .

Captain Nemo came up and gestured to me. Then, picking up a piece of chaulky stone, he walked over to a rock of black basalt and traced out a single word:

ATLANTIS. (*20,000* 419–22, IA)

In this memorable episode, Verne combines the same traditional Romantic motifs (and narrative devices) noted above with a few additional ones: the rites of initiation (where Nemo acts as the guide/mentor), the "ubi sunt" topos (with the ruins of a lost civilization serving as the catalyst), along with a well-known primordial myth (Atlantis). The first valorizes the intrinsic power of science and technology for solving historical enigmas as well as physical ones. The second underscores the ephemeral nature of human creations before the omnipotent forces of Nature. And the last dramatically brings to life one of the most ancient preoccupations of occidental civilization in its search for its own roots—a mythic reference whose tangible materialization in the text charges the scene as a whole with a kind of atavistic emotional appeal.

A fascination with the distant past is a constant narrative trait of Verne's texts, and it very often takes this form of a "search for one's origins." This recurring theme highlights the notion of continuity with one's predecessors, not only those of the familial sort (as in the case of the lost father in *The Children of Captain Grant*) or those "in the profession" (as in most of Verne's novels where the protagonists are "following in the footsteps" of previous explorers, scientists, or inventors),[1] but also in a larger evolutionary sense, that is, the origins of the human being as a species or the prehistory of the world as a whole. Take, for example, the case of the incredible Cro-Magnon giant in *Journey to the Center of the Earth* (318, IA) where Verne steps well beyond the scientific data of his time to exhibit a living specimen of the prehistoric past. Or consider the astronomic origins of the solar system as depicted in *From the Earth to the Moon* (52–57, IA) or the geological/organic beginnings of islands and atolls as explained in *Twenty Thousand Leagues under the Sea* (202–3, IA). Frequently, such contemplations of the past are both literal and all-encompassing. They depict, in museumlike fashion, the totality of the evolutionary process itself—as in the following scene from *Journey to the Center of the Earth*:

We were advancing with difficulty over these granite fragments imbedded with flint, quartz, and alluvial deposits, when we suddenly came upon a field, or rather a wide plain, covered with bones. It looked like an immense cemetery, where the generations of twenty centuries comingled their eternal remains. Great mounds of bones extended as far as the horizon, disappearing into the distant mist. There, within perhaps 3 square miles, was accumulated the entire history of animal life, a history only barely recorded in the too-recent strata of the inhabited world. . . . The lives of a thousand Cuviers would not have been enough to reconstruct all the skeletons contained in this magnificent ossuary. (303, IA)

Sometimes, however, such a spectacle is purely imaginary—a romanticized scientific reverie, brought on by speculative hypothesis but quickly metamorphosing into a kind of evolutionary hallucination. Such is the case, for instance, in Axel's paleontological "dream" in *Journey to the Center of the Earth*. This scene—dramatically reenacting the earth's entire history—once again reflects Verne's uniquely eclectic Positivist/Romantic narrative practice as he combines the technicisms of scientific pedagogy with the expressive metaphors of a spiritual pilgrimage. Verne mixes evolutionary theory with anthropomorphic religious creationism (a standard trait of his cautiously "neutral" ideological stance in all matters relating to Genesis) as he creates a sweeping vision of the origins of plant and animal life on Earth, and the cosmic birth of the very planet itself:

My imagination, however, carried me away into the wondrous hypotheses of palaeontology, and, wide awake, I began to dream. I fancied I could see floating on the water huge *chersites*, antedeluvian tortoises like floating islands. Along the dark shores there passed the great mammals of early times, the *leptotherium*, found in the caverns of Brasil, and the *mericotherium*, from the glacier regions of Siberia. . . . the pachyderme *lophiodon*, a gigantic tapir . . . an *anoplotherium*, . . . a giant mastodon. . . .

This entire prehistoric world came to life in my mind. I journeyed back to the biblical periods of creation, long before the birth of Man, when the unfinished world was not yet ready for him. Then my dream took me even further back, before the appearance of living creatures. . . . The entire life of Earth was contained in me, and my heart was the only one beating in that depopulated world. There were no longer any seasons or climates; the globe's own warmth increased steadily, becoming greater than that provided by the Sun. The vegetation grew to gigantic proportions and I walked like a ghost among aborescent ferns, treading uncertainly on iridescent marl and variegated stone. I leaned against the trunks of huge conifers and lay down in the shade of *sphenophyllas, asterophyllas* and *lycopods* a hundred feet high.

Centuries flew by like days! I went back through the long series of the Earth's transformations. Plants disappeared; granite rocks softened; solid matter turned to liquid under the action of the intense heat; water covered the surface of the globe, boiling and turning to steam which engulfed the Earth which, itself, gradually became a huge gaseous mass, white-hot, as big and bright as the Sun.

In the center of this nebula, fourteen hundred thousand times as large as the globe would someday become, I was then carried through interplanetary space. My body, in its turn, etherized and became spirit and mingled like an imponderable atom within these vast vapors that traced their flaming orbits through infinity! (259–62, IA)

"The entire life of Earth was contained in me." What statement could better epitomize the homocentric transcendentalism of the Romantic's world view? And what statement could better describe the Positivist conception of humankind as an example of Nature's most perfected species—a species in whom, biologically, "ontogeny recapitulates phylogeny" and whose scientific vision is universal?

In Verne's *romans scientifiques*, science is thus used as the logistical springboard to a Romantic contemplation of Nature, facilitating a perspective that is both totalizing and unique. Science provides the Vernian hero with the technological and/or intellectual means to attain a privileged observational vantage point, an "elevated" view of reality that is both enlightening and intrinsically poetic. Time and again in the *Voyages Extraordinaires*, the extraordinary quality of such observations is eulogized, pointing out the exclusive position of the scientist among other humans. Scientists are shown to be true trailblazers of new frontiers, not only in matters of applied empirical analysis but also in the realm of visual esthetics.

The use of science in the *Voyages Extraordinaires* as a vehicle for the poetic contemplation of Nature is paralleled by its role as a purveyor of the exotic. Satisfying the Romantic *soif d'un ailleurs*, the typical Vernian voyage may be defined in essence as a fictional journey to "otherness": other times, other places, other peoples, other customs, other forms of plant and animal life, and (more importantly) other ways of thinking. And among Verne's most favored settings in this regard are those that conform to the basic Romantic notions of exoticism: those that are far away (geographically and/or culturally), highly unusual, and picturesque. For example, the "dark continent" of Africa is intrinsically exotic,[2] as is India or the Far East.[3] Any milieu that exhibits a certain "gothic" quality fits the description[4] as does the pristine simplicity of the South Seas.[5] North America, the untamed Far West in particular, is richly exotic,[6] as are the islands of Iceland, New Zealand, and the West Indies.[7] And, of course, any geographical locale whose borders lie outside of normal human experience is quintessentially exotic—whether it be underwater, polar, subterranean, or even in outer space.[8]

But it is not enough that the overall milieu of the action be seen as an exotic locale. The text must consistently anchor such exoticism in various *effets de réel*[9] that are indigenous to that setting to enhance narrative verisimilitude and to maintain mimesis. And the *réel* depicted is most often defined according to specific reader expectations, that is, by stereotypes and clichés, as much as by accuracy of representation. Thus, there must be cannibals in Africa and head-hunters in Polynesia, Indians on the warpath in America and opium smokers in China, gauchos in Argentina and Eskimos in the Arctic. And each must exhibit life-styles, customs, and tools that correspond to their expected status as "the exotic other": villages of thatched huts and rites to pagan gods, "bowie-knifs" (sic) and death ships returning the deceased to their native land, bolas and foul-smelling igloos. Such a narrative requirement even extends to their respective languages. Verne's texts contain a veritable host of foreign tongues, ranging from the not-so-exotic (as Dutch, Spanish, Romanian), to the mildly exotic (Danish, Swedish, American English), to the highly exotic (Chinese, Arabic, the African dialect of Bambarra). There are even a number of artificial and/or invented languages like those of Nemo's crew in *Twenty Thousand Leagues under the Sea* or of the Wagddis in *The Village in the Treetops*.

But it is especially in his descriptions of the unusual flora and fauna of these various locales that Verne's scientific pedagogy becomes closely intertwined with his portrayal of the exotic. The following scene describing the prairies of Australia is a typical case in point:

> A wonderful plain, mottled with chrysanthemums, stretched beyond White Lake. The next morning at dawn, Glenarvan and his companions marveled at the magnificent landscape before their eyes. . . . Only a few distant mounds broke the perfect flatness of the ground; as far as the horizon, the prairie was covered with the erubescent flowers of spring. The blue of small flax blossoms glittered among the scarlet of acanthus. . . . Here and there, varieties of eremophilias added their bright colors. . . . The salty soil was covered with blue-green goosefoot and the beet-red colors of the hearty chenopod family—plants that are useful to industry because they make an excellent soda ash if one burns them and then washes their ashes. Paganel, who instantly became a botanist amid all these flowers, called each by name and, with his usual passion for counting everything, proclaimed that there were 4,200 known types of plants belonging to 100 different families in Australia's flora. (*Grant* 416, IA)

Or in the following episode the teeming ocean life of the Arctic's "open sea" is described in *The Adventures of Captain Hatteras*—another representative example of Verne's (somewhat enumerative) mixing of scientific pedagogy and narrative exoticism:

> Then, when his eyes left the wonders of the skies and fell to the calm surface of this ocean, he discovered species of animal life even more incredible: among others, medusas 30 feet in diameter . . . floating like islands in the middle of the algae and giant seaweed. How astonishing! And what a difference from those microscopic medusae observed by Scoresby in the seas of Greenland which this navigator estimated at approximately 11,944,000,000,000 per square mile!

Below the surface of these clear waters, the spectacle . . . was even more breathtaking. There were thousands of fish of every kind and description. . . . As legendary as the unicorn and armed with its long conical horn used to saw through icefields, a narwhale chased a timid cetacean. A host of whales spewed up tall columns of water and mucilage, filling the air with a whistling noise. The Northern with its slender tail and wide dorsal fins sped through the waves with incomparable speed, feeding on marine life as rapid as itself like the *gadus* or *scomber*. A White whale, more lethargic, peacefully munched on molluscs as slow-moving and indolent as itself. . . .

What beauty and variety! How powerful Nature is! Everything appeared so strange and awesome in these circumpolar regions! (*Hatteras* 416–18, IA)

Notice in the above passages the narrative oscillation between technicisms and anthropomorphisms, between numerical precision and hyperbole, between succinct analytical exposé and colorful impressionistic analogy. And the natural exoticism of the flora and fauna portrayed is intensified rather than diminished by the scientific nomenclature used to identify them—a consistent (if somewhat ironic) effect of the use of such specialized terminology in literary discourse, the particular "distancing" mechanisms of which are discussed in a later chapter.

MYTH, MAN, AND MAGIC

The implicit Romanticism in Verne's treatment of Nature is also evident in his treatment of science and technology. More than just a vehicle for solving problems or providing a "privileged" view of natural phenomena, science and technology are often portrayed in the *Voyages Extraordinaires* as being intrinsically poetic in their own right. This esthetic valorization is usually expressed in one of three different ways in Verne's texts: a myth-ification of the Promethean grandeur of the human conquest of the cosmos, the visual and/or tactile humanification of the technological devices involved, or the magic-fication of science itself—where it acquires the wondrous properties of sorcery.

A representative example of the first variant is the following, drawn from *From the Earth to the Moon*, where the titanic cannon called Columbiad is being created. This scene occurs in a chapter entitled *La Fête de la fonte* (The Festival of the Casting):

Twelve o'clock struck! A cannon-shot suddenly boomed and lit the air with its flame. Twelve hundred melting troughs were simultaneously opened and twelve hundred fiery serpents, unfurling their incandescent coils, slithered toward the central pit. There, they plunged down with a great roar into the 900 foot depths. It was an exciting and magnificent spectacle. The ground trembled as these molten waves, throwing billows of smoke toward the sky, evaporated the humidity of the mold, hurling it upwards through the vent-holes of the stone lining and forming a dense mist. These

artificial clouds rose in thick spirals thousands of feet into the sky. A
native, wandering somewhere beyond the limits of the horizon, might have
believed that some new crater was being formed in the center of Florida,
although there was no eruption, typhoon, thunderstorm, nor any of those
terrible conflicts between the elements that Nature is so capable of producing. No! Man alone had created these reddish clouds, these gigantic
flames worthy of a volcano, these thunderous vibrations resembling the
shocks of an earthquake, these roars that rivaled those of hurricanes and
tempests. It was his hand that hurled into an abyss of his own making this
Niagara of molten metal! (193–95, IA)

One recognizes in this passage the same themes and narrative devices used earlier
in Verne's Positivistic/Romantic glorification of Nature: vulcanism, exoticism,
the animation of the inanimate, antithesis, hyperbole, quantitative precision,
sensorial impressionism, and the alchemistic mixture of earth, fire, water, and air
images. But in this instance, the object of the "poetization" process is reversed.
Nature now provides the metaphorical means for the glorification of science and
of Man's status as Nature's rival and conqueror (instead of its contemplative
communicant).

Verne's artistic/anthropomorphic treatment of technological devices is a
frequent Romantic corollary to his detailed concern for the overall technical
verisimilitude of such hardware. As such, it serves as one of the many dealienating narrative strategies that facilitate the reader's identification with (and acceptance of) the extraordinary in these works—particularly as it relates to the products
of industry. For example, the great majority of the futuristic transportational
vehicles featured in the *Voyages Extraordinaires* are consistently de-mechanized,
either by their exterior ornamentation (making them artistic), by their Victorian
furnishings (making them homey), or by a portrayal of them as living entities
(making them user-friendly). One such vehicle that combines all three of these
essentially palliative properties is the *Géant d'acier* (Steel Giant) of *The Steam
House* (the respective names of which reflect this same juxtaposition of the
human and the industrial):

A unique engine for this convoy stood at its head. A gigantic elephant,
20 feet high and 30 long and almost as wide, moved along slowly and mys-
teriously. Its trunk was curved upwards like a huge horn of plenty, pointing toward the sky. Its gilded tusks protruded from its enormous jaw like
two scythes. On its body of dark green, strangely mottled, there was a
rich drapery of bright colors, embroidered with silver and gold, and around
the edges of which hung a richly tasseled fringe. On its back sat a kind of
highly ornate turret, domed in the Indian fashion and windowed with
thick oval lenses like the portholes of a sailing vessel.

This elephant pulled a train composed of two cars as large as houses,
like mobile bungalows, each of which was mounted on four wheels that
were sculpted at the hubs, spokes, and rims. . . .

It was really an elephant! Its coarse green-black skin undoubtedly covered one of these mighty skeletal frames that Nature had bestowed on the king of the pachyderms! Its eyes glowed with the flicker of life! Its limbs moved!

Yes! But if some curious soul chanced to place his hand on this enormous animal, all would become clear. It was only a wondrous optical illusion, an astonishing imitation, that had all the detail and appearance of being alive. In fact, this elephant was made of steel. An entire locomotive was hidden in its flanks. (70–71, IA)

Serving as a "comforting" counterpoint to the unusual exterior of this curious vehicle, the living quarters of the Steam House are equipped with the ultimate in traditional bourgeois luxury—all tastefully done so as to maintain the exotic and identifiably Indian décor while offering the full spectrum of modern Western conveniences:

The first car was 15 meters long. In the front, its elegant pilaster-supported veranda covered a wide balcony on which ten persons could fit easily. Two windows and a door opened into the living room that was lighted additionally by two lateral windows. The living room, furnished with a table, a library, and soft couches all around, was artfully decorated and walled with rich cloth. A thick rug from Smyrne covered the floor. "Tattis," a kind of wicker blind, hung over the windows and they were constantly sprayed with perfumed water, which maintained a pleasant freshness in the living room and the sleeping quarters. From the ceiling hung a belt-driven "punka," which waved back and forth automatically with the movement of the train and which, during halts, was kept in motion manually by a servant.

In the rear of the living room, a second door of precious wood, facing that of the veranda, opened into the dining room that was lighted not only by the lateral windows but also by a ceiling of frosted glass. Around the table in the middle, eight guests could be seated. Since we were only four, we were more than comfortable. This dining room was furnished with buffets and credenzas filled with all the sterling silver dinnerware, crystal glassware, and porcelaine that true English comfort requires. . . . (79–82, IA)

As with most of Verne's engineering marvels, the technological strangeness of the apparatus is compensated for by its many homey qualities, dramatized by its extreme comfort and capacity to procure a superior state of *bien-être*.

And Verne's characterization of such vehicles as living entities reaches hyperbolic proportions in this text. The steam-driven elephant eventually "dies" in dramatic fashion—heroically "committing suicide" by blowing itself up to destroy a horde of enemy bandits—and is then sorrowfully mourned by its faithful travel companions:

"Poor Géant!" commented Captain Hod. "It died to save us!" ...
Captain Hod, its fervent admirer, Banks, its ingenious inventor, and all
the other members of the expedition would never forget their "faithful
animal." They had begun to think of it as a living being. For a long time,
the echoes of the explosion that destroyed it would linger in their memo-
ries. ...

Standing before the torn body of his cherished Géant d'Acier, Captain
Hod murmured, "The poor beast!"

"We could build another ... one that would be even more powerful!"
said Banks.

"Probably," sighed Captain Hod, "but it still wouldn't be him." (517–
20, IA)

There is a certain Pygmalion flavor to the metamorphosis of such machines into
living beings, even if it is only through the imagination of the novel's fictional
protagonists. In this regard, one remembers the almost symbiotic rapport of
Captain Hatteras to his vessel: "Hatteras ... was like the soul of this vessel, at
one with it, like that of a man and a horse in a centaur" (*Hatteras* 427, IA); or
the relationship of Captain Nemo to his *Nautilus*, "I love it like the flesh of my
flesh!" (*20,000* 134, IA). Such personifications and anthropomorphisms (of
technology as, earlier, of Nature) lend both a mythic and a familiar quality to
these narratives—more effectively anchoring science to human experience.

It is in this respect that the Vernian machine often functions as a catalyst
to reader *rêverie*—a kind of dream machine—similar to the wonders of Nature
discussed earlier. Verne's machines act as fictional stepping-stones enabling the
reader's imagination to journey not only into new dimensions of geographical
space but also into new patterns of esthetic appreciation. The latter even extends
into the then-unexplored realms of modernity as the mechanical object is itself
viewed as a thing of beauty, carrying with it its own criteria of form and function: sleekness of design, precision of movement, strength of material, straight-
ness of line, amplitude of effect, and so on. It was not until Apollinaire and the
Cubists of the early twentieth century that such an esthetic was fully incorporated into French cultural standards. But it is already present in the Vernian
machines of the *Voyages Extraordinaires*—a poetic machine that, invariably one-
of-a-kind and the product of an engineer's inspiration, is a true *objet d'art*.

The poetic function of the machine in these texts is underscored by the fact
that it is never treated as an economic entity (as in Zola's works, for example):
it does not produce "surplus value" in the Marxist sense; it does not manufacture commodities; it does not create jobs, or replace them. It serves only to
make the impossible possible, the fantastic real, and the unlikely believable. Its
primary raison d'être is thus textual and imaginary. It acts as a necessary fictional device for plot progression (without which there could often be no
pedagogical "voyage" at all) and for more effective mimesis (linking the reader's
imagination to the real). And once its narrative task is fulfilled, the Vernian
machine always disappears and the status quo is firmly reestablished. For

example, after carrying him and his servant Joe across Africa, Fergusson's balloon *Victoria* is swept over the Gouina Falls in Senegal: "'Poor Victoria!' Joe lamented. Even the Doctor had a tear in his eye" (*Five* 359, IA). The *Nautilus* is first swallowed by the Maelstrom to conclude *Twenty Thousand Leagues under the Sea*, and is later permanently destroyed in a volcanic eruption at the end of *Mysterious Island*. Robur's *Albatros* disappears with its maker at the conclusion of *Robur the conqueror*, and his *Epouvante* is shattered by lightning in the final pages of *Master of the World*. And the artificial island of *Propeller Island* is torn apart by its own engines in the dénouement of that novel. Further, the striking brevity of the conclusions in such works is strongly illustrative of the central role played by machines in the overall narrative structure of the *Voyages Extraordinaires*.

It is often the Vernian machine that sustains a number of technologically perfected utopias,[10] provoking reader speculation and adding a new variant to a long literary tradition of such experimental social models from Thomas More onward. It is often the Vernian machine that, in true Romantic fashion, promotes popular revolution or fights injustice.[11] Moreover, its incredible power and its unquestioned supremacy over the constraints of Nature make of the Vernian machine a kind of sacred object—a quasi-religious miracle of applied science. The reverential epithets repeatedly used in these texts to characterize it reflect its nearly divine status: "a wonder," "a miracle," "an extraordinary machine," and the like. Also revealing is the almost religious adoration that it elicits, not only among the untutored masses—"this colossus which provoqued the superstitious admiration of the Hindus" (*Steam* 520, IA), "these ferocious savages saw it as a celestial being" (*Robur* 158, IA)—but also among the most "civilized" of Verne's protagonists. Note, for example, Captain Hod's continual litany of praise for the *Géant d'Acier* or Professor Aronnax (a scientist himself) who, when shown about the *Nautilus*, becomes "intoxicated by these marvels" (*20,000* 123, IA) and exclaims "my admiration is infinite" (259, IA). Somewhat unusual for a scientist, Aronnax accepts without question the wonders he is witnessing, saying "I am a simple observer of these facts . . . I don't attempt to explain them" (126, IA). Thus, through his identification with the leading characters (and the ever-present vox populi personages), the reader comes to share the awe and wonder generated by the Vernian machine. Concurrently, the text's overall verisimilitude is insured, its exoticism is enhanced, and its mythic overtones provide the reader with new technological holy symbols.

This third variant in Verne's Romantic portrayal of science—its metaphysical-ization or magic-ification—is perhaps nowhere more evident than in his fictional treatment of electricity in these works. Labeled alternately as "this imponderable fluid" (*Sphinx* 482, IA), "this soul of the universe" (*Propeller* 57, IA), "the soul of the industrial world" (*Robur* 69, IA), and "this energy of the future" (*Mathias* II, 58, IA), this mysterious and sublime substance not coincidentally powers the vast majority of Verne's futuristic machines. Electricity's fundamentally inexplicable nature does not diminish its practical usefulness.

On the contrary, it provides the author with a convenient and rational explanation for the many supernatural qualities of his "dream machines"—thus guaranteeing verisimilitude—while it heightens the overall magical character of these devices. And the enigmatic properties of electricity are even further emphasized by the secret of their technological utilization. That is to say, in each instance where the electrical power source of the Vernian machine is explained, the text always stops short of a complete elucidation, leaving the ultimate key to the mystery unresolved, known only to its creator. For example, consider Captain Nemo's (ostensibly) pedagogical explication of the electrical machinery powering the *Nautilus*, in a chapter appropriately entitled All by Electricity:

> "Before going any further, Professor, I must explain a few things to you," said Captain Nemo. "Please listen closely."
>
> He was silent for a few moments, then he said:
>
> "There is one source of power that is obedient, rapid, easy to handle, and flexible enough in its applications to reign supreme on board my ship. It does everything. It gives me light as well as heat, and it is the very soul of all my machinery. This power-source is electricity."
>
> "Electricity!" I cried, somewhat taken aback.
>
> "Yes, Monsieur."
>
> "But, Captain, the great speed with which your ship moves seems beyond the power of electricity. Until now, electrical power has been able to produce only a very small amount of driving force!"
>
> "Professor," answered Captain Nemo, "my electricity is not of the usual kind, and I hope you will permit me to leave the matter there."
>
> "I won't insist, Monsieur . . ."
>
> "As you can see," said Captain Nemo, "I make use of Bunzen cells instead of those developed by Ruhmkorff which would have been ineffective. Bunzen cells are few, but large and powerful, which experience has taught me is an advantage. The electricity passes back through large electromagnets, activating a special set of rods and gears which in turn transmit the power to the propeller shaft. The propeller is twenty feet in diameter and can spin up to twenty revolutions per second."
>
> "And what speed does that give you?"
>
> "Fifty knots."
>
> There was a mystery behind all this, but I didn't want to ask too many questions to clarify it. How could electricity be made to produce so much power? Where did this almost limitless force originate? Was it in the high tension generated by some new kind of coil? Was there something about its transmission that an unknown system of levers could increase to infinite proportions? I couldn't understand it. (118–26, IA)

And, in spite of the mathematics of the ensuing chapter (entitled Some Figures) where Captain Nemo continues to explain, theoretically, the principles of the *Nautilus*'s drive system, those basic questions posed by Professor Aronnax remain unanswered. The (in reality impossible) task of converting electricity stored in giant batteries into sufficient mechanical torque to propel this massive vessel is left to, as Nemo puts it, "a special set of rods and gears which . . . transmit the power." The essential mysteriousness of the process thus remains intact. For the average reader, it is enough to know that the magic of electricity propels the *Nautilus*—the remainder is assumed to be part of the uncommon engineering genius of Captain Nemo.

Another example of this secret electrical magic-ification technique is found in the cryptic explanations of Robur's flying machine *Albatros*: "neither steam nor any other liquid, neither compressed air nor any other gas, not even the successive explosions of a compression engine could provide Robur with the necessary power to keep his machine in flight. It was electricity . . . No turbines to generate it, just batteries and coils. But what substances went into the composition of these batteries? What acids activated them? That was the secret of Robur" (*Robur* 69, IA). And this same basic narrative strategy is repeated time and time again whenever Verne launches into a pseudopedagogical and verisimilitude-building exposé of how his imaginary machines operate. Almost all (with the exception of the steam-driven elephant of *The Steam House*) are animated by what the Exposition Internationale de Paris of 1900 was to call *fée électricité*: the subterranean lanterns in *Journey to the Center of the Earth*, electric underwater bullets in *Twenty Thousand Leagues under the Sea*, lighting for entire communities in *The Black Indies* and *Propeller Island*, advanced weapons systems in *Mathias Sandorf*, electric trains in *Propeller Island*, and audiovisual gadgetry in *The Carpathian Castle* and *The Day of an American Journalist in 2889*, to cite but a few.

The enigmatic nature of electricity in Verne's futuristic technology—a kind of evocative magic wand used to solve certain narrative problems in addition to purely fictional ones—is rivaled by his fanciful treatment of this same element in Nature. Portrayed as protean, wildly unbridled, and as having a mysterious life all its own, the "celestial fires" of electrical storms (particularly those at sea, for added power of antithesis) is a recurring topos in the *Voyages Extraordinaires*. But by far the most memorable episode of this sort takes place in *Journey to the Center of the Earth*, where Professor Lidenbrock, Axel, and Hans are navigating their raft across a vast subterranean ocean. Young Axel narrates their "electrifying" encounter with just such a storm:

The atmosphere grew heavy with mists charged with the electricity generated by the evaporation of the salt water; the clouds sank perceptibly lower and took on a uniform olive hue; the electric light could scarcely cut through this opaque curtain lowered onto the stage where the drama of a storm was about to take place.

I was in awe, as most living creatures at the approach of a cataclysm. . . .

. . . the rain formed a roaring cataract in front of the horizon towards which we were speeding madly. But before it reached us, the cloud's veil was torn apart, the sea began to boil, and a vast chemical reaction taking place in the upper atmosphere brought electrical forces into play. Brilliant streaks of lightning mingled with peals of thunder, criss-crossing in the

Professor Lidenbrock, Axel, and Hans aboard a storm-tossed raft
on a subterranean sea (*Journey*, engraving by E. Riou, 1864)

midst of loud crashes; the mist became incandescent, and the hailstones striking the metal of our tools and arms flashed with light; the heaving waves looked like miniature volcanoes, each containing an inner fire and crested with flame. . . .

There was a continual emission of light from the clouds' surface; electric matter was constantly being emitted by their molecules. The gaseous elements of the air had evidently been altered, countless columns of water were soaring into the air and falling back in a foaming mass. . . .

. . . a ball of fire appeared on board the raft. The mast and sail were both ripped away, and I saw them rising to an incredible height in the air—like a pterodactyl, that fantastic bird of prehistoric times.

We were paralyzed with fear. The half-white and half-blue fireball, the size of a ten inch cannonshell, moved slowly over the raft, spinning at an astonishing speed under the lash of the hurricane. It floated here and there, perched on one of the raft's support structures, jumped up onto the provisions bag, came back down lightly, bounded about, and came to rest on the powder cannister. For one horrible moment I thought we were about to be blown up, but the shining globe of fire moved away. It approached Hans, who simply stared at it; it came near my uncle, who threw himself to his knees to avoid it; it then headed towards me, pale and trembling before its brightness and heat. It pirouetted near my foot, which I tried to pull away but couldn't budge.

A smell of nitrous gas filled the air, entering our throats and suffocating our lungs.

Why couldn't I move my foot? It was riveted to the raft! Oh! the electrical fireball had magnetized all the iron on board! The instruments, tools, and arms were moving about and banging together with a clinking sound. The nails of my boots were stuck to an iron plate imbedded in the deck. I couldn't move it!

Finally, with a violent effort, I managed to pull away my foot just as the fireball was about to seize it in its gyrations and carry me away too. . . .

Suddenly there was a flash of intense light! The globe had burst! We were engulfed in flames!

Then everything went dark. I just had time to glimpse my uncle stretched out on the raft and Hans, still at the helm and "spitting fire" under the influence of the electricity with which he was saturated!

Where are we going? Where are we going? (282–90, IA)

In this near hallucinatory passage, electricity itself becomes a principal protagonist in the drama. Progressively assuming a kind of sentient corporeality, it metamorphoses from "molecules" to "matter" and ultimately becomes a fantastic incandescent "globe" that violently rips away the raft's rigging, dances about its stunned passengers, magnetizes all iron aboard, and then suddenly bursts—drowning the heroes in St. Elmo's fire. Its narrative transmutation is also paralleled by a gradual modification in the mimesis of the text itself. The initial quasi-scientific observations that such electricity was "generated by the evaporation of the salt water" and was the product of "a vast chemical reaction in the upper atmosphere" are increasingly supplanted by the conviction that "the gaseous elements in the air had evidently been altered"—textually preparing the way for the seemingly supernatural events that follow. Further, the "fireball's" capacity to magnetize metal not only gives that element a kind of living vitality of its own—riveting Axel in place—but also functions as a structurally determinative force in the novel as a whole. In altering the polarity of the heroes' compass, it skews their itinerary for the remainder of the journey, a discovery they make only at the very conclusion of the narrative. This final revelation provides a humorous *coup de théâtre* ending to the story and one last anthropomorphic depiction of electricity: in the dénouement, Professor Lidenbrock admits having been slyly duped by "electricity's practical joke!" (372, IA).

EGALITARIANISM AND HEROISM

This "Romanticization" of Nature and science throughout the *Voyages Extraordinaires* has its social and human counterpart. Serving to temper the hierarchical and authoritarian portrayal of society in Verne's novels is a certain measure of egalitarianism, where true democratic decision making and participatory governance are stressed. Although the scientist-hero's leadership and authority are never in question in these texts (he, most often, having been delegated such a responsibility), he is nevertheless shown continually consulting his followers and trying to generate a consensus before deciding upon their collective course of action. This particular scenario is most evident, for example, in Verne's *robinsonnade* narratives such as *Mysterious Island* or *The Two Year Vacation*, where microcosms of smoothly running political systems are established by the castaways. For example, in the former novel, the expressions "It was therefore agreed that" and "The plan was approved unanimously" are a standard conclusion to the many discussions among Cyrus Smith and his companions as they decide how best to survive on their remote island. And this applies both to small and relatively unimportant decisions as well as to those that are momentous: for example, whether to allow their pet dog Top to dine on the water fowl that he had retrieved from the lake—"and it was agreed that the duck would serve as Top's dinner" (211, IA)—or how to most effectively combat the pirates that had invaded the island—"This plan was unanimously agreed to by the colonists" (740, IA). The latter novel reflects the same concern for democratic procedures as the young castaways draft a constitution—"It was agreed that a program would be set up; then, as soon as it was approved by everyone, it would be scrupulously adhered to" (187, IA)—and then proceed to elect a chief executive (for a fixed term) to oversee its implementation. In both cases, there is a constant narrative awareness of (and respect for) individual human rights, regardless of one's intellectual merit or scientific knowledge.

In similar fashion, the Vernian scientist-adventurer in these texts is a great deal more than a simple paragon of Positivist rationalism. He also possesses all the qualities of the archetypical Romantic hero: courage, esthetic sensitivity, idealism, devotion to justice, humor, thirst for glory, compassion, love of freedom, and "grandeur" is general. Two of Verne's fictional personages are exemplary in this respect: Captain Nemo and Michel Ardan.

Captain Nemo, perhaps the most famous of Verne's heroes, is remembered foremost as the designer, builder, and master of the *Nautilus*. But his engineering and technical skills, although impressive, are not what truly bring him to life. It is rather his intrepid willingness "to go where no Man has gone before," his intriguing personal past shrouded in mystery, his rebelliousness, his implacable sense of social justice, and his passionate love of liberty and the sea. Nemo is the epitome of the "Renaissance man"—one who excels not only in intellectual and physical pursuits but in cultural ones as well. Note, for example, the titles of those works contained in his 12,000-volume shipboard library. One finds therein not only the great books of science, but also "all the ancient and modern masterpieces; all the best that humanity had produced in history, poetry, novels . . . from Homer to Victor Hugo, from Xenophon to Michelet, from Rabelais to Mme Sand" (*20,000* 107, IA). Or consider Nemo's magnificent art collection on board the *Nautilus*:

> The various schools of the ancient Masters were represented: a madonna by Raphael, a virgin by Leonardo da Vinci, a nymph by Corregio, a woman by Titian, a nativity by Veronese, an assumption by Murillo, a portrait by Holbein, a monk by Velasquez, two Flemish landscapes by Teniers, three little paintings by Gérard Dow, Metsu, and Paul Potter, two canvasses by Géricault and Prud'hon, and a few seascapes by Backhuysen and Vernet. Among the works of modern painting appeared those signed by Delacroix, Ingres, Decamps, Troyon, Meissonier, Daubigny, etc. as well as several reductions of marble or bronze statues, modeled after the most beautiful ones of Antiquity, which stood on pedestals in the corners of the room. . . . (109–11, IA)

Or, finally, note his more than passing interest (and talent) in music: "scores by Weber, Rossini, Mozart, Beethoven, Haydn, Meyerbeer, Herold, Wagner, Auber, Gounod, and a few others spread out near the great pipe-organ which filled the wall of the salon" (111, IA).

In the same way that Verne's mini-societies in his many *robinsonnades* are an idealized composite of civilization as a whole, Captain Nemo is an idealized composite of Verne's notions of Romantic heroism. Many of Nemo's individual character traits reappear in subsequent Vernian heroes, but nowhere in the *Voyages Extraordinaires* are they so comprehensively portrayed and concentrated in one person.

But Nemo represents only one part of the Romantic hero's total identity— the more serious (an ultimately more tragic) side. The frequently fanciful and devil-may-care dimension of this heroic prototype is incarnated in Michel Ardan of *From the Earth to the Moon* and *Around the Moon*—another memorable personality of Verne's fictional world. He is described as

> one of those "originals" that the Creator invents during a moment of fantasy and then promptly breaks the mold. . . .
>
> This amazing man lived a perpetual state of hyperbole. . . . For him, everything was larger than life—except problems and people.
>
> He was of a luxuriant nature: an artist by instinct, he was full of wit and preferred exchanging quick sardonic thrusts to impressive oratory. In arguments, he disdained logic and syllogisms in favor of a reckless "ad hominem" style all his own and could tenaciously espouse any lost cause at hand.
>
> . . . He was, in fact, an out-and-out Bohemian: adventurous but not an adventurer, a boisterous fun-lover, a Phaeton wildly driving the chariot of the Sun, an Icarus with an extra set of wings. As such, he was always in trouble, throwing himself headlong into impossible endeavors and burning his bridges behind himself. . . . (224–26, IA)

True to his compensatory role as a counterweight to the scientific solemnity of heroes such as Nemo and Barbicane, Ardan is blithely skeptical of science and its rather "fixated" practitioners, preferring the raw poetry of life to the empirical analysis of phenomena: ". . . he proclaimed himself to be a 'sublime ignoramus,' like Shakespeare, and professed supreme contempt for scientists: 'Those fellows,' he used to say, 'are only fit to mark the points scored, while we play the game!'" (*Earth/Moon* 225, IA). Such an attitude does not preclude, however, an impressive competence in purely scientific matters. Witness, for example, his skillful oratory on The Law of Progress before the members of Barbicane's Gun Club (234–63, IA), or his solving of various logistical problems in adapting their "space bullet" for human habitation (307-9, IA), or in the following passage where he once again surprises his recondite comrades in matters of basic astronomy:

> "However, this invisible side [of the Moon] is even more affected by the Sun's heat than is the visible side. I say this for your sake, Nicholl, because Michel probably doesn't understand anyway."
>
> "Thanks," responded Michel.
>
> "In fact," continued Barbicane, "this invisible side receives the most light and heat when the Moon is new—in other words, when it's located between the Sun and the Earth. In this position, as compared to when it is full, the Moon is twice as close to the Sun. This distance can be approximated as two hundredths of that separating the Earth from the Sun, or, in round figures, 200,000 leagues. Thus, this invisible side is closer to the Sun by 200,000 leagues when it is illuminated.
>
> "Correct," replied Nicholl.
>
> "On the other hand . . ." continued Barbicane.
>
> "Just a minute," Michel interrupted.

"What?" asked Barbicane.

"I'd like to continue the explanation."

"Why?"

"To prove to you that I understand."

"Go right ahead!"

"On the other hand," began Michel, imitating the tone of voice and gestures of President Barbicane. "On the other hand, when the visible side of the Moon is lighted by the Sun, the former is said to be full—in other words, it is located on the opposite side of the Earth from the Sun. The distance, in round numbers, which then separates it from that shining star increases by 200,000 leagues and the heat it receives is correspondingly less."

"Well stated!" cheered Barbicane. "You know, Michel, for an artist type, you're quite intelligent!"

"Ah yes," Michel said nonchalantly, "we are all like that down on the Boulevard des Italiens!" (*Moon* 196–97, IA)

But Ardan's principal function in these texts is less to valorize scientific knowledge per se than to bring a humorous vox populi element to the learning of it: in other words, humanizing the many technical discussions through satire, wit, and fantasy. Ardan brings them "down to earth," one might say—more effectively dealienating them for easier assimilation by the lay reader. In so doing, Ardan constantly pokes fun at the incomprehensible esotericism of his companions' scientific jargon: "'Ugh!' said Michel, 'one half of the "v" zero squared . . .! Speak so that we can all understand, o algebraic men!'" (*Moon* 95, IA). And he voices his continual frustration over his companions' scientific "objectivity" and apparent lack of concern for the human ramifications of their theorizing:

Nicholl and Barbicane paid no attention to Michel's jokes. They were embroiled in a scientific discussion. What the trajectory of the projectile would be—that's what excited them. One of them defended the hyperbola, the other fought for a parabola; each was armed with proofs bristling with x's. Their arguments were presented in a language that was maddening for Michel. And neither of these two adversaries would give up his own theory of predilection.

This continuing scientific dispute began to exasperate Michel who said:

"Dear Messieurs Cosinus, when are you going to cease waving these hyperbolas and parabolas around my head? I wish to know only one thing—the only really important thing in this entire discussion. We will follow one of your two trajectories. Granted. But *where* will each of them take us?"

"Nowhere," answered Nicholl.

"What do you mean, nowhere?"

"It's obvious," added Barbicane. "These are unclosed trajectories. They extend to infinity."

"Oh, you scientists!" exclaimed Michel. "You're truly incredible! What matter these parabolas and hyperbolas to us if they both take us into the infinity of space?"

Barbicane and Nichol couldn't keep from smiling. They had just been practicing "Art for Art's Sake!" (*Moon* 213–14, IA)

And Ardan repeatedly extols to his savant friends the virtues of metaphorical analogy over denotative fact when discussing such technical matters, once again, for more effective lay comprehension. One passage where he clearly demonstrates this approach is the following, where Barbicane is attempting to explain the (erroneous) existence of "ether" in space:

"Ether, my friend, is an agglomeration of mysterious atoms which, in proportion to their dimensions (according to works of molecular physics), are as far away from each other as celestial bodies in space. This distance, however, is smaller than one three millionths of a millimeter. These atoms produce light and heat by their vibrations of 430 trillion waves per second at four to six ten thousandths of a millimeter amplitude."

"Billions of billions!" exclaimed Michel Ardan. "Has someone measured and counted these vibrations? All these, my dear friend Barbicane, are scientists' numbers. They astound the ear and say nothing to the mind."

"But it is nevertheless necessary to count . . ."

"No, it's better to compare. A trillion doesn't mean anything. An object for purposes of comparison means a great deal. For example, when you say that the volume of Uranus is 73 times larger than Earth's, that Saturn's is 900 times, that Jupiter's is 1,300 times, and the Sun 1,300,000 times, I will still not have really understood. I prefer, by far, those old comparative models . . . which say very simply: the Sun is a pumpkin two feet in diameter, Jupiter is an orange, Saturn a lady-apple, Neptune a small cherry, Uranus a large cherry, Earth a pea, Venus a small pea, Mars a large pinhead, Mercury a mustard seed, and Juno, Ceres, Vesta, and Pallas tiny grains of sand! At least, in that way, you know where you stand! (*Moon* 86–87, IA)

Ardan's sensitivity to language in general, and to the "science" of rhetoric in particular, highlights his role as a fictional *porte-parole* for the author's lifelong fascination with puns, double entendres, and other forms of semantic wordplay. As such, Ardan exemplifies Verne's own legendary *esprit de boutade* —concerning which one of his contemporaries at the Paris stock market once remarked that he "had more success at witticisms than at business . . . always ready with a come-back, a joker, a cunning sceptic."[12] But, more importantly perhaps, Ardan's character also serves to inject yet another measure of self-reflection into these works, that is, where the text suddenly becomes conscious of its own materiality. For example, time and again Ardan offers esthetic commentary on his own or his companions' choice of words and/or phraseology—showing as much a concern for style as for meaning and clarity. Witness his reaction, for example, to Barbicane's comparative exposé of what life must be like on the light versus the dark sides of the moon:

> "I would add," continued Barbicane, "that, in contrast, an inhabitant of the visible side is particularly favored by Nature to the detriment of his brothers on the invisible side. The latter, as you can see, has long nights of three hundred and thirty four hours where not a single ray of light penetrates the darkness. The former, on the other hand, enjoys the Sun for fifteen straight days, and when the Sun finally drops below the horizon, he sees another splendid star rise up along the opposite horizon—the Earth, thirteen times larger than the Moon that we see; the Earth, which rises at a 2 degree angle and shines with a light thirteen times more intense than moonlight; the Earth, which disappears only at the moment when the Sun reappears once again!"
>
> "A nice sentence!" said Michel Ardan. "A bit academic, perhaps."
> (Moon 195–96, IA)

One almost imagines Verne murmuring to himself the final line of this passage, as he continually oscillates between the two narrative poles of poetic description and scientific explication—trying to reunite in his texts a utilitarian Positivistic vision of the universe with a carpe diem Romantic one, an ideology of conquest with one of contemplation, and an awareness of language as information with language as style. More than any other perhaps, it is this "voyage" in Verne's works that is the most *extraordinaire* of all.

These, then, are a few examples of Verne's complementary brand of textual Romanticism, those that serve to enhance and anchor (but not devalorize) his Positivistic science. But during the late 1880s, the entire tone of his *Voyages Extraordinaires* changes. This transformation was neither unilateral nor without precedent in Verne's previous works. As already pointed out, even the earliest of his novels (the ones he is most remembered by) were very heterogeneous in this respect, mixing Positivist proselytism with Romantic ribbing, for example, the tongue-in-cheek satire of Michel Ardan, or the various absentminded scientists like Paganel or Cousin Bénédict—so totally "fixated" in their scientific studies that they lose track of the details of everyday living. But the overall ideological balance of these texts was never open to question. Such poking fun was always lighthearted and was intended to more fully humanize (rather than criticize) the scientist and the science depicted, thereby facilitating the pedagogical implantation.

PESSIMISM

The second half of Verne's novelistic production is very different from the first in its general ideological focus. Such a change can most simply be described as a slow but steady metamorphosis away from the overall optimism of a Positivistic world view. And, correspondingly, one discerns a more frequent

Jules Verne, age 76 (photo 1904)

foregrounding of a generally pessimistic, cynical, and vehemently antiscience outlook. As might be expected, the scientific pedagogy within these particular texts grows less and less central to the plot structures—becoming progressively more abridged, watered down, or cut out altogether. Questions concerning environmental protection, human morality, and social responsibility are more often raised. Humor either disappears entirely or is recentered in irony and/or acidic satire. And the scientists themselves are increasingly portrayed as crazed megalomaniacs—using their technological know-how for purposes of world domination or fabulous wealth.

The underlying reasons for this palpable change of tone in Verne's works are very complex and the result of a variety of factors in the author's own life as well as in the social fabric of late nineteenth-century France. During a time in which he was experiencing serious problems with his rebellious son Michel,[13] as well as growing financial worries,[14] Verne also had to cope with the successive deaths of three individuals who were very close to him: his mistress Madame Duchêne in 1885, his editor and *père spirituel* Hetzel in 1886, and his mother in 1887.

Further, an event still cloaked in mystery took place on March 9, 1886. Verne was attacked at gunpoint by his nephew Gaston and was shot in the lower leg. Lodged in the bone of his ankle, the bullet could not be removed. As a result, Verne remained partially crippled for the rest of his life. In December of the same year, he confessed to Hetzel fils: "As for the rest, I have entered into the darkest part of my life. But I am unwilling to let it conquer me. Believe me when I say that I take these things very philosophically. The future is rather threatening for me because of the business that you already know about, and I confess that if I couldn't take refuge in hard work, which pleases me, I would indeed be in a pitiful state" (Martin 240, IIC). But a few years later, Verne seems to have grown less philosophical about such matters. In two letters to his brother Paul, he confides: "All that's left for me . . . are these intellectual distractions. . . . My character is profoundly changed, and I have received blows from which I will never recover . . ." (Martin 236, IIC) and "my dear Paul, you are happy. Remain happy. As for me, I am rarely so any more . . . All told, I'm finishing up badly" (Martin 237, IIC).

This growing pessimism in Verne's private life had its counterpart in the French social climate of the 1880s and 1890s. A severe long-term economic crisis lasted from 1882 to 1895, provoked in part by a series of agricultural disasters, a depressed manufacturing industry, skyrocketing unemployment, and a series of bank failures. Political strife worsened, precipitating the Boulangiste "uprising" and the fall from power of Jules Ferry. These and other occurrences created in the French public a general mood of disillusionment and frustration with the Positivist policies of the past. It was during this period that Verne began to serve as an elected official for the city of Amiens, putting him into constant confrontation with such matters as he and his fellow councilmen grappled with the local impact of these national issues.

It also seems far from coincidental that these same decades witnessed the rise of modern capitalistic imperialism and the frenetic rivalry among the various industrialized nations of the Western world to colonialize (and exploit) a greater and greater number of unexplored and/or undeveloped countries around the globe—particularly in Africa, the Far East, Indonesia, and the South Seas. And concurrently, on the domestic front finance capital came increasingly to replace industrial capital as the springboard for economic growth—intensifying the hegemonic power of banks, profit-conscious investors, and moneylenders in the politics of France's decision making.

Finally, this period also saw the birth of the modern military-industrial complex, where the advances of technology were unilaterally applied to the production of ever more lethal weapons systems. National military budgets soared, as France and the other industrialized powers of the world sought to consolidate their geo-strategic holdings through the practice of conscription (used by Prussia before the Franco-Prussian War of 1870) and the latest in advanced military hardware: iron-clad warships, land mines, machine-guns, poison gas canisters, long-range artillery, and more. Science and technology were increasingly becoming the handmaidens to international warfare—not only in the military confrontations with one's rivals, but also in the bloody repression of insurrections within one's own colonies.

Whether such developments directly affected the fundamental tone of his *Voyages Extraordinaires* is no doubt debatable. But Verne *was* undeniably a witness to, and very conscious of, these profound transformations in the overall tenor of his times. And the ideological texture of his novels *does* change during this period. Whether it be the product of the events in his own life or those in the world around him (or a combination of both), Verne's pessimism becomes much more palpable in these latter texts. His science turns increasingly misanthropic and his technology often verges on the satanic. And the idealistic Byronic Romanticism of his work becomes progressively tinged with overtones of Baudelarian *spleen*, of Huysmans-like introversion, or of Jarry-esque derision.

In illustrating how this change of ideological orientation manifested itself in the thematic makeup of Verne's fiction, the gradual shift in his portrayal of the scientist is especially suggestive. Viewed schematically, there are four types of scientists in the *Voyages Extraordinaires*: the heroic, the eccentric, the incompetent, and the dangerous. The first two types are positive (in both senses of the word); the latter two are negative. And their respective appearance in these works is usually mutually exclusive and successive in nature.

The first (and earliest) characterization of the Vernian scientist is unsparingly laudatory—albeit one-dimensional—where his courage and knowledge are exceeded only by his personal integrity and altruism. This sort, as previously discussed, is typified by such individuals as Dr. Fergusson of *Five Weeks in a Balloon*, Cyrus Smith of *Mysterious Island*, or Dr. Clawbonny of *The Adventures of Captain Hatteras*. One might be tempted to say that Captain Nemo of *Twenty Thousand Leagues under the Sea* also belongs to this category of heroic scientist.

But Nemo's solitary nature, his moments of brooding silence, and his thirst for vengeance make him much less one-dimensional as a fictional character and infinitely more intriguing—his mysterious and oxymoronic personality identifying him as a quite unique specimen in Verne's roster of protagonists.

The second type of scientist—still quite heroic (often inadvertently) but also very fallible—combines scientific expertise with comical personality quirks: for example, the excited stuttering of Professor Lidenbrock in *Journey to the Center of the Earth*, the "distracted" foibles of Paganel in *The Children of Captain Grant*, or the pedantic idiosyncracies of Palmyrin Rosette in *Hector Servadac*. Each is what the author invariably calls "an original" and is depicted as a kind of *grand enfant*: adorably naïve and amusingly unconventional. And each, as mentioned, becomes so engrossed in his science that he fits the description of the proverbial absentminded professor—respected and competent in his field, devoted to his "students," but totally inept in the mundane matters of day-to-day living.

The third type is similar to the second but without the heroism, the scientific virtuosity, or the compassion. These scientists are treated with humor, but it is bitingly satirical and pejorative. They are shown to be narrow-minded, fastidious, egocentric, insensitive, verbose, and unproductive. Aristobulus Ursiclos of *The Green Ray* epitomizes this brand of quack-scientist (his name reflects his character), as well as William Falsten of *The Chancellor* whom Verne classifies as "the kind of scientist who thinks only of machines, who is so absorbed by mechanics and mathematics that he sees nothing beyond that" (15, IA). A number of statisticians throughout the *Voyages Extraordinaires* also belong to this group, such as Cokburn of *The Floating City* or Poncin of *The Amazing Adventure of the Barsac Mission*—professional mathematicians whom Verne considers not true scientists at all, but rather, in the words of Michel Ardan, individuals "who keep score while we play the game" (*Earth/Moon* 225, IA).

The fourth type of scientist grows more prevalent in Verne's later works: the mad scientist, the irresponsible scientist, the scientist who presents a serious danger to Nature, to society, and to humanity as a whole because he chooses to compromise his wisdom for power or money. There is no humor in these portrayals. There is neither heroism nor compassion. And "pure" scientific research (as exemplified by the naming and classifying topoi described earlier) is no longer the driving force behind these scientists—just as the activities of exploration and discovery are no longer the ultimate goals of their "voyage." The majority of these wayward scientists are inventors, using their technological genius to create apocalypse-machines. They are shown to be uncommonly erudite and technologically brilliant, but also greedy, misanthropic, vainglorious, arrogant, and often insane.

The first novel in which this particular brand of scientific villain appears is *The Begum's Fortune* (1879), a text that is often cited as Verne's only technological utopia/dystopia. Two scientists, one French and one German, inherit a vast fortune from a distant and fabulously rich relative who was a sultan in India. Each decides to build the city of his dreams in the newly explored American

territory of Oregon. The former constructs France-Ville, a harmonious prototype of perfect urban hygiene (reflecting the scientific specialty of its creator,
Dr. Sarrasin). The latter constructs Stahlstadt—meaning the City of Steel—an
immense and militaristic industrial complex devoted to the production of can-
nons and explosive shells that contain a variety of poison gases (the specialty of
its Krupps-like creator, Herr Schultze). Schultze succeeds in revolutionizing
modern warfare with his gigantic artillery and lethal missiles, and, needless to
say, does a thriving business by providing the major powers of the world with
potent new weapons. But his *idée fixe* is neither wealth nor political prestige; it
is racial supremacy for the Germanic people. The narrator explains:

> The professor had heard of his rival's intention to build a French city
> where the physical and spiritual hygienic conditions would improve all the
> qualities of the race and create generations of young people who were
> strong and valiant. To him, this enterprise seemed both totally absurd and
> destined to fail because it was contrary to the laws of Progress—laws which
> dictated the fall of the Latin race, its subsequent servitude to the Saxon
> race, and, finally, its total disappearance from the face of the Earth . . . It
> was obvious that he was called upon by the creative and destructive force
> that is Nature to wipe out these pygmies who dared oppose her wishes. . . .
>   Besides, this project [Stahlstadt] was of secondary importance to Herr
> Schultze. It was only a small part of a much greater plan to destroy all
> those who refused to merge with the German people and become united
> with the Vaterland. (55–57, IA).

Incarnating French attitudes toward Germany during the postwar years of the
1870s and foreshadowing certain events of the twentieth century, Herr Schultze
is Verne's first truly evil scientist. As pointed out earlier, his vision of Nature and
humanity is focused uniquely on relationships of force, as dictated by cold
analytical logic. Identifiably Nietzschean in his evolutionary beliefs[15] and
reflecting a kind of scientific social Darwinism, Schultze lectures the young
Marcel Bruckmann in the manner of Zarathustra, saying:

> "My dear young man," answered Herr Schultze, "there appears to be in
> your otherwise very organized head a collection of Celtic ideas that would
> be of great harm to you, if you were to live very long. Good and evil, right
> and wrong are purely relative things, simple human conventions. Nature's
> laws are the only absolute. The law of competition is like the law of gravi-
> tation. Fighting against it is senseless; accommodating oneself to it and
> then acting according to its dictates is both wise and reasonable. And that
> is why I will destroy Doctor Sarrasin's city." (124, IA)

Herr Schultze represents the dark underside of Verne's object-ive rationalism and
the growing awareness on the author's part that, in Rabelais's words, "science

without conscience leads to the ruin of the soul."[16] It is significant in this respect that Schultze's scientific totalitarianism is ultimately foiled at the last moment by a kind of deux ex machina gas leak in his secret laboratory and he is instantly frozen solid—a form of justice that is doubly poetic given his lack of human warmth. But, quite characteristic of Verne's later works, it is this intervention of Providence that defeats him in the end, not the human forces of morality. This outcome aptly illustrates the twofold nature of Verne's growing pessimism: that science in the hands of evil people becomes evil, that it is all-powerful in its own right and, when misused, can be stopped only by supra-human means.

But science can also corrupt good people. Even the most morally resilient of scientists can fall prey to the supreme omnipotence it offers. One excellent case in point is the metamorphosis of Robur from his initial appearance in *Robur the Conqueror* (1886) to his death in *Master of the World* (1904). In the final episode of the former novel, Robur is portrayed as a heroic *oberman* of the skies who, from the deck of his invincible *Albatros*, warns the general public of the potential dangers of science:

> "Citizens of the United States!" he said. "My experiment is completed. But my opinion is, as of now, that nothing should be rushed, not even Progress. Science must not get ahead of social customs. Evolution, not revolution, is what's needed. In a word, everything in its own time. My arrival today is much too early to overcome your contradictions and divisiveness. The nations of this world are not yet mature enough for unity.
>
> So I am leaving you, and I am taking my secret with me. But it will not be lost to humanity forever. It will belong to you the day that you become wise enough to use it constructively and never abuse it. Farewell, citizens of the United States! Farewell!" (246–47, IA)

Contrary to what occurs in Verne's earlier novels, the fruits of the scientist's discoveries are no longer bequeathed to humanity as a whole. The scientist himself judiciously decides that the human species is not yet fit to possess such technology and he disappears from sight, taking his secrets with him. But all is not lost—Robur promises to return someday—and there is still hope for the future. Thus, at this stage, Verne's pessimism is somewhat attenuated by the wisdom of Robur himself and by the assumption that Man will, at some point in time, be capable of using (but not abusing) the science that Robur symbolizes.

But the Robur of *Master of the World* breaks that promise and, with his new car-boat-plane vehicle called *Epouvante* (*Terror*), he begins openly to intimidate humanity for the pleasure of proving his superiority. Industrialized nations from around the world, seeing in this apparatus an incomparable military weapon (an increasingly frequent motif in Verne's later works), offer him millions for it, to which he defiantly responds:

Proposals coming from the diverse nations of Europe as well as those lately received from the United States of America can expect no other answer than the following:

I categorically refuse any offer for the purchase of my vehicle. This invention will be neither French, nor German, nor Austrian, nor Russian, nor English, nor American. The machine will remain my property, and I will do with it as I please.

With it, I have control over the entire world. No human power exists, under any circumstances, that is strong enough to resist it.

Do not try to take it from me. It is and will continue to be beyond your reach. Any harm that you attempt to do me will be repaid a hundred-fold.

As for the price I am offered, I have no interest whatsoever. I have no need of your millions. Besides, the day where I might wish to have millions or even billions, I would need only to reach out my hand for them.

Let it be known on both the New and the Old Continents, they can do nothing against me—and I can do everything against them.

This letter, I sign it: Master of the World. (102, IA)

As the narrative continues, a young, inexperienced, and somewhat hapless Inspector Strock attempts to track down Robur. Predictably, he succeeds only in finding himself a prisoner aboard the *Epouvante*. Upon face-to-face encounter, Strock realizes that the once-heroic Robur is now totally insane.

We were face to face, two feet apart. With folded arms he looked at me, and I was shocked by his gaze. . . . It was not that of a sane man, a gaze that seemed to have nothing human left in it! . . .

Obviously, Robur was obsessed. This gesture, that I had already observed when he was walking around the campsite, this gesture, he did it again . . . his arm raised and pointing to the sky . . . It was as if some irresistible force was drawing him toward the upper reaches, as if he no longer belonged on earth and was destined to live in space, a perpetual guest of the higher atmosphere. . . . (189–90, IA)

Robur's loss of reason is accompanied by a complete loss of communicativeness: an arrogant mutism in sharp contrast to his previous incarnation where he had proved to be surprisingly loquacious—explaining the details of *Albatros* to his (also) unwilling passengers, giving speeches before public assemblies, sounding his trumpet above all the major capitals of the world, and so on. In this text, however, it is Strock who communicates his observations to the reader. And such secondhand descriptions create an even greater "distance" between the identifying reader and the erstwhile hero, as well as severely undercutting the authoritativeness of the (very rare) passages of scientific pedagogy present in the novel.

The climax of *Master of the World* has Robur defiantly flying his *Epouvante* into the heart of a lightning storm, with dire consequences:

With eyes blazing, the impassible Captain flew directly into the storm—*face to face* with it, as if to defy its power and to show that he had nothing to fear from it. To avoid the storm's fury, the *Epouvante* would need to immediately dive—a manoeuvre which Robur apparently had no intention of doing.

No! He maintained his exalted bearing like a man who, in his intractable pride, believed himself above or outside all of humanity! To see him thus, I fearfully wondered if this man wasn't some fantastic being escaped from some supernatural world!

Then he spoke, and amid the roaring of the storm and the crashing of the thunder I heard:

"I . . . Robur . . . Robur . . . Master of the World! . . ."

At that moment, all of my instincts and my sense of duty suddenly came to the fore. . . . Yes! it was totally crazy, but I had to try to arrest this criminal whom my country had outlawed, who was threatening the entire world with his terrible invention. I had to somehow handcuff him and bring him to justice! . . . Was I or was I not Strock, police inspector? . . . And, forgetting momentarily where I was, one against three above a seething ocean, I rushed toward Robur and, with a voice that could be heard above the storm's din, I shouted "In the name of the Law, I . . ."

Suddenly, *Epouvante* shuddered as if jolted by a powerful electrical shock. Its members shook violently like those of a human when electrocuted. Its frame shattered, the machine broke into pieces and fell.

The *Epouvante* had just been struck by lightning. With wings broken and turbines smashed, it plummeted from an altitude of more than a thousand feet into the depths of the ocean! (197–98, IA)

Once again it is the hand of Providence that succeeds in striking down the otherwise indomitable scientist and his technological marvel. Once again, the secrets of its construction disappear with its inventor—this time forever. And once again, the helplessness of humanity (and its reliance on supernatural intervention) is dramatically underscored: Strock's attempts at lawful arrest are upstaged by a higher law that takes matters into its own hands.

The Icarus-like moral to this story could be taken from any number of Verne's later texts. But it is important to realize that this particular lesson is not unique to these texts. It is present in the great majority of Verne's works, from the earliest of his *Voyages Extraordinaires* to the last. What is different, however, is that such an explicit challenge to the established order of things is now the central thematic element around which the entire plot unfolds. Earlier, it was always implicit—an unemphasized corollary to the many scientific explorations and discoveries portrayed, usually evoked in passing as the hero momentarily wondered: "Wasn't he walking on forbidden ground? Wasn't he, in this voyage, trying to overstep the limits of the impossible? Hadn't God reserved for some later century the knowledge of this continent . . .?" (*Five* 207, IA). But such fears, although serving to highlight the religious humility of the hero in question (and to heighten the suspense), were usually shown to be groundless and were quickly forgotten. If present at all, Providence was shown to be infinitely benevolent and a reliable source of "just-in-the-nick-of-time" assistance whenever the heroes found themselves in a tight spot: for example, saving Fergusson and companions from a ferocious lion attack (*Five* 231-32, IA), rescuing the survivors of the Hatteras expedition (*Hatteras* 470, IA), providing the castaways of Lincoln Island with a grain of wheat to begin their crops (*Mysterious* 264, IA), answering Dick Sand's call for help in fighting cannibals (*Boy* 438, IA), and so on. Thus, the deus ex machina leitmotif is quite common throughout all of the *Voyages Extraordinaires*. But its use for the violent destruction of the hubris-filled scientist and his futuristic machine marks a new twist in the author's narrative practice, and one that would be utilized again and again throughout his later novels.

Among Verne's "dangerous" scientists, there exists yet another variant: the one who, although not crazed, is totally irresponsible and either refuses to understand the threat posed by his inventions or simply doesn't care. The final novel in the trilogy of *From the Earth to the Moon, Around the Moon,* and *Topsy Turvy* is a good case in point. Barbicane, Maston, and company (but not Michel Ardan for obvious reasons) are once again brought into the limelight. But this time it is to construct a giant cannon, which, when fired, will alter the earth's rotational axis. The rationale is that, once straightened, the earth's polar caps would partially melt, exposing hundreds of thousands of square miles of new land and access to fabulously rich coal and mineral deposits. Representing the commercial interests of the United States (a reflection of the author's changing attitudes toward America during the latter years of his life), they first "purchase" the Arctic at an international auction. Then Maston is charged with working out the mathematical formulae to accomplish the task. Finally, Barbicane and the remainder of the newly formed North Polar Practical Association begin construction of the cannon in central Africa near Mount Kilimanjaro (picked for its capacity to withstand the recoil of such a blast). During this time, however, the probable global effects of such an operation are calculated by civilian engineers and printed in newspapers around the world:

> In two of the sectors, situated opposite one another in the northern and southern hemispheres, the seas would withdraw and would flood the other two sectors of these hemispheres.
>
> In the first sector: the Atlantic Ocean would dry up almost totally . . . Consequently, between America and Europe vast new lands would emerge . . . But it must be noted that, with the drop in the water level, the breatheable atmosphere would also drop proportionately. Thus, the coasts of Europe and America would be at such a great altitude that even cities located at twenty or thirty degrees would have at their disposition only the air normally found at an altitude of four kilometers. Hence, to take only the principal cities of New York, Philadelphia, Charleston, Panama,

Lisbon, Madrid, Paris, London, Edinburg, Dublin, etc. . . . absolute impossibility of living there.

Same effect in the opposing sector, which includes the Indian Ocean, Australia, and a quarter of the Pacific Ocean. . . .

In the sector of the Northeast . . . Petersburg and Moscow on the one hand and Calcutta, Bangkok, Saigon, Peking, Hong Kong, and Yeddo on the other . . . these cities would disappear underwater. . . .

In the sector of the Southwest . . . the disasters would be somewhat less severe . . . However, large territories would still be submerged by this artificial flood. . . . (139–41, IA)

Or, as the narrator blithely sums it up, with tongue undoubtedly in cheek and *humour noir* in full array (albeit with a certain amount of bitterness showing through the seams):

Those threatened were divided into two categories: the asphyxiated and the drowned. . . .

On the side of the asphyxiated, there were the Americans of the United States and the Europeans of France, England, Spain, etc. The prospect of annexing new territories on the ocean floor was not sufficient to make them accept the modifications involved. . . .

On the side of the drowned, there were the inhabitants of South America, then the Australians, Canadians, Hindus, New Zealanders . . . Ah! If it had only been a question of burying under new seas the Samoyeds or the Lapons of Siberia the Fuegans, the Patagonians, the Tartars, the Chinese, the Japanese or a few Argentinians, perhaps the civilized States would've accepted this sacrifice. But too many Powers had too large a share of these catastrophes to not protest. . . . (143–44, IA)

But turning a deaf ear to the cries, the pleas, and the threats of their brethren from around the world, Barbicane and company complete their project. Their huge cannon is subsequently loaded and, with great ceremony, fired. As the peoples of all nations hold their collective breath and await the impending cataclysm, it quickly becomes evident that the attempt has failed. Why? Because of an unnoticed error in Maston's mathematics—an error that occurred at the outset of his complex algebraic formulations and that was caused (predictably?) by a deus ex machina intervention in the form of a lightning bolt:

In fact, when the famous secretary of the Gun Club took as a base for his equations the circumference of the Earth, he marked it as forty thousand meters instead of forty thousand kilometers—which skewed the solution to the problem. . . .

Yes! Three zeroes forgotten in the measurement of the Earth's circumference!

Suddenly J. T. Maston remembered. It was at the beginning of his work, when he had just closed himself up in the study of Ballistic Cottage. He had correctly written the number 40,000,000 on the blackboard. . . .

At that moment, the telephone rings! J.-T. Maston heads towards it . . .
He exchanges a few words with Mrs. Evangelina Scorbutt . . . And then a
lightning bolt strikes the lines, knocking him off his feet and toppling his
blackboard. . . . Then he gets up . . . He begins to rewrite the half-erased
number on the blackboard . . . He had barely written 40,000 . . . when the
phone rings a second time . . . And when he gets back to work once again,
he forgets to add the last three zeroes to the measurement of Earth's
circumference! (175–76, IA)

Once again humanity is saved from science by the intercession of Providence.
And once again the text concludes on the following (somewhat awkward, given
the scathingly satiric narrative voice used up to this point) moralizing note:
"To change the conditions by which the Earth moves is an effort well beyond
those permitted to humanity. Man cannot alter the order of the Universe as
established by the Creator" (178, IA).[17]
Many other examples of this brand of irresponsible scientist can be seen in
Verne's later works: Orfanik of *The Carpathian Castle*, for instance, or Thomas
Roch of *For the Flag*, or Wilhelm Storitz of *The Secret of Wilhelm Storitz*,
among others. All are partly or totally deranged, all are a serious menace to
society, all are seemingly invincible, all are ultimately foiled by Providence, and
all are a testament to their creator's growing obsession with the dangers of advanced technology. But one "mad scientist" in particular merits special attention: Marcel Camaret of *The Amazing Adventure of the Barsac Mission*. This
work is, quite appropriately, the very last novel of the *Voyages Extraordinaires*
and was at least partially written by Verne's son Michel. But what is of importance is that, in his portrayal of Camaret, Verne directly addresses the question
of the scientist's "responsibility" for the technical marvels that he brings into
the world.
The scenario is as follows: the principal protagonists of the story have ven-
tured deep into Africa in search of the lost brother of their organizer Jane
Buxton. They are captured by men on strange flying machines and taken to the
secret city of Blackland, located somewhere in the Sahara. Established by its
tyrant "king" Harry Killer (another very appropriately named protagonist),
Blackland is an international criminal "utopia"–a highly advanced technological
haven for escaped murderers, rapists, and thieves from all countries around the
world:

> It was a very strange city. Built on perfectly flat land . . . it formed an
> exact semi-circle . . . Its area of approximately one hundred and thirty
> acres, was divided into three sectors of unequal size. . . .
> In the first lived the aristocracy of Blackland. . . .
> In the third lived the Civil Body, those White Men who could not enter
> the first sector. . . .
> Located between the first and the third, the second sector . . . took up
> the remainder of the city. It was the slaves' compound.

On the north corner, adjacent to the public gardens, was a huge quad-
rangular building surrounded by parapeted walls . . . the Palace, as it was
commonly called, where lived Harry Killer and nine of his early associates,
now promoted to the rank of advisors . . . Located in front of the Palace
was the Factory.

The Factory was like an autonomous and independent city into which
this dictator continually poured money . . . If it were he who had initially
conceived of Blackland, it was the Factory that had created it for him and
had furnished it not only with all the modern conveniences but also with a
host of extraordinary inventions that Europe would not come to know
until several years in the future. (239–45, IA)

A modern Sodom and Gomorrah, Blackland is portrayed as a city of consumate
evil. And the rapacity of its inhabitants is exceeded only by the wonders of its
futuristic technology—climate-control devices, electric flying machines called
planeurs, telephones, electric lighting, and automated agricultural machinery—all
provided by the creative genius of the director of the Factory, the scientist
Marcel Camaret.

In contrast to his surroundings, Camaret is portrayed as a quiet and timid
man, soft-spoken and dreamy-eyed, but "endowed with unlimited energy"
(248, IA) as well as a prodigious intellect. Typical of Verne's "eccentric" scientists, he is so absorbed in the abstractions of his craft that he has totally lost contact with the world around him:

Marcel Camaret was the only inhabitant of the Factory who could leave it
at will and wander the streets or the neighboring countryside of Blackland.
Although he often took advantage of this liberty to stroll his daydreams
around the city, it must not be concluded that he was any better informed
than his workers about the unusual customs of Blackland—he was totally
unaware of them, and even of the name of the city itself.

One day, a worker asked him about the city's name. Camaret thought
about it for a moment, and, to the astonishment of his subordinate, he
replied hesitantly:

"My word . . . I'm not sure. . . ."

Never, until that very instant, had he thought to inform himself about
this detail. Nor did he think any more about it afterwards. (247–48, IA)

But where the rapt preoccupations of Verne's earlier "eccentric" scientists had
led to burlesque situations of slapstick comedy, that of Camaret leads to human
suffering and tragedy. He is completely unaware of the unscrupulous nature of
his benefactor Harry Killer and the sinister use the latter has made of his
inventions:

Camaret . . . lived in a perpetual feverish state. All his dreams, he had
managed to materialize them one after the other. After the rain-making
machine, his brain produced a hundred other inventions which benefited

Harry Killer, without their creator ever knowing how the latter made use of them.

As for how his comrade might utilize such machines, the idea never entered Marcel Camaret's head. A being of pure abstraction, he had seen them only as problems to be solved. He never concerned himself with their practical application or with the origin of the materials put at his disposition for their construction. . . . He had asked, he was supplied. To him, nothing was simpler. (250–51, IA)

Driving this moral point home even further, the narrator continues:

Of course, an inventor cannot be held responsible for the evil for which he was, indirectly, the cause. It would never occur to anyone, for example, to accuse the man who invented the revolver for all the crimes committed by this weapon—crimes which would have not taken place without it. But, nonetheless, the creator of such an instrument is aware that it can and must kill: it was with this goal in mind that he created it.

Nothing of the sort in the case of Marcel Camaret. If he had ever had the idea of inventing a cannon that was larger and whose bullet was heavier than any in existence, he would have happily calculated the form of the piece, the weight and profile of the projectile and the necessary powder charge without ever considering this work as anything but an exercise in ballistics. He would have been greatly surprised to learn that his brain-child could, given the chance, be a brutal killer. (250, IA)

Quite obviously, the main ideological thrust of Verne's fiction has shifted. No longer a simple question of using science as a kind of narrative springboard to adventure and pedagogy, it is rather the social implications of science and the moral role of the scientist himself that now occupy center stage in the author's text, forming the thematic kernel around which his entire plot revolves. It is no longer a simple question of science in the hands of an evil or indifferent scientist who threatens the safety of the world, but rather of the responsibility of those who—innocently naïve though they may be in their own right—nevertheless create the means whereby such crimes can occur. The lesson is clear: scientists not only have a moral obligation to educate society (as pointed out earlier), but also to safeguard society from the fruits of their own labor.

It is significant in this regard that, unlike in his earlier pessimistic novels, it is not Providence that intervenes at the last moment to rescue the protagonists—it is Marcel Camaret himself. And it is not a bolt of lightning from the heavens that ultimately destroys Blackland and its corrupt inhabitants—it is, once again, Marcel Camaret. Upon finally learning the truth of how he had been manipulated and of the use to which his miraculous inventions had been put, Camaret's gentle madness turns into insane wrath and—likening himself to the vengeful God of the Apocalypse—he triggers a fiery holocaust that consumes the entire city, reducing it to lifeless rubble:

"God has condemned Blackland! . . ."

In his mind, God was obviously himself, judging by the gestures accompanying his shouted death-sentence. But before anyone could restrain him, Camaret had fled, screaming over and over again:

"God has condemned Blackland! . . ."

He closed himself up in the tower . . . Almost immediately, the first explosion was heard . . . The explosions continued without interruption, and even accelerated in number. . . .

Blackland, blown to pieces by the one who had created her, was nothing more than ruins and debris. Of the admirable but dangerous handiwork of Marcel Camaret, absolutely nothing remained. (429–39, IA)

Thus, Verne's treatment of the scientist seems to have traveled full circle. Initially, the scientist's status in his works was that of a "constructive" and salutary agent of human progress and knowledge (often aided by God). He then turned into a proud, unconquerable, and potentially destructive threat to humanity (and punished by God). And now, in his final incarnation, he appears as a well-intentioned but betrayed—and ultimately tragic—figure whose constructive genius is perverted by others, and who chooses to destroy (by his own hand) both them, himself, and his potentially humanitarian creations in a fit of remorseful rage. From saint to titan to angel of death, the metamorphosis of the scientist in the *Voyages Extraordinaires* says a great deal about Verne's evolving ideological stance concerning the fundamental relationship of science to human endeavor.

But the detrimental social effects of science are not limited to the corruption or megalomania of scientists or to the dangers that these misguided individuals represent to humanity. The industrial applications of science are also shown to pose grave threats to the human habitat and to the quality of life on this planet— a concern that increasingly haunts the pages of Verne's later novels. For example, one preferred image that the author begins to use in these texts when characterizing industry (and in sharp contrast to his portrayal of it in earlier works) is that of a "coal-eating monster." In *The Black Indies*, it is called "the monster of a million gullets that is industry" (23, IA), and in *Topsy Turvy* he states, "The stomach of industry thrives on coal; it will not eat anything else. Industry is a 'carboniverous' animal" (51, IA). Industry's incessant hunger for more coal— provoking such rash attempts as that depicted in *Topsy Turvy* to procure new sources—is paralleled by its need for other natural resources to construct and maintain its machines or to manufacture its goods. And the resulting negative impact on the environment is shown to take a variety of forms. Among those cited by Verne is the near extinction of certain species of animals that have industrial uses, such as whales (for their oil) or elephants (for their ivory). Of the former he repeatedly warns: "for some years now . . . abusive destruction has reduced their number" (*Sphinx* 12, IA), and "It must be noted in passing that

. . . whalers have all but abandoned the seas of the northern hemisphere. Due to excessive hunting, whales are becoming rare" (*Sphinx* 177, IA). Of the latter, he predicts: "However plentiful they are, the species will eventually disappear. Since an elephant can bring in one hundred francs of ivory, they are hunted without mercy. Each year, according to the figures of M. Foa, no less than forty thousand of them are slaughtered on the African continent, which produces seven hundred and fifty thousand kilograms of ivory shipped to England. Before fifty years goes by, there will be no more of them, in spite of their long life expectancy" (*Village* 31-32, IA).

Another such environmental concern is that of air pollution. Consider, for example, the following passage from *The Last Will of an Eccentric*, where the hero Max Réal is traveling through the state of Ohio and describes the impact of the many petroleum refineries located there:

> From Cleveland, I went to Warren, an important city in Ohio and very rich in petroleum. A blind man would recognize it by smell alone; its air is sickening. One could easily believe that it would ignite if a match were lit. And what a countryside! On the flatlands, as far as the eye can see, nothing but oil derricks and wells, and even on the hillsides and along the edges of creeks. All these, like so many oil lamps fifteen to twenty feet high . . . all that's lacking are the wicks! (344, IA)

But perhaps the most frequent criticism of modern industry in these texts is an esthetic one. That is to say, in ravaging Nature's resources and "making way" for progress, such industrialization destroys the beauty, the exoticism, and the natural poetry of the landscape. As Max Réal expressed it in a letter to his mother:

> You see, dear Mother, this region doesn't equal our poetic prairies of the Far West, nor the wild valleys of Wyoming, nor the distant views from the Rockies, nor the deep horizons of the Great Lakes and the Oceans! Industrial beauty is fine; artistic beauty is even better; natural beauty, nothing to match it! . . .
>
> So I continued heading southwest. Many stations paraded by on either side of the train: cities, burgs, villages, and, throughout this entire district, not a single corner of Nature that was left alone! Everywhere the hand of Man and his noisy machinery! . . . One day, the trees themselves will be made of metal, the prairies of felt, and the beaches of iron filings! . . . that's progress. (344 -47, IA)

The considerable difference, for instance, in Verne's portrayal of locomotives and railroads between his earlier works and his later ones is especially revealing in this regard. Traditionally, Verne has been remembered as a Saint-Simonian apologist of progress who continually sang the praises of those "noble engines" and the gleaming "ribbons of steel" spreading gloriously across the land. And passages such as the following from *Around the World in 80 Days* served to validate these beliefs about him:

> The locomotive, glistening like a reliquary, with its large lantern throwing out tawny beams of light, its silver-plated bell, its "cow-catcher" that protrudes like a spur, blended its hisses and rumbles with those of the rivers' torrents and cascades and twisted its smoke into the black boughs of the fir trees.
>
> Few, if any, tunnels; nor any bridges along the route. The railroad hugged the flank of the mountainsides, not seeking by the straight line the shortest distance between one point and another, and not violating Nature. (229, IA)

But in his later works, the kinetic poetry of the locomotive and its harmonious integration into Nature are conspicuously absent. In a complete change of perspective (both narratologically and ideologically), the author now describes the many experiential disadvantages of train travel. Among others, it "alienates" the voyagers from personal contact with the countryside and the towns through which they travel. Also, railways tend to homogenize everything located along their routes, wiping out local color and the exotic "otherness" of foreign milieus:

> Yes! blinded by the smoke, the steam and the dust, and, even worse, by the rapidity of transport. . . . insulated within the compartment of a car, with no more field of vision than that offered by a tiny window . . . stopping only at train stations that all look alike, seeing of cities only their outside walls or the tips of their minarets, listening to the constant noise of the rumbling of the locomotive, the hissing of the boiler, the creaking of the rails and the screeching of the brakes, is *that* what you call traveling? (*Steam* 17, IA)

> So what can be done? During this end-of-the-century era, we always arrive too late, and the marvels of the Oriental countryside, their curious customs, the masterpieces of Asiatic art are now only memories or ruins. Railroads will eventually homogenize all the countries through which they pass, forcing them down to the same level, to the same likeness. (*Bombarnac* 152, IA)

This loss of exoticism due to industrial progress (and to its political counterpart—colonialization) is most succinctly described in Verne's Polynesian "voyage" entitled *Propeller Island*. The sudden influx of European industriousness into these once pristine island cultures is shown to have brought with it the full panoply of Western customs, dress, and religious practices—all but replacing those more exotic conventions that were indigenous to these locales. This esthetic loss constitutes a major disappointment to the protagonists of this novel. But the worst effect of such industrial progress on these Shangri-Las, according to Verne, is neither its negative effect on their unspoiled environment nor its destruction of those esthetic pleasures enjoyed by tourists. Rather, it is its catastrophic impact on the heretofore happy and healthy natives of such cultures. As the artificial island of *Propeller Island* navigates from one South Seas archipelago to the next, its passengers begin to hear a sadly familiar refrain:

> Since they have begun to dress more "decently," the Nouka-Hivians and other natives have lost their original vitality as well as their natural gaiety. They are bored now, and their health has suffered. Before, afflictions such as bronchitis, pneumonia, and consumption were unknown to them. . . . (125, IA)

> At the time of Dumont d'Urville, the number of Nouka-Hivians had grown to eight thousand inhabitants . . . but since, their numbers have steadily declined. What is the cause of this decrease? Extermination by war, kidnapping of the males for plantations in Peru, abuse of hard liquor, and— why not admit it?—all the evils brought by . . . "civilized" races. (122, IA)

Thus, the lesson of these later *Voyages Extraordinaires* is quite clear: in much the same fashion as science corrupts the individual with its forbidden fruit of knowledge, industry corrupts the idyllic innocence of Nature. Neither is immune from what Verne now calls "this minotaur called Progress" (*Thompson* 272, IA). And in both instances, the consequences of such corruption are necessarily and invariably the same--death.

Finally, the object-ive rationalism and analytical logic of Verne's earlier novels finds its opposite here as well. Human instinct is continually valorized as an effective problem-solving tool. But one must be careful to differentiate between two separate sorts of instinct in Verne's protagonists: the kind that has been learned (more often evoked in his earlier texts), versus the more atavistic kind that is a vestige of our animal ancestry (the benefits of which are portrayed more often in his later texts). The former is the product of experience, like the archetypal veteran sea captain who can foretell abrupt changes in the weather or, without the aid of his instruments, sense the ocean currents beneath his vessel.[18] Or consider the young Dick Sand who, according to his captain, has already learned those nautical instincts necessary to becoming a truly fine sailor:

> "Look at him now, Mistress Weldon," continued Captain Hull. "He's at the helm, his eyes fixed on the top of the mainsail. No inattention on the part of this young sailor, and no lurching of the vessel! Dick Sand already has the sureness of a seasoned helmsman! A good start for a young seaman! Our trade, Mistress Weldon, is one that must be started as a young child. He who has not served as cabin-boy will never become a complete seaman, at least in the merchant marine. Everything must be a lesson, and thereby be both instinctive and well thought out in a good seaman—both the resolution made and the manoeuvre executed." (*Boy* 44, IA)

In these two instances, it is practical experience that provides these heroes with an "instinctual" feel of their respective ships. This brand of instinct is a physical (and somewhat mechanical) attribute: a product of hands-on learning over a long period of time, and of the continual repetition of certain cause-effect relationships. Such instincts are developed through trial and error, are subordinate to reason's commands, and are measured by one's dexterity or deftness of movement in the execution of those commands.

In Verne's later works, in contrast, instinct is often portrayed as replacing reason in problem-solving situations, and superior to it. For example, take the case of the scientist Jeorling who is the narrator of *The Ice Sphinx*. At one point in the narrative, when all other means of analysis fail to account for the unusual magnetic phenomena that he and the crew of the *Halbrane* encounter in the Antarctic, he offers an hypothesis, saying: "It was in this way . . . that I came to explain the occurrence, by instinct" (484, IA). Or note the recurring premonitions among the heroes of *Little-Fellow* (276, 302, IA), *The Secret of Wilhelm Storitz* (80, 142, 144, 198, IA), and *The Thompson Travel Agency* (33, IA). Or note the narrator's comments in *Mistress Branican* where he praises women's intuition: "Whereas a man relies on direct observation of fact and the consequences that derive from it, it is certain that a woman often has a clear vision of the future thanks to her intuitive qualities. It's a kind of inspiration that guides her and gives her a certain prescience about things" (150, IA). Or, finally, consider the following example, taken from *The Village in the Treetops*, where the lost protagonists must rely on the natural instincts of their African guide Khamis to lead them through the unexplored forest:

> In fact, a kind of instinct like that of animals—an inexplicable sixth sense that is found in some races of men—permits the Chinese, among others, and several tribes of Indians of the Far West to guide themselves by hearing and smell more than by sight, and to recognize direction by certain signs. Khamis possessed this faculty to a rare degree. He had many times proven it beyond a doubt. In a certain measure, the Frenchman and the American could put their entire trust in this ability . . . [that was] not prone to error. (52, IA)

Instinct is thus "not prone to error"—unlike the analyses of its rationalistic counterpart (see Maston's math error in *Topsy Turvy* or Lidenbrock's false compass headings in *Journey to the Center of the Earth*, among others). Thus, it is important to note that Verne's pessimism concerning the essential character of the human species is *not* unilateral in its applications. It is only humanity's acquired scientific nature that is in question in these texts and its blind faith in object-ive rationalism.

As a fitting conclusion to this chapter the following discussion concerns a text that is very emblematic of this ideological shift in Verne's portrayal of science. This particular short story is, appropriately, one of the author's final pieces of fictional writing. It was published posthumously in 1910 and was undoubtedly much revamped by his son Michel. It is entitled *Eternal Adam* and carries a footnote at the bottom of the title page informing the reader that it was "Written by Jules Verne in his final years and until now unpublished, this short story is somewhat unique in that it offers conclusions that are pessimistic—contrary to the proud optimism that animates the *Voyages Extraordinaires*. M.J.V." (*Yesterday* 213, IA). Aside from being an obvious attempt to validate the authenticity of this short story as being from the pen of his father, Michel's commentary also reflects (mistaken) public opinion in France during this period concerning the overall character of the *Voyages Extraordinaires*—a collection of which, in truth, only the earliest titles could be called "proudly optimistic." But the myth of Jules Verne as the "technological prophet" was already, in 1910, an established institution—so much so apparently that the publishers of this posthumous work felt the need for this explanatory note on the title page.

As for *Eternal Adam* itself, it is a story within a story. In the distant future, a scientist named zartog Sofr-Ai-Sr (note the resemblance with Nietzsche's Zarathoustra, as first pointed out by Marcel Moré)[19] is shown grappling with the theoretical details of human evolution. He is an inhabitant of the only land mass on Earth—an island continent called Hars-Iten-Schu, a kind of future Atlantis and occupying precisely the same geographic position as its prehistoric ancestor. Zartog Sofr-Ai-Sr is a true Positivist and the most highly respected archeologist of this advanced civilization. At one point during his rather Saint-Simonian musings, he states:

> Yes, comparing Man when he first appeared on the Earth naked and unarmed to what he has become today, one can only admire him. For centuries, despite his hatreds and his warring on his brothers, he has never retreated from his ongoing struggle with Nature and has ceaselessly increased his margin of victory over her. At first somewhat slow, his conquest has, during the past two hundred years, accelerated at a phenomenal pace. His achievement of political stability and universal peace has resulted in vigorous scientific growth. Humanity has learned to live by its brain and no longer by its limbs alone. Man has learned to think. That is why, during these past two hundred years, he has made so much progress in understanding and domesticating matter. . . .
>
> Yes, Man is great, greater even than the immense universe—a universe which, in the very near future, he will rule over. . . .
>
> So, in order to know the entire truth of his ascendancy, one last problem remains to be solved: "Exactly who is he? Where did he come from? Toward what mysterious end point is he evolving?" (218–20, IA)

But the hero of this tale encounters a fundamental problem in the evidence produced by his archeological excavations. Contrary to all logic, there seems to be no ascending continuity in human evolutionary development—at least according to the artifacts he unearths. In fact, hundreds of centuries of growth appear to alternate successively with rapid periods of de-evolution and degeneration in the human species. And what is even worse, at its highest point of development, ancient civilization seems further advanced than that of Sofr-Ai-Sr's own day!

> A conscientious examination of these sacred ruins was enough to remove all doubt: the men who lived during this ancient era had already acquired a cerebral development much superior to their successors, greater even than that of zartog Sofr's contemporaries! There had obviously been, during some one hundred and sixty or one hundred and seventy centuries, a period of drastic regression followed by a long slow period of regrowth. . . .
>
> "What?" he murmured to himself. "Admit that, some forty thousand years ago, Man had attained a level of civilization comparable to—if not superior to—the one that we now enjoy? That his knowledge and his possessions suddenly disappeared without a trace, forcing his descendants to begin over from nothing as if they were pioneers on a world that was uninhabited before them? . . . But, to admit this would deny all hope for the future! It would brand all our efforts as useless, all progress as uncertain and precarious as a tiny soap bubble floating on an ocean's waves! (223–25, IA)

Predictably, the remainder of the narrative goes on to prove this very fact. During a fortuitous moment at the dig, Sofr uncovers a partially disintegrated aluminum canister containing ancient manuscripts written in an unknown language (French), which he spends the ensuing two years deciphering. Much to his surprise and chagrin, he finds himself face-to-face with the astonishing truth of the matter: it is a diary, written approximately 20 thousand years before by the sole survivor of a planetary cataclysm. This journal recounts the end of humankind, the abrupt disappearance of the known continents, and the subsequent social and intellectual retrogression of those few individuals remaining who had managed to find refuge on a large island that suddenly rose up in the mid-Atlantic.

This "discovered" narrative constitutes the story within the story of *Eternal Adam*—reiterating, in *mise-en-abȳme* fashion via the text's very format, the major lesson of the tale as a whole.[20] Ironically, the author of this diary was likewise a successful and very "positive" mining executive during his own era (dated "2 . . ."). And just prior to the first earthquake tremors, he and his dinner guests were engaged in the following conversation—strangely reminiscent of Sofr's own panegyric to progress:

> Then, coming back to their topic of discussion, the two rivals agreed that, whatever his origin, Man was an admirable creature and had attained the highest level of civilization ever known. They proudly enumerated his conquests. All areas of endeavor were mentioned. Bathurst praised chemistry . . . Moreno delivered an encomium to modern medicine . . . They paid tribute to the machines of industry, each more ingenious than the next, each doing the work of a hundred men . . . They especially praised

electricity, that incredible power-source which was so docile and whose properties and very essence were now so well understood. . . .

In all, it was a real dithyramb—and one in which I contributed no small share myself. We all agreed that humanity had reached a pinnacle of intellectual development never achieved before our time, one which assured Man's imminent and total victory over Nature. (232–34, IA)

The biting irony of the lesson is not lost on the zartog Sofr-Ai-Sr. *Eternal Adam* concludes with his (Verne's?) reactions to this irrefutable proof of the meaningless transience—and vanity—of all human effort:

a kind of dread gripped his soul . . . Sofr's optimism was washed away forever. If the manuscript presented no specific technical details, its general indications were abundant. And it proved without a doubt that humanity had, much earlier, progressed to a higher state of knowledge than it had since. . . .

Reading this narrative from beyond the grave, Sofr imagined the terrible drama that was perpetually unfolding in the universe, and his heart was full of pity. Feeling the pain of those who had suffered long before, crushed beneath the weight of so much effort, in vain, throughout the infinity of time, the zartog Sofr-Ai-Sr slowly and sorrowfully came to realize the eternal cycle of all things. (262–63, IA)

Thus concludes the final entry in Verne's epic to "homo rationalis," one of the final journeys of his *Voyages Extraordinaires*. Perhaps extraordinary in the mimetic sense of the term, it is nevertheless a succinct and fitting resumé to Verne's own ideological evolution since the 1880s—a recapitulation of his growing pessimism regarding the true status of science and of men and women living in a universe that exceeds their comprehension.

Seen in the context of his entire oeuvre, this work marks the end of an ideological "voyage" that parallels the majority of Verne's fictional ones in its essential circularity. Prior to 1862 and his first contract with Hetzel to initiate the series to be known as the *Voyages Extraordinaires*, Verne (as mentioned) wrote a number of essays, plays, and short stories, among the latter *Master Zacharius* (1853). Like some of his earliest writings, this particular short story is Romantic in the extreme, but (in contrast to them) the variant used here is à la Hoffmann. It features a mad scientist/clockmaker who, in true Faustian fashion, barters his soul for the secrets of science. He achieves wealth and glory as the creator of the best timepieces in the world. But, as the years pass, his pride grows to insane proportions: "No! I cannot die! No more than the Creator of this universe—a universe that abides by His laws! I have become His equal! I have shared his power!" (*Ox* 146, IA). Suddenly, throughout the land, Zacharius's clocks begin to tick erratically and, one by one, grow silent. Zacharius comes down with a strange illness and, soon after, perishes miserably as the last of his marvelous timepieces stops ticking.

When viewed in this diachronic perspective, the overall ideological orientation of Verne's *Voyages Extraordinaires* seems to follow a distinctly cyclical pattern—similar to that of humanity in *Eternal Adam*. From the initial "generic" Romanticism of those texts dating from his early years (1850s-62), it then evolves into the proudly optimistic Positivism of what might be called his Hetzel-period (1862-86), to subsequently (re)become the sometimes trenchant anti-Positivist Romanticism of his later works (1886-1919).

The circle is thus closed. The journey is completed where it began. And the true unity of this oeuvre lies in its oscillating heterogeneity as it travels from one ideological pole to the other and back again.

NOTES

1. V., for example, Arne Saknussemm in *Journey to the Center of the Earth* (39 ff.), various aeronautic pioneers in *Robur the Conqueror* (31–32), the voyagers eulogized in *The Ice Sphinx* (234), previous explorers of the Arctic in *The Adventures of Captain Hatteras* (20–21, 48–49, 93–95, 106–11), etc.

2. In *Five Weeks in a Balloon, The Boy Captain,* and *The Amazing Adventure of the Barsac Mission.*

3. In *The Steam House* and *The Tribulations of a Chinaman.*

4. In *The Carpathian Castle.*

5. In *Twenty Thousand Leagues under the Sea* and *Propeller Island.*

6. In *Master of the World, The Last Will of an Eccentric,* and *From the Earth to the Moon.*

7. In *Journey to the Center of the Earth, The Children of Captain Grant,* and *For the Flag.*

8. In *The Adventures of Captain Hatteras, Journey to the Center of the Earth,* and *Around the Moon.*

9. Roland Barthes, "L'Effet de réel," *Communications* 11 (1968), 84–89.

10. V. *Twenty Thousand Leagues under the Sea, The Begum's Fortune,* and *Propeller Island,* for example.

11. V. *Twenty Thousand Leagues under the Sea* and *Robur the Conqueror,* for example.

12. Félix Duquesnel, cited in Martin, p. 113, IIC.

13. For example, repeated bankruptcies, costly amorous escapades, divorce from his first wife, and difficulties with the law.

14. It was during this period that Verne was even forced to sell (at a sizable loss) his beloved yacht.

15. This prescience on Verne's part is all the more extraordinary because Nietzche was still relatively unknown at this time and his most controversial texts were yet to be written (e.g., *Beyond Good and Evil* in 1886, *The Geneology of Morals* in 1887, and *The Will to Power* in 1889).

16. F. Rabelais, *Pantagruel,* Chap. 8. In *Oeuvres complètes* (Paris: Gallimard, "Pléiade," 1955), p. 206.

17. Cf. a similar passage at the conclusion of *Propeller Island*: ". . . to create an artificial island, an island that moves across the surface of the seas, is not such

an act going beyond the limits assigned to Man, and is it not forbidden for Man to so rashly usurp the powers of the Creator?" (317).

18. V. Captain John Mangles in *The Children of Captain Grant* (351–58).

19. Marcel Moré, *Le Très Curieux Jules Verne*, p. 229.

20. Although it was André Gide who coined the expression "mise-en-abŷme," G. Genette has termed this particular narrative structure a "récit métadiégiétique" in *Figures III* (Paris: Seuil, 1972), 238 ff.

The dual nature of Verne's pedagogical discourse, as noted above, functions as what might be called an alienating-dealienating signifying structure. In other words, time after time in these texts, a thematic or semantic "novum" is initially presented and its qualities of exotic "otherness" are purposely enhanced. Immediately thereafter, it is dealienated for the reader using a variety of overtly didactic strategies along with certain emotional buffers—both of which allow the novum to become fully assimilated into the reader's common experience. Such a novum can take the form, for example, of a futuristic piece of technology, a foreign locale, a rare (or simply unusual) species of plant or animal, an odd phenomenon of Nature, or any other object, idea, or linguistic term to which the average nineteenth-century reader would be unaccustomed. The hermeneutic task of the didacticism is to explain it cognitively. The buffers serve to reduce its emotional threat and to provide (sometimes subliminal) reader security throughout this pedagogical process. Occasionally the novum in question is the esoteric nature of the scientific explanation itself—which requires an additional set of didactic devices and buffers to ease its acceptance. Such, for instance, is the function of much of the satire, irony, and vox populi humor in these texts. Finally, having fulfilled its (pedagogical and narratological) task, the novum disappears and the mimetic status quo is once again reconstituted.

The Russian formalists' notion of *ostranenie*,[1] used to describe the singular character of certain poetic constructs, or Brecht's use of the term "alienation effect"[2] when speaking of the goals of his drama are both derivatives of the novum technique, in other words, that which produces cognitive estrangement via the unusual, the strange, or the seemingly nonmimetic. In contrast to their respective practices, however, Verne's narratives not only seek to create such estrangement in the reader, but also to conquer it. Of course, one might contend that the semiotic structure of SF as a whole involves the creation and conquest of a novum/ostranenie/alienation effect. But the procedure in most SF is *implicit*—that is, through forced participatory cognition on the reader's part, where he or she is constantly required to fill in absent paradigms in order to recuperate meaning.[3] In the Vernian variant, the text itself does the work—such is the role assigned to the scientific didacticism in these narratives. Thus, it is the *explicitly* pedagogical signifying structure of Verne's basic narratological recipe that serves to differentiate his "scientific novel" from most modern SF.

But before considering the actual textual mechanics of Verne's pedagogy, a few words need be said concerning "scientific" versus "literary" discourse in general. Viewed as speech acts, these two types of discourse, in their hypothetically "purest" manifestations, appear to be diametrical opposites in many ways. This seems readily apparent if one examines, for instance, their respective subject matters (fact versus fiction), their goals (conceptual knowledge versus esthetic pleasure), implied readers (specialists versus generalists), their discursive time frames (abstract and generalized present versus event-specific past, present, and future), as well as their functional and/or institutional place in society as a whole (applicative versus autotelic). The dichotomized

nature of these two linguistic phenomena is further reflected not only in the preferred lexicon of each (technicisms and mathematics versus metaphors and similes)
but also in their hermeneutic structures—referential, emotive, phatic, conative,
and so on.[4] For example, scientific discourse is highly mimetic, taxonomically
reductive (presupposing a higher and rationally ordered "system"), and necessarily one-dimensional in its referentiality. Literary discourse, in contrast, often
expresses the nonmimetic, is paradigmatically expansive (more accepting of principles of relativity and uncertainty), and is most often multi-dimensional in its
referentiality. The French critic Roland Barthes has outlined what he sees as the
essential identifying features of these two brands of discourse in the following
terms:

> According to the discourse of science ... knowledge is an enunciated
> statement. In writing, knowledge is enunciation. The enunciated state-
> ment, object of linguistic study, is viewed as the product of an absent
> enunciator. Enunciation, on the other hand, highlights the place and the
> energy of the speaking subject ... [it] aims at the reality of language
> itself. ... words are no longer deceptively thought of as simple instru-
> ments ... Writing makes a festival of knowledge. (*Leçon* 20, IIIA)

According to Barthes, literary discourse is distinguishable from scientific discourse principally by its self-referentiality—where the emphasis is less on language as instrumentality than language aimed at itself. Each tends to generate a
very different kind of "meaning"—denotative versus connotative, analytic versus
esthetic, and so on. In other words, in seeking to "objectively" explain the
exterior world, scientific discourse (unlike literary) endeavors only to be true or
false—determinable by experimentation and observation. As such, it limits its
interpretive possibilities to questions of right versus wrong, correct versus incor-
rect, and provable versus unprovable. The primary goal of scientific discourse is
intelligible coherence and empirical noncontradiction. Further, its value as an
effective didactic tool is proportionate to the extent to which it can depersonify
the language process itself. For example, by eliminating the narrator as a medi-
ating presence between the reader and the text, it strives to maintain a single,
autonomous, authoritative, and machinelike narrative voice whose sole function
is to communicate factual information. In so doing, it seeks to reduce the para-
digmatic to its lowest common denominator in favor of the "pure" referent.
In the words of Aldous Huxley:

> The aim of the scientist is to say only one thing at a time, and to say it
> unambiguously and with the greatest possible clarity. To achieve this, he
> simplifies and jargonizes. In other words, he uses the vocabulary and syn-
> tax of common speech in such a way that each phrase is susceptible to
> only one interpretation ... At its most perfectly pure, scientific language
> ceases to be a matter of words and turns into mathematics. (*Literature and
> Science* 12, IIIA)

As Michel Foucault (among others) has pointed out, this particular ideal of a pure scientific discourse was an important *episteme* of Verne's historical milieu—a period that witnessed dramatic (albeit still Newtonian) changes in the basic premises of scientific methodology. The cognitively object-ive outlook (deemed prerequisite to valid scientific inquiry) was increasingly extended into the realm of language itself. This fundamentally altered what had been the traditional relationship of language to knowledge:

> From the 19th century onward, language begins to turn in upon itself, to acquire its own substance, to deploy its own history, to claim for itself certain laws and an objectivity that it never had. . . . To know a language was no longer to come closer to knowledge. . . .
>
> This demotion of language to the status of an object was compensated for, however . . . by the fact that it was a necessary medium for any scientific knowledge . . . Hence, two concerns became paramount during the 19th century. One consisted of wanting to neutralize and to "polish" scientific language so that, emptied of all its identifying features and purified of all its linguistic accidents and improprieties . . . it could become the perfect reflection, the exact double, the crystalline mirror of a knowledge that was not of the verbal kind. Such was the Positivists' dream: a language that would function only in terms of what was known, a kind of "picture-language" . . . i.e., when confronting mute things, scientific discourse would be the "picture" of them. . . . (*Les Mots et les choses* 309, IIIA)

As institutionalized linguistic phenomena, literary and scientific discourse also require two very different kinds of reading "competence," as Jonathan Culler has termed it (*Structuralist Poetics* 113-30, IIIA). The former presupposes an awareness of and sensitivity to certain recurrent topoi, tropes, and other literary/cultural conventions for a maximum recuperation of meaning. The latter presupposes familiarity with a very different set of codes that are axiomatic, mathematically derived, and syllogistic in nature—codes that are geared to the rational explanation of physical phenomena (as opposed to the poetic portrayal of human perceptions). In fact, the very notion of scientific discourse is misleading, implying bidirectionality and reciprocity via the medium of language. Unlike literary discourse where the reader-text relationship is richly dialectical, scientific discourse is not dialogic by nature. It seeks only to inform. In other words, its discursive character mirrors the procedures inherent in scientific inquiry itself. As Mikhail Bakhtin explains:

> Mathematical and natural sciences do not acknowledge discourse as a subject in its own right. In scientific activity one must, of course, deal with another's discourse—the words of predecessors, the judgments of critics, majority opinion and so forth. One must deal with various forms for transmitting and interpreting others' words. . . . But all this remains a mere operational necessity and does not affect the subject matter itself of the science, into whose composition the speaker and his discourse do not, of

course, enter. The entire methodological apparatus of the mathematical and natural sciences is directed toward mastery over *mute objects, brute things,* that do not reveal themselves in words, that do not *comment on themselves.* Acquiring knowledge here is not connected with receiving and interpreting words or signs from the object itself under consideration. (*The Dialogic Imagination* 351, IIIA)

There are at least two fundamental problems inherent in any discussion attempting to compare scientific with literary discourse. The first has to do with the near total absence of typological studies of the former in terms of its specific structure as an encoded signifying system, particularly when compared to the vast amount of critical attention given the latter during the twentieth century.[5] As one contemporary literary critic has described it:

> narrative analysis has been created to describe the functioning of *figurative* speech. And this fact has influenced the nature of the theory itself—both via the categories that it selects and the definitions that it offers. . . .
> Whether it be the result of inattention and/or of censure, scientific or technological texts have not at all been described scientifically. . . . (Rastier 175, 179, IIIA)

The second problem has to do with the seemingly oxymoronic presence of scientific discourse *within* literary discourse—a fundamental characteristic of Verne's *romans scientifiques.* In the majority of Verne's texts, science is not presented via the accepted discursive codes of the literary tradition, that is, as satire (à la Flaubert), impressionistic obscurantism (à la Villiers de l'Isle-Adam), or as an amorphous backdrop justifying certain social structures or human behavior (à la Balzac or Zola). For each of these authors, the scientific serves simply as a narratological handmaiden to plot development and/or character portrayal—often for purposes of increased verisimilitude. And it is usually articulated in these texts through a type of narrative discourse that is itself literary rather than scientific in nature. In contrast, Verne's novels—popularizations as they are—*science is presented as science,* for its own sake and in its own terms. And the resulting tension in Verne's narratives between these two forms of discourse—each contributing to the very identity of this new genre—sometimes has an effect on the reader similar to that produced by Lautréamont's juxtaposition of an umbrella and a sewing machine. In other words, it creates a kind of estrangement that the narrative must find a way to overcome to be effective pedagogically.

Thus, in Verne's novels, pedagogy becomes the door through which scientific discourse is inserted into literary discourse. And the mechanisms of its integration vary greatly in nature and form. They range from simple passing references to known scientists, to anecdotal remarks, to passages of scientific knowledge inserted en bloc into the text, to substitutions of scientific terminology for literary ones in a variety of tropes, to the hermeneutics of the reading process itself where the decoding procedures intrinsic to scientific methodology are reproduced in the text. But such mechanisms are always buffered so as to maintain reader identification with traditional literary motifs and plot structures (for example, the heroic quest or *roman d'apprentissage* format, the melodramatic Manichean struggle of good versus evil, and so forth) and with stylistic procedures common to normal literary usage (for example, humorous wordplay, maxims, standard poetic metaphors, references to well-known authors, and excerpts from their works). In this way, the texts' discursive balance is maintained and the effectiveness of the pedagogy is both strengthened and made more palatable.

Chapters 6 and 7 examine in greater detail the narrative components of Verne's scientific didacticism, *not* attempting to judge them in terms of their intrinsic *littérarité*, but simply to show how they function. Their basic alienating-dealienating character, I believe, make them texts that are noteworthy not only in a sociohistorical context (as instruments for nineteenth-century social adaptation) but in a narratological one as well.

NOTES

1. V. V. Chklovski, "L'Art comme procédé" and B. Eikhenbaum, "La Théorie de la 'méthode formelle,'" in T. Todorov, *Théorie de la littérature* (Paris: Seuil, 1965), pp. 83, 45.

2. B. Brecht, "A Short Organum for the Theatre," in *Brecht on Theatre*, trans. John Willett (New York: Hill & Wang, 1979), p. 182.

3. V. D. Suvin, *Metamorphoses of Science Fiction* (New Haven: Yale University Press 1979), pp. 3–15; also M. Angenot, "The Absent Paradigm: An Introduction to the Semiotics of Science Fiction," *Science-Fiction Studies* VI:17 (1979), 9–19.

4. V. Roman Jakobson, *Questions de poétique* (Paris: Seuil, 1973) and "Linguistics and Poetics" in *Style in Language*, E. Sebeok, ed. (Cambridge: MIT Press, 1960), pp. 350–77.

5. This situation, however, is now showing signs of improvement in the 1980s. See, in particular, the on-going work of The Society for Literature and Science—a scholarly organization devoted to fostering research and discourse on the relations between literature and various scientific disciplines. See also Harry Garvin, ed., *Science and Literature* (Lewisburg: Bucknell University Press, 1983); Wilda C. Anderson, *Between the Library and the Laboratory* (Baltimore: Johns Hopkins University Press, 1984); N. Katherine Hayes, *The Cosmic Web* (Ithaca, N.Y.: Cornell University Press, 1984); and Walter Schatzberg et al., eds., *The Relations of Literature and Science* (New York: MLA, 1987), among other recent studies.

CHAPTER 6

Narrative Exposition and Pedagogy

As already noted, the pedagogical elements in Verne's fictions seem to occur wherever there is a need to rationalize the unusual or come to grips with the unaccustomed. Science is thus portrayed as a privileged instrument for decoding the experiential usually through the processes of identification, localization, and assimilation. The textual mechanisms in the *Voyages Extraordinaires* that convey such pedagogy can perhaps best be divided into three main groups, according to the overt presence or nonpresence of a fictional narrator, narratee, or other mediators between the text and the reader. Let us call the first format *direct exposition*, the second *semidirect exposition*, and the third *indirect exposition*. In the first, the pedagogy is totally unmediated: the information and/or lesson is offered directly to the reader by the text itself, that is, there is no identifiable narrator, the only narratee is the reader himself, and the role played by such pedagogy is tangential to (or completely detached from) the action. In the second, it is partially mediated: the text's omniscient narrator intrudes periodically to offer clarifications, commentary, or documentation, sometimes even correcting the observations of the fictional characters. The third variant is almost wholly mediated: the pedagogy is no longer addressed directly at the reader but, rather, to one of the protagonists in the narrative—usually a vox populi figure or a young man who is a kind of apprentice or acolyte. It almost always originates from the learned scientist of the group—the lesson itself being closely tied to developments in the plot at that moment (for example, serving to identify what they are observing, to rescue them from imminent danger, and so on).

Finally, there exist a number of ancillary devices in Verne's texts that aid in the didactic implantation. These may be grouped into four general types: *reiterators*, which repeat the essentials of the lesson; *animators*, which enrich the lesson with drama, humor, or wordplay; *valorizors*, which emphasize the value of the lesson learned; and *buffers*, which facilitate the lesson's "emotional" assimilation. These are discussed in detail in Chapter 7.

The bulk of Verne's scientific pedagogy is generally reducible to these few narrative strategies. Each lesson is a composite of one or more of these textual features and, as one would expect, their usage depends in part on the difficulty and/or complexity of the scientific lesson itself. For example, simple technical nomenclature or geographical-historical "backgrounding" are most often done via direct exposition. Scientific updates, particularly in narratives supposedly taking place in the past, are usually added by a meta-narrator via semidirect exposition. Mechanical explanations or taxonomic identifications are done via character dialogue in a show-and-tell format, and so forth. Reiterators and animators are normally used in specific instances to aid in the remembering of a particular term, fact, or theory. In contrast, valorizors and buffers occur throughout the text as a whole and act as an omnipresent pedagogical support structure to it.

Now let us examine in more detail each of these didactic strategies in Verne's narratives and see how each functions as part of the overall educational project of the *Voyages Extraordinaires.*

DIRECT EXPOSITION

Among those "unmediated" pedagogical passages in Verne's works, one finds four general types: en bloc insertions (in the indicative, negative/question, or conditional modes), en passant explanations (appositive, parenthetical, and the like), extratextual references (footnotes), and nonlinguistic devices (illustrations, maps, and realia).

An en bloc insertion occurs when a relatively lengthy piece of pedagogy is spliced directly into the narrative without any special fictional accommodation for it. In other words, the syntagmatic flow of the narration abruptly halts, a change of register takes place, and the text (communicating with the reader in what might be called one-to-one address) begins to provide extensive scientific information and/or documentation about the subject matter in question. There is no attempt to use the fictional characters as *porte-paroles*. There is no identifiable narrator, no "subjectification" of any sort. This variant constitutes a kind of *cas-limite* in Vernian pedagogical discourse in terms of its textual autonomy and narrative simplicity. And it can be articulated in three different ways: indicatively, negatively, or conditionally vis-à-vis the action at hand. An indicative en bloc insertion acts as a context builder, "filling in the blanks" between what the protagonists already know (but don't express) and what the reader presumably does not know. It may take the form, for example, of a comprehensive inventorylike listing of the supplies that accompany the explorers/scientists, each item documented as to its purpose, its inventor, and its particular properties and function.[1] Or it may serve to provide the reader with the necessary historical or geographical background to the events portrayed in the novel (heightening the latter's verisimilitude by localizing them either chronologically or spatially).[2] In the most extreme cases, it may constitute an entire chapter intercalated between two successive stages of plot progression, often introduced by an explanatory statement indicating why such a lengthy clarification is needed and concluding with a statement like "Such, then, were the circumstances." This is the case, for instance, in the third chapter of *The Steam House* where the history of India is briefly outlined (20 pages) in order to provide a "real" historical setting for the ensuing story (such chapters of pure didacticism invariably occur near the beginning of the narrative, for obvious reasons): "The following few words will provide a summary of what India was like at the time of this narrative, and, in particular, the facts concerning the bloody rebellion of the Cipays ... Such was the administrative and military situation on the peninsula at that time ..." (*Steam* 33, 35, IA).

Or consider the novel *From the Earth to the Moon*, where 14 pages of basic astronomy are offered early in the novel under the suggestive title of *Le Roman de la Lune* (Novel of the Moon). In this chapter, which mixes both the indicative and the conditional approaches, a hypothetical celestial observer is evoked as a kind of secondhand witness to convey a detailed scientific exposé of the origins of the universe, the solar system, and the moon (a narrative strategy very common in Verne's pedagogy, and one discussed later in this study):

A hypothetical observer, endowed with infinite vision and placed at the center of the universe during its slow birth, would've seen untold numbers of atoms whirling through space. But, little by little, as the centuries passed, a change took place. Obeying the laws of gravitation, these atoms began to combine chemically to produce molecules, creating nebulae. . . .

Among these five thousand nebulae, there is one which Man has come to call the Milky Way. It contains eighteen million stars, each one of which is the sun to its own solar system. . . .

The Sun seems almost lost in the immensity of this stellar field . . . Around it gravitate eight planets, each one having spun off from its core during the early moments of Creation. They are . . . Mercury, Venus, Earth, Mars, Jupiter, Saturn, Uranus, and Neptune. . . .

Among these children of the Sun, kept in their elliptical orbits by the laws of gravitation, there are some who have satellites of their own. Uranus has eight, Saturn eight, Jupiter four, Neptune as many as three perhaps, and Earth has one—the latter, one of the less important in the solar system, is called the Moon. . . .

Such was the accumulated knowledge about the Moon which the Gun Club was proposing to perfect in all its aspects, cosmographic, geological, political, and moral. (*Earth/Moon* 52–66, IA)

There is a fundamental difference between what I have termed an "indicative" as opposed to a "negative/question" or a "conditional" treatment of such direct, unmediated pedagogy. Whereas the former never utilizes the actual protagonists of the narrative as didactic intermediaries, the latter two, although not placing such pedagogy directly in their mouths, nevertheless identify it as something the protagonists either did *not* observe or *would have* observed under different circumstances. The information conveyed is thus not completely autonomous (vis-à-vis the fictional characters), and the omniscient narrator's presence is somewhat more palpable.

A typical example of en bloc insertion using negation is the following passage taken from *Around the World in 80 Days*. In this novel, Verne has at his disposal what would seem to be the perfect narrative vehicle for teaching geography—a trip around the world. But two factors continually hinder its exposition. First, the purpose of the journey itself is speed (not tourism). Second, the hero Phileas Fogg, intent as he is on winning the wager, is portrayed as one who "did not travel, he simply circumscribed" (*80* 71, IA), that is, he pays very little attention to those countries through which he passes. Caught between the dual necessities of character verisimilitude and geographical didacticism, Verne solves this narrative problem through negative exposition. The city of Bombay, located along Fogg's route, is a good case in point:

> Consequently, Phileas Fogg never thought to visit these marvels of Bombay, neither the city hall, nor the magnificent library, nor the fortresses, nor the docks, nor the cotton market, nor the bazaars, nor the mosques, nor the synagogues, nor the Armenian churches, nor the splendid pagoda of Malebar Hill surmounted by two polygonal towers. He would contemplate neither the masterpieces of Elephanta, nor its mysterious hypogea hidden south-east of the outer roads, nor the Kanherie caverns of Salcetta Island, these admirable remains of Buddhist architecture. . . .
>
> No, nothing! When leaving the passport office, Phileas Fogg went directly to the train station. . . . (64, IA).

The following is an example of this same negative mode strategy, but it utilizes a series of interrogatives for the same purpose:[3]

> But, at this hour, where were the habitual strollers of Top-Hane's Square? Those Persians coquettishly coiffed in their astrakhan bonnets, Greeks elegantly balancing their fustanellas, Circassians always dressed in their military uniforms, Georgians still attired in their Russian tunics even when beyond their own borders, Arnauts . . . Turks . . . Yes! where were they? (*Kéraban* 2, IA)

Finally, en bloc pedagogy in the conditional mode fulfills the same narrative need—allowing the narrator to elaborate on what the protagonists "would have" seen had they visited certain locales. For example, note its use in the following case where the author wishes to describe the state of Pennsylvania without having his protagonists actually travel there:

This state of Pennsylvania owes its name to the illustrious English Quaker William Penn who, towards the end of the seventeenth century, acquired a vast amount of land along the border of Delaware. . . .

Harris T. Kymbale would've undoubtedly told this story, along with many other anecdotes about the country, if luck had only given him a couple of weeks in the Pennsylvanian region. With what vivacity and suppleness of style he would've described this territory! It was rather like Ohio, with the picturesque Alleghanys bisecting it from south-east to north-west . . . He would've first evoked its general topographical aspects, those justifying the latter half of its name: its vast forests of oak, beech, chestnut, walnut, elm, ash, and maple . . . With measured and melodious prose, he would've then praised the spacious fields where the mulberry groves prosper and the vineyards flourish. . . .

Even Max Réal, usually so scornful of industrial regions, would've found in Pennsylvania more than one lovely site that would've tempted his artist's brush. . . .

But neither the first nor the fourth game-player had been chosen to go there . . . and it will be an eternal regret to posterity. (*Last Will* 353–54, IA)

It might be added that such an "eternal regret to posterity" is largely mitigated by Verne's *own* in absentia descriptions of these regions, inherently accenting the social value of his efforts to fill what would have otherwise been a pedagogical void in the narrative.

What differentiates the above en bloc pedagogical insertions from the en passant brand is their comparative length. Whereas the former occupy anywhere from a paragraph or two to an entire chapter in the text, the latter are quite brief, usually a few words added to clarify a technicism or a foreign term, a numerical reference for purposes of comparison, or a short explanatory anecdote. But similar to the en bloc passages of direct exposition, they too are unmediated and autonomous vis-à-vis the fictional characters and/or plot. And they too do not betray the presence of an intrusive narrator.

Several variations on the en passant pedagogical strategy are evident throughout Verne's novels. One of the most frequent utilizes the mechanism of apposition, as in the following example: "The saddle was made of 'pelions,' sheep-skins tanned on one side and fleecy on the other, which were held in place by a wide and intricately embroidered girth" (*Grant* 102, IA).

Another variant is quite similar, but usually introduced with a phrase like "in other words" or "a kind of": "Then, proceeding by hypotypose, in other words by using lively and animated description, he proceeded" (*Steam* 313, IA); "An hour later, Kin-Fo was sleeping peacefully with his arms wrapped around this 'tchou-fou-jen,' a kind of split bamboo pillow which helps Chinese beds to remain cool very appreciated in these hot climates" (*Tribulations* 58, IA).

Others are contained in short parenthetical statements, frequently used for measurement conversions (assisting those readers accustomed to metric calibrations, at the same time maintaining narrative verisimilitude): "At six o'clock in the morning, the thermometer reading was 26 degrees (-3 Centigrade), at six o'clock in the evening 29 degrees (-2 Centigrade), and at midnight 25 degrees (-4 Centigrade); the wind was blowing lightly from the south-west" (*Hatteras* 102, IA).

Finally, there are those en passant pedagogical references that are directly integrated into the discursive structure of the passages of which they form a part. Such references usually take the form of a quick aside that more fully localizes the item in question—often through taxonomic classification: "Zirone, without wondering about which of the one hundred and seventy-six species of pigeons now accounted for by ornithologists this bird might belong, saw only one thing: it had to be one that was of the edible variety" (*Mathias* 16, IA).

Fulfilling the same function as the en passant explanations, one finds in Verne's texts a continual usage of "extratextual" references such as footnotes. Almost exclusively in direct exposition (whereas en bloc and en passant passages need not be), footnotes are one of the main staples of unmediated pedagogy in the *Voyages Extraordinaires*, with well over 700[4] of them throughout this series. And, interesting to note (in the context of Verne's evolving narrative practices), nearly half of such footnotes occur in the first six novels of this 64-work collection; that is, those works that are the most overtly Positivistic, the most scientifically didactic, and, incidentally, the most popular during the author's own lifetime.

The majority of Verne's footnote references serve to explain unusual terms of vocabulary, to provide additional documentation, or to enhance the narrative's internal verisimilitude. The most common are simple measurement conversions or translations/clarifications of foreign or technical words located in the text:

> it carried two kegs of water containing twenty-two gallons each (1). . . .
> (1) Approximately one hundred liters. A gallon, which contains eight pints, is equivalent to 4.453 liters. (*Five* 47, IA)

> The next morning Glenarvan and his companions reunited in the plain: the first estancias (1) adjacent to the Sierra Tandil were in sight. . . .
> (1) The word "estancias" designates those large cattle ranches on the Argentinian plains. (*Grant* 219, IA)

When used in this fashion, the footnotes serve to guarantee the reader's comprehension of the text's sometimes difficult lexicon. In doing so, they reduce the intrinsic exoticism of such terminology by restating it in lay language that is familiar and easily understandable—all the while maintaining the *effet de réel* integrity of the text itself. Within the format of direct exposition (with no narrator present), this particular use of footnotes constitutes one of the strongest phatic devices in Verne's pedagogy, not only directly addressing the reader, but reformulating the text's very signifying structure to "bring it down to his level." That is to say, in order to fulfill its role as effective pedagogy, the lexicon of Verne's fictions must simultaneously straddle two registers of usage: that determined by the narrative itself (for exoticism but also for verisimilitude and precision) and that of his implied reader (for its immediate dealienation).

When offering additional documentation, such footnotes can often seem gratuitous. But they serve a number of important functions. They not only expand the scope of the pedagogical lesson, but also validate and augment the authority of the text itself as a pedagogical instrument. This can take place, for example, through a simple mention of a known scientist's or historian's authoritative textbook on the subject matter in question:

> Then during the 15th and 16th centuries, Copernicus and Tycho Brahe (1) fully explained the nature of the solar system and the role played by the Moon among these celestial bodies. . . .
> (1) V. *The Founders of Modern Astronomy*, an admirable book by Monsieur J. Bertrand of the Institute. (*Earth/Moon* 60, IA)

Or they may be considerably more prolix in nature, providing a detailed explanation of the item noted, along with an historical overview of its importance. The following example, from *Journey to the Center of the Earth*, is intended to fully document a portable electric lantern called a Ruhmkorff apparatus that the heroes will carry with them in their underground quest:

> (1) The device of M. Ruhmkorff consists of a Bunzen battery, powered by potassium bichromate, which gives off no odor. An induction coil connects the battery to a specially constructed lantern; inside this lantern is located a vacuum tube containing a trace of carbonic gas or azote. When the device is switched on, this gas glows and produces a steady white light. The battery and coil are carried in a leather pouch attached to the traveller's bandolier. The lantern, placed externally, is sufficient to light up even the most opaque of darknesses. It permits the traveller, without fear of explosion, to walk through normally flammable gases, and it does not become extinguished even if submerged in water. M. Ruhmkorff is a very learned and talented physicist. His great invention was the induction coil which permits the production of high voltage electricity. In 1864, he earned the award of 50,000 Francs which France had reserved for the most ingenious application of electricity. (96–97, IA)

Finally, when used to enhance the narrative's internal verisimilitude, such pedagogical footnotes do not seek to translate a difficult term, cite an authoritative reference, or explain the complex functioning of a piece of technology. Rather, they serve to comment on the characters' actions in the text itself. This occurs in a number of different ways throughout the *Voyages Extraordinaires*— and relatively infrequently, as compared to the other brand of footnotes described above. For example, they may attempt to more fully anchor the narrative (and its protagonists) in real historical events, as in the case of *The Children of Captain Grant* where a French explorer named Guinnard is shown to be a colleague of Paganel: "(1) Monsieur A. Guinnard was, in fact, a prisoner of the Poyuche Indians for three years, from 1856 to 1859. With great courage he survived the terrible ordeal and eventually escaped through the Upsallata pass in the Andes. He returned to France in 1861, and he is now one of Paganel's colleagues in the Société de Géographie" (231, IA).

Or they may serve as an intertextual device, recalling the events or personages from other *Voyages Extraordinaires* and presenting them as historically real. For example, when the hero-narrator of *The Ice Sphinx* passes near to—but is unable to approach—the South Pole, a footnote on that page explains: "(1) Twenty-eight years later, something which M. Jeorling could not have foreseen, another explorer did see the Pole and stepped onto this point of the globe on March 21, 1868. . . . He took possession of this continent in his own name, unfurling above it a flag embroidered with a large gold 'N.' Nearby floated a submarine called the *Nautilus*, and his name was Captain Nemo" (404, IA).

Clearly, this latter type of footnote usage is quite different from the translation or documentation variety. Here the purely pedagogical becomes entwined with self-referential mechanisms of verisimilitude, as the inherent "authority" of the footnoting procedure itself is redirected toward fictional ends rather than didactic ones. This particular use of footnotes (as one might expect) tends to increase as the overall pedagogical dimension of Verne's texts decreases, and especially from the mid-1880s onward (as earlier discussed). It is significant in this regard that the novel containing the greatest number of such intertextual footnotes is *Topsy Turvy* (1889) where the characters and events of five different *Voyages Extraordinaires* are cited: not only those of *From the Earth to the Moon* and *Around the Moon* (whose Gun Club members become the heroes—or antiheroes—of this narrative), but also *The School for Crusoes, Hector Servadac,* and *The Adventures of Captain Hatteras.* The latter reference is the most amazing as the footnote itself performs a double reversal—both underscoring the historical reality of Hatteras (in the manner of the Nemo reference cited above) and at the same time denying it: "(1) In this list of the explorers who have attempted to reach the North Pole, Barbicane has left out the name of Captain Hatteras whose flag might be seen planted at the eighty-second latitude. This is understandable, given that Captain Hatteras was, in all likelihood, only an imaginary hero" (*Topsy* 78, IA). The tongue-in-cheek use of "in all likelihood" (*vraisemblablement*) in this footnote is a glimpse of things to come in Verne's growing penchant for wordplay, satire, and humorous self-reflection—all very common throughout his later texts. His concern for scientific pedagogy becomes more frequently replaced with a concern for *écriture* in its own right. And as a result he more often calls into question those novelistic boundaries separating the real from the imaginary.[5]

The final group of pedagogical devices classifiable under the heading of direct exposition are nonlinguistic in nature. They are the many maps, illustrations, and what might be called realia that regularly punctuate these narratives. As direct visual representations of the text's content, they enhance both its didacticism and its fictional immediacy by adding a pictorial dimension to the text's signifying structure.

The maps of the *Voyages Extraordinaires* are particularly effective in this respect. One might easily imagine the youthful reader tracing his or her own fictional "voyage" with the aid of such maps—around the world as well as through the narrative itself—and one cannot help but recall another such youngster in the opening lines of a more metaphoric "voyage," the one concluding Baudelaire's *Les Fleurs du Mal*: "For the child, fascinated by pictures and maps, the Universe matches his vast appetite" (155, IIIA). The Vernian map serves first to reduce the geographic abstraction of the text's language—fully concretizing it and providing a conceptual stepping-stone to mimesis. In the same way as language itself might be considered a representational map of both the real and the imaginary, Verne's cartography is a kind of diagrammatic language that depicts both real and imaginary locales. Witness, for example, not only those detailed atlaslike maps of Africa, the Arctic, South America, northern India, the Mediterranean, Ireland, the United States, Scotland, and other countries or continents,[6] but also those of such wholly fictional places as Lincoln Island (*Mysterious* 287, IA) or Chairman Island (*Vacation* 195, IA).

Further, in their respective production, drawing a map and writing a novel can be seen as two sides of the same semiotic coin, particularly in Verne's case. Two observations tend to support this assertion. First, there exist several maps in the *Voyages Extraordinaires* drawn by the author himself (like those in *The Adventures of Captain Hatteras* and in *The Children of Captain Grant*, for instance). Second, consider the fact that one of the principal features of most of Verne's texts (both in terms of the geography portrayed as well as in the narratological sense) is the continual need to "fill in the blanks." That is to say, the Vernian voyage is the fictional means whereby the process of global mapping is transformed into narrative discourse, and vice versa. This implicit twofold geo-graphic function is perhaps nowhere better expressed than in *The Children of Captain Grant* where Paganel states:

> Is there, indeed, a greater satisfaction, a pleasure more real than that of a navigator who inks in his discoveries on a sea-chart? He sees entire lands take shape before his eyes; island by island, headland by headland, they emerge from the empty waters! . . . Then the isolated discoveries fit together to form a whole, the lines merge, the marked dots join to form a pattern . . . Ah! my friends, a discoverer of new lands is a veritable inventor! He feels all the same emotions, savors all the same surprises!" (81, IA)

In these lines, one almost hears echoes of Barthes's *Le Plaisir du Texte*: "a space for pleasure is thereby created" (11, IIIA). Thus, as localizing devices, the many maps in Verne's *Voyages dans les mondes connus et inconnus* are significant in three ways. They constitute a narratological support structure to the didacticism in these works. They provide a spatially defined framework for the action portrayed. And they serve as an additional (encoded) signifying system that parallels—in its reading as well as in its writing—the semiological dynamics of the text itself.

Whereas the maps in each Vernian novel constitute a macroscopic reference point around which the narrative as a whole is constructed and with which it interacts, the illustrations in these texts (some 4,500 throughout the *Voyages Extraordinaires*, an average of more than 70 per novel) are keyed either to individual protagonists, to the technological device that is the vehicle of their journey, or to a single, specific scene or event encountered along their route.

In the first two instances, the illustrations serve primarily as portraits. In providing the reader with a mental picture of the heroes and their unusual mode of transport, they act as mimesis builders and facilitate referentiality. Further, the Vernian machine itself is often depicted against a backdrop that highlights its extraordinary character—either by the unique panoramas that it affords (for example, undersea spectacles such as coral forests, famous sunken vessels, and Atlantis, or bird's-eye views of entire cities, lakes, and mountain ranges, or even the earth as a whole) or by its capacity to do the seemingly impossible (racing with a locomotive, outpulling a team of elephants, conquering the South Pole, and so forth). Such illustrations anchor the textual novum to the real world— dealienating it via contextualization and emphasizing its useful (albeit exotic) nature.

As for the remainder of the illustrations—those that function not as simple identity portraits but depict various scenes from the narrative itself—the question of *which* passages are chosen for such pictorial representation often seems decided less by their importance to the overall plot than by their pedagogical value and/or their potential for enhancing the text's local color, verisimilitude, or metaphoric content. For example, such key scenes as the explosion of the *Géant d'Acier* in *The Steam House*, the mysterious Dr. Antékirtt revealing his true identity as Mathias Sandorf, or the near-collision with a comet in *Around the Moon* are not represented. Conversely, in those same novels, dozens of relatively unimportant scenes (to the narrative as a whole) are: for example, the Indian snake charmers of Guzarate (*Steam* 227, IA), Cap Matifou and Pescade's gymnastic feats (*Mathias* 193, IA), and the moon portrayed as the goddess Phoebe (*Moon* 160, IA).

But it is the recurring didactic function of such illustrations that is of special interest. Two variants are the most frequent: those simple "postcard" type scenes that reproduce the various cities, topography, monuments, flora and fauna, and unusual sights and peoples encountered by the heroes (and drawn as seen through their eyes), and those scenes that supplement specific lessons in zoology, astronomy, geology, aviation, and such (sometimes as observed by the heroes, but most often not). Examples of the first, by far the most numerous throughout the *Voyages Extraordinaires*, include the following: sketches of the many Asian cities located along the route of Claudius Bombarnac in the novel of the same name (9, 51, 107, 116ff., IA), of the Himalayas in *The Steam House*

(270, IA), the tomb of Louis IX in *Hector Servadac* (105, IA), a eucalyptus forest and kiwi birds in *The Children of Captain Grant* (494, 706, IA), a "cannibal-tree" in *Five Weeks in a Balloon* (166, IA), and an eskimo village in *The Adventures of Captain Hatteras* (75, IA).

The second group is relatively limited in number and includes such pedagogical aids as illustrations of those diverse species of fish enumerated by Conseil in *Twenty Thousand Leagues under the Sea* (147, 150, IA), of the phases of the moon in *From the Earth to the Moon* (57, IA), of hot air balloons and dirigibles in *Robur the Conqueror* (19, IA), and of the planet Saturn and its moons in *Hector Servadac* (416, IA). More than a simple *effet de réel* or a means to enhance the picturesque qualities of the narrative, these illustrations attempt to be instructive. Thus, the postcard brand of illustration helps the reader to "see" in the visual sense, the instructive brand in a more cognitive one. But the manner in which they do so is also noteworthy.

In the postcard illustrations, precision of representation is the key. In the instructive ones, this concern for exactitude is sacrificed for the sake of clarity and comprehensiveness. A particularly good example of this difference is shown by the progressive substitution in Verne's later works of actual photographs for the postcard type when portraying cities, lakes, and mountains (*The Brothers Kip, A Second Homeland, Master of the World*)—yet another instance where science is incorporated into Verne's *romans scientifiques*, this time via their published format. But in those same works the pedagogical type of illustration (where present) continues to remain diagrammatic and handdrawn. Further, the elements of each such scene are carefully composed for maximum pedagogical impact, even at the risk of a loss of verisimilitude. For example, in those illustrations depicting the many species of fish observed by Professor Aronnax and Conseil in *Twenty Thousand Leagues under the Sea* (147, 150, 376, IA), there are no two fish of the same type in the same patch of ocean; each occupies its own space in the drawing (with very little if any overlap), and each is portrayed along the same vertical axis and at the same distance from the viewers (the skates and flounders even standing upright to better show their anatomy). And the illustration of the hot air balloons and dirigibles in *Robur the Conqueror* (19, IA) reflects the same concern for condensed multiplicity and orderly arrangement, regardless of the nonmimetic artificiality of such a portrayal.

Finally, the textual location of such illustrations vis-à-vis the narrative is also significant. Although differing from edition to edition, they generally precede their narrative counterparts by at least a page or two, arousing the curiosity of the reader, inciting him or her to continue reading, and foreshadowing locales and events to come. Narratologically, such a strategy creates suspense. Didactically, it creates needs that the narrative subsequently satisfies and, as such, functions as a preliminary support structure to the lesson. That is to say, the reader immediately "recognizes" the passage in question when encountering it in the text, effectively implanting it in memory.[7]

Before moving on to those didactic strategies in Verne's works that are partially mediated via a narrator and fall under the category of semidirect exposition,

An illustration of fish species (*20,000*, engraving by A. de Neuville, 1870)

a few words should be said about Verne's use of "realia." These are normally integrated into the text itself, and—in pictorial fashion—reproduce such difficult-to-describe narrative items as medieval runes (*Journey* 13, 18, IA), stone inscriptions (*Journey* 324, IA), cryptogram grids (*Mathias* 70-78, IA), and game boards (in *Last Will* 168-69). Although not very frequent throughout the *Voyages Extraordinaires* (perhaps due to their difficulty in typesetting), such realia, where present, tend to diversify the signifying structure of these texts, further illustrating how "a picture is worth a thousand words."

Much more common in Verne's novels, however, are those nonliterary linguistic passages such as encoded messages, fragments of letters (usually half erased and quasi-illegible), graphs and charts, billboard signs, newspaper bulletins, rebuses, crests and logos, and the like. Midway between pictures and words, they serve principally as *effets de réel*, typographically reproducing the item under observation by the protagonists. And their overall effect is to strengthen the reader's identification with the latter. As a rule, both variants of realia increase the *lisible* qualities of the Vernian text. They address the mind's eye with patterns and images as well as with words—periodically interrupting the syntagmatic flow of the text with visual "rest breaks" to avoid monotony—and they effectively enhance the verisimilitude of the narrative itself. Such insertions in Verne's prose often give one the impression of reading an encyclopedia or of deciphering a treasure map (both profoundly "Vernian" activities) or even of witnessing what Bahktin once called "heteroglossia" (*The Dialogic Imagination* 262-63, IIIA), as the text's different communicative registers interact one with the other. Thus, the thematic diversity of the huge mapping project (geographical, scientific, ideological, and so on) of Verne's *Voyages Extraordinaires* is closely matched by the wide variety of signifying systems used for its expression. And, as most literary critics are quick to point out, narrative form *is* meaning.

SEMIDIRECT EXPOSITION

The narratological heterogeneity of the *Voyages Extraordinaires* is perhaps nowhere more clearly evident than in the narrative voice of these texts. As Michel Foucault has observed, it is a strangely multiple one:

The narrative process is continuously breaking up. It changes signs, inverts itself, distances itself, comes from somewhere else as if from another speaker. Narrative voices emerge from nowhere, silencing those that preceded them, offering for a moment their own discourse, then suddenly disappear, to be replaced by another one of these nameless faces, these grey silhouettes. It is an organization very different from that of *A Thousand and One Nights*. In the latter, each narrative, even if it is recounted by a third party, is linked to the one who actually lived the story—each fable has its own voice, each voice its own fable . . . In Verne's works, there is one fable per novel, but recounted by many different voices—voices that are intertwined, obscure, and contesting one another. ("Arrière fable" 6, IID)

As previously discussed, the direct exposition pedagogical format used in Verne's works included *no* visible narrator—the historical, geographical, or scientific information was conveyed via nonlinguistic devices such as maps and illustrations or via what Foucault calls elsewhere in the same article "this anonymous, mono-tone, and slick voice . . . the frozen voice . . . of scientific discourse" (11, IID). Conversely, what I later call indirect exposition will be its opposite—the strong-est possible mediation by a narrator, for example, first-person narration by one of the fictional characters of the text or sustained dialogue among several of them. But located between these two extremes is another type of didactic dis-course in the Vernian text. It might be called semimediated or semidirect and is characterized by the palpable presence of an extrafictional meta-narrator or invisible authorial voice who is the source of the information presented.

The primary role of this particular type of narrator, as one might expect, is to control the fictional development of the narrative. It is he who (usually through indirect discourse) provides the reader with descriptions of what the var-ious protagonists are doing at any given moment, what they are seeing, what they are feeling, and so forth. It is he who situates the narrative in a specific time and place. It is he who gives overviews and summaries of pertinent events occurring prior to, adjacent to, and sometimes even after those of the text's present. But what distinguishes Verne's brand of meta-narrator is his lack of fix-ity. Constantly oscillating between objective omniscience and feigned ignorance, between noninvolvement and direct intrusion into the fiction itself, and between a narrative position of *trompe l'oeil* (illusion, deception) and *clins d'oeil* (author-ial "winks," collusion),[8] the Vernian narrator is forever shifting his intratextual stance. For example, to establish a kind of phatic complicity with the reader, the narrator continually sprinkles his text with first- and second-person plurals—even going so far as an occasional *"entre nous"*—as in the following passages from *Around the World in 80 Days* and *Little-Fellow*: "But he was destined to once again make the acquaintance of this honest lad, simply because of the circumstances. How? We shall soon see" (*80*, 129, IA); "Just between us, who would've dreamed of taking on this little abandoned child with no family?" (*Little* 57, IA); "Our young lad resembled a macaw of the tropics . . . If you had only seen him" (*Little* 219, IA).

Other modes of direct narrator-reader address include a number of chapter titles appearing throughout the *Voyages Extraordinaires*. They often betray the meta-narrator's ubiquitous presence in the text as well as his somewhat tongue-in-cheek humor. The following titles are drawn from *Hector Servadac*, for ex-ample: "I:4– Which allows the reader to multiply to infinity exclamation points and question marks" (24, IA); "I:5–Which requests the reader to follow Captain Servadac during his first exploration of this new land" (42, IA); "II:2–The final word of which will tell the reader what, undoubtedly, he has already guessed" (288, IA).

Or, finally, consider those instances where the meta-narrator explains quite frankly to the reader why he is choosing a particular narrative methodology, why certain clarifications or lengthy asides are necessary, which characters are worthy of close attention, or which passages are important to remember: "Where was he heading? It doesn't matter. He is only a passing figure in this narrative. He won't be seen again" (*Castle* 19, IA); "And, as a moral conclusion, here is what is important to retain from this story" (*Vacation* 520, IA). As is rather obvious, the intent of such passages is extremely didactic. But, instead of science or geography, the subject matter of this particular kind of didacticism is the actual content and/or mechanics of the fictional narrative per se.

This repeated "exterior" contact with the reader is paralleled by the Vernian meta-narrator's frequent "interior" contact with the fictional protagonists themselves. He often addresses them personally—chastizing them, encouraging them, correcting them, or even forewarning them of impending danger. Note, for example, his exhortation in *Little-Fellow* for Grip to remain with the hero rather than returning to sea: "Come on, stay Grip! Stay with them!" (335, IA). Or, in *Propeller Island*, where he applauds the brave words of one Barnumlike character: "Well said, Calistus Munbar!" (277, IA). Or in *The Tribulations of a Chinaman*, where the narrator addresses Kin-Fo, warning him that his lesson is not yet completed: "No, friend Kin-Fo! Not yet!" (161, IA). Although purely rhetorical in nature (at no time do the fictional characters actually acknowledge the meta-narrator's existence), this textual strategy is nevertheless quite effective as a builder of both reader complicity and verisimilitude. The characters almost seem to have a life all their own, making their own decisions independently of the narrator who (like the reader) alternately observes them from afar or shares the immediacy of their experiences.

But, on the other hand, wherever it is a question of scientific pedagogy, the Vernian meta-narrator (as pedagogue) almost *never* directly addresses the reader or his own protagonists. He consistently prefers to channel his didacticism through the fiction, while remaining discreetly distant. His intervention into the narrative in order to instruct only takes the form of an after-the-fact validation or an (often footnoted) correction of some statement uttered by one of his fictional protagonists. Variants of the former are plentiful throughout the *Voyages Extraordinaires*. They generally follow a lengthy pedagogical dialogue between two characters and are confined to brief remarks such as "Paganel spoke the truth" (*Grant* 671, IA), "Captain Servadac was not mistaken" (*Servadac* 59, IA), or "All that he recounted was rigorously exact" (*Black* 72, IA). Through such a validation procedure, the implicit authority of the pedagogical lesson (as well as that of its fictional *porte-parole*) is substantially increased. In so doing, the meta-narrator serves primarily to legitimize such didacticism—not only as regards the accuracy of such information as it exists "in the real world" but also (due to his twofold complicity with both the reader and the characters) as regards the very presence of such nonfiction in the body of the fiction itself.

When correcting his protagonists' pedagogy (which, for fear of undercutting his heroes' authority, understandably occurs much less frequently throughout these works), the function of the Vernian meta-narrator is quite different. He "sets the record straight" about the facts in question (usually via a footnote), at the same time emphasizing the human fallibility —and therefore believability—of his fictional protagonists. For example, consider the following footnote in *From the Earth to the Moon* where the meta-narrator corrects an error made by the normally reliable Barbicane who, to placate the fiercely chauvinistic Maston's demand for an American inventor involved in cellulose research, mistakenly cites a certain Maynard from Boston:

> NOTA—In this discussion, President Barbicane claims that one of his countrymen invented collodion. This is untrue, with all due deference to J.-T. Maston, and the error comes from the similarity of two names:
> In 1847, a medical student in Boston named Maynard had the idea of using collodion for the treatment of open wounds, but collodion was already known in France in 1846. The honor of this great discovery belongs to Louis Ménard, a distinguished scientist who was a painter, philosopher, and Hellenist as well as a chemist. (119, IA)

The compensatory nature of this correction is twofold: on the one hand, the historical accuracy of the information in question is re-established, but, on the other, Maston's pro-American chauvinism is also countered by the discernible pro-French chauvinism of the meta-narrator himself (creating an additional level of phatic complicity with his—presumably French—reader). Thus, this particular passage communicates on several different signifying levels: didactically as a piece of scientific history, narratologically as a character enhancer, ideologically as a kind of *clin d'oeil* of shared nationalism, and even (highly typical of Verne) rhetorically as a homonymic play on the words *Maynard* and *Ménard*. And it is quite possible—even probable—that the latter constitutes the real raison d'être of this footnote, knowing Verne's penchant for puns, anagrams, and the like.

Thus, the invisible meta-narrator in Verne's works does aid (albeit indirectly) in the educational project of these texts. He acts as an intermediary between the reader and the protagonists; he builds complicity with the former, increases the believability of the latter, and constantly varies the text's point of view. But, as mentioned, he is rarely the actual mouthpiece of the scientific pedagogy, except to validate or correct that of his protagonists. Instead, he functions mostly as a facilitator of the narrative process itself. That is to say, he is a kind of hermeneutic stepping-stone that permits the reader both a macroscopic view of the narrative action (what Genette has called *focalisation totale*), a contiguous one (*focalisation externe*), and an internal one through the eyes of the protagonists themselves (*focalisation interne*).[9] And it is especially within these latter two character-mediated modes that Verne conveys the bulk of his scientific didacticism—a narrative format that I term indirect exposition.

INDIRECT EXPOSITION

One of the most determining factors governing the success or failure of Verne's didactic discourse—and the *roman scientifique* itself as a pedagogical genre—is the reader's perception of the authority of the narrative's fictional pedagogue. Can he be believed; not only in terms of the accuracy and reliability of his information, but as a person? In direct exposition, because of the complete absence of a recognizable narrator, the problem does not arise. In semidirect exposition, the problem is mitigated by the inherent textual authority of the meta-narrator. But in indirect exposition, where the pedagogy is closely intertwined with the fiction itself and its medium is an imaginary protagonist, the problem becomes fundamental.

One solution to the problem, of course, is to have the fictional character continually quote nonfictional sources: for example, authoritative scientists, historians, geographers, and the like. This narratological strategy does periodically occur throughout the *Voyages Extraordinaires* and does add a measure of expertise and believability (as well as an *effet de réel*) to the narrative structure of those novels in which it appears. The following example, although somewhat lengthy for its kind, is quite typical. The fictional first-person narrator of *Twenty Thousand Leagues under the Sea* (the scientist Pierre Aronnax) quotes the American oceanographer Maury when explaining the origin of the Sargasso Sea:

And, why such marine plants come together in this peaceful region of the Atlantic is as follows, according to the scientist Maury, author of *Physical Geography of the Earth*:

"It seems to be the result," he says "of a phenomenon familiar to everybody. If bits of cork or chaff, or any floating substance, be put into a basin, and a circular motion be given to the water, all the light substances will be found crowding together near the center of the pool, where there is the least motion. Just such a basin is the Atlantic Ocean to the Gulf Stream, and the Sargasso Sea is the center of the whirl."

I share Maury's opinion, and I was able to study the phenomenon at its very source, where sailing vessels rarely venture. (442, IA)

But such a narrative tactic, although useful, cannot be maintained for very long or repeated too frequently in these texts without violating the reader's novelistic expectations. Further, such quotations tend to decrease the immediacy of the fictional experience for the reader. It momentarily breaks his or her contact with the narrator-protagonist through whom the reader witnesses "firsthand" such phenomena and with whom he or she can share the emotional as well as the purely intellectual impact of such observations.

The narrative dilemma posed here—central to the very nature of Verne's *roman scientifique*—is one of subjective versus objective, fiction versus fact, suspension of disbelief versus cognition, in other words, reader *entertainment* versus reader *instruction*. On the one hand, the text must encourage the reader to accept unquestioningly the illusion of the narrative, in order that it may "live its own life in the reader," as Georges Poulet once expressed it ("Criticism and the Expression of Interiority" 46, IIIB). On the other hand, it must force the reader to think scientifically. In order to accomplish this balancing act, the narration must constantly maintain above a certain "threshold of functional relevance"[10] two very different signifying codes (novelistic/scientific) to maximize the reader's involvement in both the fiction itself and in those various nonfictional mini-lessons that are embedded in it. That is to say, in order to both amuse and instruct the reader effectively, the ideal narrative format would need to find a way to commingle the authoritative (but reader alienating) discourse of science with the personal (and reader identifying) discourse of fiction. Two options are available to do so. The discourse of science can be somehow personalized without destroying its integrity (as earlier discussed—by humanizing the machines, incorporating humor and vox populi personages into the scientific explanations, highlighting the Romantic or magical properties of science, and so on). Or the scientific authoritativeness of the fictional narrator himself can be somehow enhanced without destroying his novelistic appeal or his capacity to function as a surrogate for the reader's identity displacement, a narrative strategy discussed in the following pages.

As mentioned, the use of first-person narration is itself an effective verisimilitude builder. It rivals in its implicit authority the meta-narrator's use of the *passé simple* in conveying the impression of real actions. Unlike the *passé simple*, however, it allows the reader to share personally the immediacy of the protagonist's experiences. But, of course, the first-person narrator must himself be totally trustworthy (unlike those, for example, of Henry James in *The Turn of the Screw* or of Maupassant in *Le Horla*), especially if he is to maintain his credibility not only as a witness but also as a pedagogue. It is undoubtedly for this reason that Verne seems consistently to prefer two professions above all others for the majority of his first-person narrators: scientists/engineers and reporters/journalists. Both are (ostensibly) chroniclers of objective facts. Neither is (ostensibly) subject to whimsy or undue flights of fancy. Both professions are "serious," pragmatic, depend on first-hand observation, and—above all else—are devoted to the pursuit of truth. A few examples from the *Voyages Extraordinaires* include Pierre Aronnax in *Twenty Thousand Leagues under the Sea*, Claudius Bombarnac in the novel of the same name, Jeorling in *The Ice Sphinx*, and Amédée Florence in *The Amazing Adventure of the Barsac Mission*, among others. But there is a built-in ideological determination in the choice of such narrators. To maximize their acceptability to the nineteenth-century implied readers of these texts, they are invariably male, white, middle class, relatively wealthy, politically conservative, and very cultivated, in other words, the epitome of "trustworthiness." Finally, in those instances where the text's narrator does not closely conform to all of the above specifications (for example, young Axel in *Journey to the Center of the Earth*), he is not usually selected as the mouthpiece for the text's scientific didacticism, and another more "authoritative" figure (such as Axel's uncle, the geologist Dr. Lidenbrock) fills this particular role.

Next in importance in establishing the credibility of the narrator (as well as that of the narrative itself) is the ubiquitous presence of the diary journal in which the chronicler methodically records the events of the "voyage" and his personal impressions, observations, and reactions to them—all for the sake of "posterity" (and future publication, of course). Quite often, the narrative itself assumes the actual form of successive journal entries, usually preceded by an explanatory-justificatory note, such as "I will confine my remarks here to a simple reproduction of my daily notes, written at the time of the events in question, in order to give a more exact account of our crossing" (*Journey* 256, IA), and concluding with another such note as the narrative resumes its normal pattern, like: "Here ends what I have termed my 'ship's log,' luckily saved during the shipwreck. I now shall continue my story as before" (291, IA). Each day is logged in chronologically and, using first-person present tenses, the narrator recounts his experiences as he lives them. But unlike its use by other late nineteenth- and early twentieth-century authors (Maupassant, Gide, Mauriac, and others), the diary journal in Verne's works functions not only as a narrator verisimilitude builder, but also as a support structure to the pedagogy present in these texts. It is treated as an additional data entry for the ongoing scientific inquiry—a written attestation of observational fact helping both to factualize and to humanize the empirical investigation in question.

Similar to its use in third-person narratives—where the meta-narrator reproduces various entries from the protagonist's diary—the journal technique is highly effective in conveying actuality and immediacy (building complicity between the reader and the narrator) and in more fully "fleshing out" the fictional character who is its source. There are, however, some inherent problems with using it as a device for verisimilitude—problems, moreover, that parallel those of any first-person, present-tense narrative. First of all, the narrator is often portrayed as dutifully entering data in his journal at moments when such an activity is patently impossible. One rather hyperbolic example of this occurs in *Journey to the Center of the Earth* where the hero Axel is shown faithfully recording his experiences in the dark while clinging to a tempest-tossed raft in the middle of an underground sea! Second, the journal-manuscript itself is always miraculously rescued from destruction at the end of the "voyage"; even if, as in *Journey to the Center of the Earth, The Adventures of Captain Hatteras, Mysterious Island, Twenty Thousand Leagues under the Sea,* and a host of other Vernian novels, the heroes themselves barely escape with their lives.[11] Last—although generally overlooked by the average reader who "plays along" with such novelistic conventions—is the constant internal contradiction of a first-person, present-tense narrative that, although admittedly written after-the-fact (from journal notes), nevertheless pretends to be totally unaware of future events. Of course, such dissimulation is essential if the suspense, excitement, and melodramatic qualities of the story itself are to be safeguarded. But the contrast between the reader's realization that the text itself was "remembered" and the reader's continual perception in the text of what Barthes has called *leurres, blocages,* and so forth[12] (feigned ignorance on the part of the narrator, false solutions, delayed *coup de théâtre* endings, and so on) is often striking.

To mask such implausibilities, the Vernian text makes use of a variety of compensatory devices to strengthen the verisimilitude of its first-person narration. Two general types are of particular note: those that serve to underscore the normalcy of the narrator's perceptions (and thereby increase the reader's identification with him) and those that enhance the narrator's "scientificity" as an authoritative witness. In the former case, for example, the text continually emphasizes the physical limitations of the given narrator-observer—restricting his descriptions only to what he could feasibly be expected to see under the circumstances. Consider, for instance, Professor Aronnax's first underwater excursion in *Twenty Thousand Leagues under the Sea*:

> I could see objects clearly at a distance of a hundred meters. Beyond that, they were tinted with fine shades of ultramarine and a darker blue as the distance increased, to finally disappear into the misty shadows. . . . Above me, I could see the calm surface of the sea. . . .
>
> At a depth of three hundred feet, I could still make out the sun's rays, but only barely. Their brilliant intensity had given way to a kind of reddish dusk, halfway between day and night. Nevertheless, we could still see enough to continue. . . .
>
> The ground was still sloping down, and its angle steepened to take us deeper and deeper. . . . I say five hundred feet, although no instrument allowed me to determine the exact depth. But I knew that, even in the clearest water, the sun's rays could penetrate no deeper. The darkness was becoming impenetrable. Objects were not visible ten feet away. I was groping my way along. . . . (171–81, IA)

Each of Verne's first-person narrators is endowed with only "average" physical abilities. None can see in the dark (like Paganel of *The Children of Captain Grant*), none are exceptionally strong (like Hans of *Journey to the Center of the Earth*), none possess unusual gifts of precognition (like Cyrus Smith of *Mysterious Island*), or hypnotic powers (like the hero of *Mathias Sandorf*). They are first and foremost "normal"—as befits their status as surrogates through whom the reader experiences the action. Their relationship to their physical environment is thus highly mimetic, and like the reader they need to be constantly located in what one critic has called "transparent locations"[13] in order to narrate their observations effectively. This helps to explain the frequency and thematic importance throughout the *Voyages Extraordinaires* of such "strategic" narrative vantage points as gigantic portholes,[14] mountaintops, spacious underground caverns, crystal-clear ocean water, flying machines, large nonpartitioned rooms (with many windows), and other such locales.

"Normal" also are their occasional lapses of memory, like Aronnax admitting: "My memory doesn't allow me to capture all of the impressions" (*20,000* 68, IA). Or the repeated ellipses in their journals, as in Axel's in *Journey to the Center of the Earth* (286–87, 290, IA). Or periods of anxious questioning, like those of Kazallon when lost at sea: "Where are we? Towards what part of the Atlantic has the raft been carried?" (*Chancellor* 215, IA). Or even their occasional fainting during moments of high drama (leaving a lapsus in the narrative) like Aronnax during the Maelstrom (*20,000* 612, IA), Axel when stranded in an underground tunnel (*Journey* 227, IA), or Kazallon during a shipwreck (*Chancellor* 155, IA). All are recognizably "human" characteristics that serve to strengthen the verisimilitude of the first-person narrator.

But one such limitation device is particularly potent: the one that shows the first-person narrator as painfully aware of being unable to express the vividness of his experiences with simple words. Most often, this brand of journal-entry results in a kind of hyperbolic Mallarmean silence, as in the following: "I cannot begin to describe Marthe's astonishment and Grauben's joy upon our return" (*Journey* 369, IA), "What a scene! What writer's pen or artist's brush could ever succeed in depicting it?" (*City* 161, IA), "let those who read this understand all that my pen cannot begin to express here!" (*Chancellor* 173, IA), or "I cannot hope to describe the effect that it produced on me . . . There exist certain impressions that neither pen nor spoken word can adequately render" (*Sphinx* 484, IA).

These passages are especially frequent in the pages of *Twenty Thousand Leagues under the Sea*, where Professor Aronnax laboriously struggles to be both scientifically accurate and emotionally expressive in his prose. Among such self-conscious Vernian narrators, Aronnax is by far the most candid and self-effacing in matters of writing style, as he demonstrated immediately after the giant squid attack: "None of us will ever be able to forget that terrible scene of April 20th. I wrote it down while in a state of violent emotion. Since then, I've reread my account of it. And I've read it to Conseil and to the Canadian. They found it to be exact as to the facts but insufficient as to the overall effect. To depict such scenes, one would need the pen of our most illustrious poet, the author of *Travailleurs de la Mer*" (563–64, IA). This passage is narratologically significant as a verisimilitude builder not only to the extent that it humanizes Aronnax but also because of the way in which it effectively shifts the reader's attention away from the contradictory "remembered" status of the text as a whole—highlighting the immediacy of the journal-writing process itself and the stylistic difficulties encountered by its author. The reader is thus put into the position of witnessing the actual generation of the manuscript. Further, the reality of the narrator is additionally bolstered by the reference to Victor Hugo—"the most illustrious of *our* poets"—a highly phatic *effet de réel* comparison that, by proxy, increases Aronnax's own believability. But there is yet another (more "meta") level of reader-text interaction here: one that, again by proxy, paradoxically strengthens

Attack of the giant squid (*20,000*, engraving by E. Riou, 1870)

Aronnax's verisimilitude as a writer while underscoring his purely fictional status. That is to say, one easily imagines the narrator as a mouthpiece for Verne himself, and the former's critical comments a reflection of the author's *own* feelings regarding this—same—piece of narrative. Such an impression is intensified even further if one takes into account two facts. First, the Hugolian novel cited is, indeed, the intertextual source of the scene in question. Knowing this, the reader can see that Verne is not only acknowledging that debt, albeit indirectly, via the fiction itself, but is also offering self-reflective commentary on it. Second, and even more convincing, is the fact that Verne consented to use himself as portrait-model for the only illustration of Professor Aronnax that figures in *Twenty Thousand Leagues under the Sea*!

As pointed out, the first-person Vernian narrator-pedagogue must not only be normal and believable, but scientifically credible as well. For Aronnax or Jeorling of *The Ice Sphinx*, both of whom are scientists—the former even having to his credit a (totally imaginary but nonetheless) "authoritative" text entitled *Mysteries of the Underwater Depths*—the question of scientific credibility is obviously less problematic for the reader. But what of those narrators who are simple lay persons and visibly unaccustomed to the rigors of scientific method and/or object-ive rationalism? Two narrative strategies are used to strengthen their authority as reliable witnesses, what I call on the one hand the "doubting Thomas" effect, and on the other, the "vaccination" effect.

In the first case, each such narrator is portrayed as being intensely skeptical and as continually doubting the reality of what he is observing. Not prone to being deceived by illusions or trickery, he repeatedly exclaims: "I didn't want to believe my eyes!" (*20,000* 280, IA) or "No! It's impossible! Our senses were being deceived, our eyes couldn't see what they were seeing!" (*Journey* 329, IA). The reality of his experience is usually then "proven" by one of two means in most texts: the narrator either points out that many others are witnessing the same incredible sight, or (in true St. Thomas fashion) he attempts to convince himself by "touching" it. For example, when confronted with the unlikely presence of a ghost at a marriage ceremony, the narrator of *The Secret of Wilhelm Storitz* justifies his observations by saying: "And here is what I saw, what a thousand other persons saw as well . . . And, at that moment, here is what I heard. A thousand others heard these same words" (160, IA). Or, when shown by Captain Nemo a giant pearl being cultivated inside a truly gargantuan oyster on the Indian Ocean seabed, Professor Aronnax exclaims: "Overcome with curiosity, I reached out my hand to grasp it, to judge its weight, to feel it!" (*20,000* 322, IA).

This doubting Thomas credibility building procedure is paralleled in its efficacy by a similar vaccination narrative tactic (as first mentioned by Barthes in *Mythologies*).[15] It is designed to short-circuit the reader's questioning of the text's verisimilitude by relocating it in the person of the narrator himself. That is to say, the narrator is depicted as being very much aware of the unbelievability of his story and openly admits it to the reader, thereby defusing it as a potential menace to the narrative process while strengthening his own position as a reliable witness. For example, at the conclusion of his tale, Axel affirms that the public will never believe it: "Here is the conclusion of a story that most skeptical people will never believe. But I am already prepared for such incredulousness" (*Journey* 368, IA). Or, at the very outset of *The Ice Sphinx*, Jeorling states quite frankly: "Undoubtedly, nobody will believe this story titled *The Ice Sphinx*. But that doesn't matter because, in my opinion, it needs to be published. People can believe it or not, as they choose" (1–2, IA). Through such assertions, the narrative's credence before the general public is shown to be of no great importance. It is the "facts" of the story itself that must be presented, for the sake of science and posterity. The reader is not urged to believe in it; the reader is *dared*. By assuming a "scientific" outlook—one that concedes the existence of heretofore inexplicable phenomena and seemingly impossible occurrences—then the reader too, the text implies, can set himself apart from the average public and join the privileged elite of those explorers and scientists who continually experience the extraordinary.

Once the first-person narrator's credibility has been established (as a person as well as a reliable witness), the stage is set for the narrative to convey its scientific pedagogy. This is usually done in one of two ways: either through direct address (narrator to reader) or through third-person dialogue (transcribed by the narrator). In momentarily switching to an objective voice, the former often resembles the didactic narrative formats of direct exposition or semidirect exposition as it makes use of the present tense, the impersonal subject "one," and so on. But in contrast to them, here the fictional narrator is always sure to make his presence known before the end of the passage:

> It was a kingdom of coral.
> Within the phylum of zoophytes and the species of Alcyonaria, there is the order of Gorgonaria which contains the three classes Gorgonaria, Isidae, and Coralliae. It is within this last group that coral belongs, this strange substance that was first classified as a mineral, then as a vegetable, then finally as an animal. To the ancients it was a medicine; in modern times it is considered jewelry. It was only in 1694 that Peysonnel from Marseilles definitively identified it as part of the animal kingdom.
> Coral is a cluster of microscopic animals gathered on a brittle, rock-like polyp. These polyps sprout the little microorganisms and, while partaking of this communal existence, also have a life of their own. Thus, it is a kind of natural socialism. I was familiar with the latest work that had been done on this strange zoophyte which, as the naturalists have observed, slowly petrifies into treelike shapes. Nothing, therefore, could have been more interesting to me than to visit one of these petrified forests that Nature has planted at the bottom of the sea. (*20,000* 277, IA)

In solidly anchoring the pedagogical lesson in his own personal experience (hopes, expectations, and the like), the fictional narrator adds to it an additional dimension of relevancy for the reader. Further, the "odd" nature of the subject matter itself (defined according to the narrator's expertise in these matters) serves to make it even more intriguing—and, of course, exotic. In both ways, the first-person narrator facilitates the pedagogical implantation of the lesson through what might be called emotional enhancement.

In the dialogue variant, however, the pedagogy is more conversational: the narrator either instructs one of his (normally less competent) companions or is himself taught by another (more authoritative) protagonist. In both instances, the reader continues to be directly involved in the pedagogical process through his or her identity link with the first-person narrator. But, in this case, the reader is not the addressee but rather a third-person witness to the exchange. The following example, where Professor Aronnax talks to Ned and Conseil about the nature of pearls, is rather typical:

Ned and Conseil sat down on the couch and the Canadian first said to me:
"Monsieur, what exactly is a pearl?"
"My dear Ned," I answered "for the poet, a pearl is a tear of the sea; for the Orientals, it is a drop of hardened dew; for women, it is an oblong jewel with a glassy sheen which they wear on their finger, around their neck, or on their ear; for the chemist, it is a mixture of calcium phosphate and calcium carbonate with a bit of gelatin; and, finally, for the naturalist, it is merely an abnormal secretion from the same organ which produces mother-of-pearl in certain bivalves."
"Subphyllum of mollusks, class of Acephala, order of Testacea," added Conseil.
"Exactly, my knowledgeable Conseil. Now among these Testacea the abalones, turbos, tridacnae, and pinnae marinae—in other words all those which secrete mother-of-pearl, that blue, violet, or white substance which coats the inside of their valves—are capable of producing pearls."
"Mussels too?" asked the Canadian.
"Yes, the mussels of certain rivers in Scotland, Wales, Ireland, Saxony, Bohemia, and France sometimes produce pearls."
"Well! I guess I'll have to be more careful from now on!" answered the Canadian. (*20,000* 307, IA)

Such passages of pedagogical dialogue in the *Voyages Extraordinaires* generally follow the same basic format: a novum is encountered by the fictional protagonists, its clarification is requested of the "resident expert" by a vox populi character, the information is conveyed through a friendly give-and-take discussion (as opposed to a lengthy lecture), and it is punctuated with bits of humor to offset the serious educational tone. The latter component is usually the product of the interlocutor's "reduction" of the lesson to his own frame of reference (Conseil's penchant for taxonomies), his naïve incredulousness (Ned Land's interjections), or his idiosyncratic—and wholly pragmatic—applications of what he sees to be the lesson's message ("Well! I'll have to be more careful from now on!").

Where the dialogue occurs between two scientists, however, the format is quite different. The vox populi humor is all but absent and, replacing it as the animating phatic device in the narrative, is an element of confrontation and competition—what might be called a contest dialectic. Notice, for example, the intellectual sparring of Professor Aronnax and Captain Nemo in the following somewhat lengthy (but quite typical) pedagogical passage:

"That's all very well, Captain, but now we come to the real problem. I understand how you can cruise just beneath the ocean's surface. But when you go deeper, won't your submarine encounter a pressure that will push it upward, a force equal to one atmosphere for every thirty-two feet of water, or almost fifteen pounds per square inch?"

"That's true, Monsieur."

"Then, unless you fill the *Nautilus* completely, I don't see how you can make it dive deep into the ocean's depths."

"Professor," replied Captain Nemo, "you must not confuse static and dynamic, otherwise you risk making errors. It requires very little effort to reach the great depths of the ocean because an object develops a 'sinking' tendency. Please follow my reasoning."

"I'm listening, Captain."

"When I wanted to calculate the increase in weight I had to give to the *Nautilus* in order to dive, I only had to concern myself with the greater density of water at increasingly lower depths."

"That's obvious," I answered.

"Now, even though water is not absolutely incompressible, it is at least compressible only to a very small degree. As a matter of fact, according to the latest calculations, this reduction in volume amounts to no more than a proportion of four hundred and thirty-six ten-millionths per atmosphere, or for each thirty-two feet of depth. So if I wish to go down to a depth of thirty-two hundred feet, I take into account the reduction in volume at a pressure equivalent to that of a column of water thirty-two hundred feet high, or in other words a pressure of a hundred atmospheres. The reduction in volume would therefore be four hundred and thirty-six hundred-thousandths. Hence I would have to increase the weight of the vessel from 1507.2 tons to 1513.77 tons. The increase would therefore be only 6.57 tons."

"That's all?"

"That's all, Monsieur Aronnax. And the calculation is easy to verify. But I have supplementary tanks capable of taking on a hundred tons. I can therefore dive to considerable depths. When I wish to resurface, I need only to get rid of this water and empty all the tanks. The *Nautilus* will lose one-tenth of its weight and rise."

I could not argue with his reasoning, based as it was on solid mathematics. (*20,000* 130–31, IA)

The primary characteristic of such dialogue is its quantitative argumentation and its object-ive rationalism. The pedagogy is embedded in a contest format—the winner of which is decided by *force de raison* (and demonstrable mathematics). This parry-and-thrust approach is an effective didactic strategy in a variety of ways: it animates the otherwise dry theoretical discussion in question, it humanizes Aronnax as a scientist who does not have all the answers (facilitating continued reader identification with him), and it encourages emulation of those analytical capabilities—scientific method—that enabled Captain Nemo to win such a confrontation. This particular narrative configuration is quite common throughout the *Voyages Extraordinaires* whenever two or more scientists are brought into contact to convey a pedagogical lesson. And its use is not restricted to first-person narratives. In fact, it occurs more frequently in texts of direct or semidirect exposition such as *From the Earth to the Moon* and *Around the Moon*, where entire chapters are devoted to such theoretical jousting matches.[16]

Finally, there is a third variant to Verne's dialogue-based didacticism, one that combines the two preceding formats while giving them a special twist. In this type, the confrontation is between the scientist and his acolyte—the latter serving as the first-person narrator (and reader surrogate) in the text. And, contrary to expectations, it is the acolyte who ultimately wins the exchange (much to the gratification of the reader). The following passage from *Journey to the Center of the Earth* is a good case in point:

"Uncle," I replied, "I agree that all your calculations are exact, but allow me to draw a conclusion from them."

"Go ahead, my boy."

"At the latitude of Iceland, beneath which we are now located, the radius of the Earth is about 4,749 miles, isn't it?"

"4,750."

"Let's say 4,800 in round figures. And out of 4,800 miles, we have done forty-eight?"

"As you say."

"And this at a cost of 213 miles diagonally?"

"Exactly."

"In about twenty days?"

"In twenty days."

"Well then, forty-eight miles are one hundredth of the Earth's radius. If we continue as we are, it will take us two thousand days, or nearly five and a half years to reach the center!"

The Professor didn't answer.

"Not counting the fact that if we go two hundred miles horizontally for every forty vertically, we will come out at some point on the Earth's circumference long before we ever reach its center."

"To blazes with your calculations!" shouted my uncle angrily. "To blazes with your hypotheses! What are they based on? How do you know that this corridor doesn't go directly to our destination? Besides, there's a precedent for what I'm doing. Another man has done it, and where he has succeeded I shall succeed!"

"I hope so, but after all, I'm entitled. . . ."

"You're entitled to hold your tongue, Axel, instead of talking such nonsense."

I saw that my uncle was about to rebecome the ominous Professor, and I decided to let the matter drop. (205, IA)

In this delightful passage, the irascible Professor Lidenbrock is caught in his own scientific web. Continually admonishing Axel to be more methodical, logical, precise, and less emotional in his thinking, he then becomes his nephew's first victim as Axel clearly demonstrates—via mathematics—the total impracticality of their quest. The humor of the passage comes from Lidenbrock's stubborn unwillingness to accept proven fact, especially when it runs counter to his heart's desire (their heroic trek to the center of the Earth) and even more particularly when such a rational deduction comes from the mouth of his youthful subordinate. In portraying such an ironic reversal of roles, Verne has aptly provided his younger readers (who identify even more fully with Axel as the first-person narrator) with yet another motivational incentive for learning geology and math, that is, to be in a position to challenge the scientific authority of their elders—on their own terms!

Thus, through the narrative strategy of indirect and fully mediated exposition, Verne's didactic discourse is effectively dealienated in two ways: via reader identification with the speaking subject and via reader involvement in the conversations among the various protagonists as reported by the first-person narrator. The pedagogical novum to be explained and then assimilated by the reader—the origin of pearls, sea pressure and buoyancy, the diameter of the Earth, the nature of coral, and so forth—is first "naturalized" through the reader's shared immediacy of the phenomenon itself as he experiences it along with the narrator. It is then valorized by its evident capacity not only to solve specific problems, but also to influence interpersonal relationships, in other words to win contests, to elicit humor, to question authority, and so on. Thus, it is shown to be an eminently useful acquisition on many different levels—intellectually, emotionally, and socially.

In fact, one could reasonably argue that the more such didacticism is mediated through the fictional characters of these texts (that is, presented via indirect exposition), the more direct is its impact on the average reader—and, ultimately, the less polarized the two realms of science and fiction themselves.

NOTES

1. V. such inventories, for example, in *The Adventures of Captain Hatteras* (16, 29, 243), *Journey to the Center of the Earth* (95–99), *From the Earth to the Moon* (328–30), *Around the Moon* (54–55), *The Boy Captain* (156–57), among others.

2. Direct en bloc history and geography lessons are far too numerous throughout the *Voyages Extraordinaires* to list in any comprehensive way. But note, for example, those of *The Adventures of Captain Hatteras* (49–51, 93–95), *The*

Children of Captain Grant (87, 688–89), *Mathias Sandorf* (27–28), *Propeller Island* (103–5, 140–41, 178–79), and *Little-Fellow* (1–3, 59–60, 80–81, 228–29).

3. Many other examples of such negative/question pedagogy occur throughout the *Voyages Extraordinaires*, for instance, in *Hector Servadac* (100–1), *The Black Indies* (16), *Little-Fellow* (229, 231), *The Green Ray* (136), and *The Last Will of an Eccentric* (356).

4. Other examples of this sort include those in *Hector Servadac* (166) and *Little-Fellow* (294).

5. For this and other pertinent information concerning Verne's use of footnotes, v. Daniel Compère's excellent (although somewhat taxonomic) article entitled "Le Bas des pages," *Bulletin de la Société Jules Verne* 68 (1983), 147–53. See also Shari Benstock's "At the Margins of Discourse: Footnotes in the Fictional Text," *PMLA* XCVIII:2 (March 1983), 204–23.

6. In *Five Weeks in a Balloon* (252), *The Adventure of Captain Hatteras* (104), *The Children of Captain Grant* (215), *The Steam House* (81), *Mathias Sandorf* (283), *Little-Fellow* (190), *The Last Will of an Eccentric* (338–39), *The Green Ray* (66), respectively.

7. V. the following studies on the maps and illustrations in Verne's texts: Edmondo Marcucci, *Les Illustrations des Voyages Extraordinaires de Jules Verne* (Bordeaux: Société de Jules Verne, 1956); Georges Borgeaud, "Jules Verne et ses illustrateurs," *L'Arc* 29 (1966), 43–45; Jean Chesneaux, "Les Illustrations des romans de Jules Verne," *BSJV* 37–38 (1976), 114–15; and D. Compère, "Fenêtres latérales," *Jules Verne IV: texte, image, spectacle*, ed. François Raymond (Paris: Minard, 1983), pp. 55–72.

8. V. Simone Vierne, "Trompe l'oeil et clin d'oeil dans l'oeuvre de Jules Verne," *Jules Verne et les Sciences Humaines*, colloque, Cerisy-la-Salle (Paris: 10/18, 1979), pp. 410–40.

9. Gérard Genette, *Figures III* (Paris: Seuil, 1972), pp. 206–11.

10. S. Heath, "Structuration of the Novel-Text," *Signs of the Times* (Cambridge: Granta, 1971), pp. 52–78. Cited in Jonathan Culler's *Structuralist Poetics* (Ithaca, N.Y.: Cornell University Press, 1975), pp. 141–42.

11. V. Christian Robin's excellent article entitled "Le Récit sauvé des eaux: du *Voyage au centre de la Terre* au *Sphinx des glaces*—réflexions sur le narrateur vernien." In François Raymond, ed., *Jules Verne II: L'Ecriture vernienne* (Paris: Minard, 1978), pp. 35–50.

12. R. Barthes, *S/Z* (Paris: Seuil, 1970), pp. 215–16.

13. V. Philippe Hamon, "Qu'est-ce qu'une description?" *Poétique* 12 (1972), 473.

14. V. Thomas A. Sebeok, "Captain Nemo's Windows: Semiotics of Windows in Sherlock Holmes," *Poetics Today* III:1 (1982), 110–39.

15. "The collective imagination is immunized with a small innoculation of recognized evil; in so doing, the risk of a widespread infection is minimized." In R. Barthes, *Mythologies* (Paris: Seuil, 1957), p. 238.

16. V. in this regard Chap. 20 of *From the Earth to the Moon*, appropriately entitled *Attaque et riposte*, p. 249.

CHAPTER 7

Ancillary Didactic Devices

In the preceding pages, this work has focused on what might be called the more presentational aspects of Verne's didactic discourse—such matters as exposition, narrative voice, and characterization. Within this overall narratological format, there exist a number of specific textual mechanisms that make such didacticism more effective. I call them ancillary didactic devices and group them into four categories according to function: *reiterators*, which repeat the lesson; *animators*, which enrich the lesson with drama, humor, or wordplay; *valorizors*, which continually emphasize the value of the lesson learned; and *buffers*, which provide emotional security throughout the process.

REITERATORS

In constantly repeating a fact, theory, or scientific formula, the role of the reiterators is to successfully implant such pedagogy in the reader's consciousness through simple persistence. In its most elementary textual manifestation, the in toto duplication of the material to be learned is repeated throughout several chapters of a novel. This may be done in a number of different ways in order to avoid the impression of redundancy (the major drawback of this narrative strategy). For example, such information may be replicated at relatively infrequent intervals, particularly if it is quite general in nature and can relate to the plot at almost any juncture—as in the recurrent mention of the difference in seasons between the northern and southern hemispheres in *Mysterious Island*:

> It was the 6th of May, a day which corresponds to the 6th of November in countries located in the northern hemisphere. (203, IA)

> The season of winter truly began with the month of June, which corresponds to the month of December in the northern hemisphere. (257, IA)

> However, winter arrived with the month of June, which is December in northern climes, and the greatest concern was the making of warm and sturdy clothing. (449, IA)

> The month of November at this latitude corresponds to the month of May in northern zones. (670, IA)

Most of these entries are located at the beginning of chapters that are spaced quite far apart from one another—periodically reminding the reader of the noncontradiction between the dates cited and the weather and/or activities of the protagonists on those days. But there is another reason why the repetition of this information in the text does not seem redundant. Due to the original *feuilleton* format of lengthy novels like *Mysterious Island*, such chapters are not only set apart spatially for the reader but in time as well.

Such pedagogy is also often repeated from novel to novel throughout the *Voyages Extraordinaires*. For example, the difference in seasons discussed above reappears in *Robur the Conqueror* (167, IA) and in several chapters of *The Two Year Vacation* (154, 209, 289, IA). Other examples include an Indian vehicle called a palki-ghari that is first explained in *Around the World in 80 Days* (116–17, IA) and later in *The Steam House* (86, IA). The condition whereby one is able to see at night (*nyctolopie*) is explained twice in *The Children of Captain Grant* (53, 290, IA) and once again in *Claudius Bombarnac* (21, IA). Bowie-knifes (sic) are defined first in *From the Earth to the Moon* (13, IA), then in *Twenty Thousand Leagues under the Sea* (71, IA) and yet again in *Robur the Conqueror* (49, 52, IA). And this pattern of novel-to-novel repetition occurs throughout most of Verne's works. Ironically (given the serial nature of these novels), each narrative presumes no prior learning on the reader's part from earlier ones.

Another strategy of pedagogical repetition utilizes footnotes. They normally recall an earlier in-text explanation and serve temporarily to jog the memory of the reader until such time as the lesson has been fully digested. Take, for example, the repeated mention of pemmican in *The Adventures of Captain Hatteras*:

> they also put on board a very large provision of this Indian food called pemmican which concentrates a great amount of nutrients in a small volume. (16, IA)

> However, in widening the circle of his search, the Doctor managed to locate and gather up about fifteen pounds of pemmican (1) . . .
>   (1) A condensed meat product. (244, IA)

> the weary men allowed themselves the luxury of a little heat, something that they had not been accustomed to for a long while. Some pemmican,

a few biscuits, and several cups of coffee soon put them into better spirits.
(259, IA)

When first introducing this technicism, the text fully explains it. Many pages
later, the explanation is briefly reiterated in a footnote to anchor it in the reader's memory. Finally, the term is used thereafter without explanation—the
assumption being that the reader has, by now, fully assimilated it into his or her
working vocabulary.

A similar didactic strategy for dealienating technicisms uses quotation marks.
Notice, for example, the rapid integration of the word *creek* into the narrative
of *The Two Year Vacation*—a word already having been defined in *From the
Earth to the Moon* (164, IA) and in *Mysterious Island* (148, IA) via footnotes:
"It was 2 o'clock when they halted in the middle of a narrow clearing with a
small stream running through it—what North Americans call a 'creek.' The
crystal-clear water in this creek was gently flowing along a bed of blackish
rocks" (113, IA). Or note the same phenomenon in *Voyage to the Center of
the Earth*, where the term in question had never before been used:

> "It's called 'surtarbrandur,' or fossilized wood."
> "But then, like lignite, it must be rock-hard and cannot float."
> "Sometimes that does occur. Some woods eventually harden into
> anthracite, but some others, like this kind, has only just begun to fossilize.
> Look here." My uncle tossed a piece into the sea.
> The wood disappeared into the water then bobbed back to the surface
> and rocked in the waves.
> ... The following evening, thanks to the ability of their guide, the raft
> was finished. It was ten feet long and five feet wide. The logs of surtar-
> brandur, bound together with strong ropes, provided a solid deck and, once
> launched, this improvised vessel floated gracefully in the waters of the
> Lidenbrock Sea. (251–52, IA)

In both instances, the unusual (and somewhat exotic) lexical item first appears
in the text with quotation marks—signaling its difference to the reader—and is
immediately followed by an en passant definition. When used again, it is a normal (unmarked) word, fully integrated into the narrative. Of course, such a pedagogical tactic has its limitations. If the latter unquoted technicism is located too
distant from its quoted and defined counterpart, the risk is great that the reader
will not immediately recognize it. In most of Verne's texts, they are most often
located within a paragraph or two of each other.

The use of reiterators throughout the *Voyages Extraordinaires* is extensive
and quite effective as a pedagogical narrative technique. But, as noted, they rely
exclusively on rote memorization and do very little to render the lessons intrinsically memorable. Much more potent in this regard are those didactic strategies
that I call animators.

ANIMATORS

When discussing the various "animating" devices in Verne's didactic discourse, it is necessary to distinguish between those that are primarily contextual and those that are keyed specifically to the passages of pedagogy. For example, such traditional narrative formulae as cliff-hanging chapter endings, death-defying acts of heroism, scenes of emotional pathos, *coup de théâtre* revelations, catastrophism,[1] cloak-and-dagger suspense, in-the-nick-of-time rescues, and the many other melodrama-building plot structures used throughout the *Voyages Extraordinaires* all provide a highly charged motivational context for the didacticism in these texts—particularly when the "lesson" in question directly affects the outcome of the story. But there are a number of other such narrative devices used within the pedagogical sequences themselves that serve to enliven their otherwise textbooklike demeanor.

One such strategy involves the selection of the lesson itself. If not a close derivative of the action (originating the "voyage," providing last-minute salvation from danger, locating the lost protagonists, and so on), they are usually chosen according to their qualities of unusualness, exoticism, rarity, or singularity—at least by the standards of the average late nineteenth-century French reader. For example, consider the flora and fauna most often chosen for explanation and elaboration in these texts—eucalyptus trees, phosphorescent mushrooms, bread fruit, baobabs, whales (a Vernian favorite), ostriches, jaguars, kangaroos (another favorite), seals, elephants, sharks, condors, and the like. Or consider the often incredible foods that our heroes sample in their travels—often minutely described as to their proper preparation—such as raccoons, opossums, armadillos, llamas, ants, monkeys, bat eggs, penguins, whale milk, iguanas, or flamingos.[2] Or note the customs of various foreign peoples that are selected for analysis and discussion—cannibalism (a recurrent topic), igloo building, taboos, harums, bride shopping, non-Western dress of all sorts, hookas, snake charming, tattooing, animal worship, dueling techniques, among others. In all cases—whether or not they are totally "normal" within their own milieu—the topics chosen for pedagogical exposition are almost always *extraordinary* in nature (from a nineteenth-century French society viewpoint).

Another animating technique involves continually varying the medium of the pedagogy itself. As mentioned, the Vernian scientist is most often the vehicle of instruction in these works and his encyclopedic memory the source of the information conveyed—normally through dialogue with his companions. But such is not always the case. Various textbooks, logs, newspapers, dictionaries, letters, and other items also frequently serve as the textual stepping-stones for presenting such information. For example (as excerpted in an earlier chapter), witness Max Réal's seven-page letter to his mother describing in detail his passage through Maryland, Virginia, West Virginia, Ohio, and Illinois in *The Last Will of an Eccentric* (343–50, IA). Frascolin of *Propeller Island* is dubbed the Larousse of the Tropics because of his constant quoting from a dictionary of the same name (105, 149, IA). And in addition to the many direct quotations from the works of famous scientists, explorers, historians, and geographers such as Camille Flammarion, Sir William Parry, Michelet, and Elisée Reclus, lengthy excerpts from reference books such as Vorepierre's *Dictionnaire illustré* are reproduced in their entirety when defining certain technical terms (*Boy* 112-13, IA), as well as passages from scientific journals like the popular *Tour du Monde* (*Boy* 295, IA). Finally, one must not forget the central role played by the many ship's logs and personal diaries throughout the *Voyages Extraordinaires*.

A variety of rhetorical devices and tropes also serve to animate Verne's more didactic passages. "Scientific" comparisons and metaphors such as the following from *The Children of Captain Grant* are common in these texts—the unique structure of which is a quite fascinating illustration of how one might go about combining scientific and literary discourse, while simultaneously giving it a peda-gogical thrust: "The day star, like a metal disk gilded by the Ruolz process, emerged from the Ocean as if from an immense voltaic bath" (48, IA). Or, re-maining within the same time-honored topos of sunrises, note the following variant from *The Green Ray*:

> However, the perimeter of the sea grew brighter along the eastern horizon. It gradually unfolded the full gamut of colors contained in the solar spec-trum. The faint red of the early mists at sea-level progressively transmuted into violet at the zenith. Second by second, the colors took on more intensity. The pink became red, the red became fiery. Daybreak occurred, at the point of intersection between the diurnal arc and the circumference of the sea. (185–86, IA)

Passages such as these clearly illustrate how Verne's scientific pedagogy operates on two distinct levels. In addition to constantly "reducing" science to common lay terminology (explaining technicisms via footnotes, apposition, and the like), he also periodically injects scientific nomenclature directly into his literary rhetoric, substituting technical terms for the traditional poetic ones anticipated by the reader.

Such a strategy, although effective pedagogically and quite fascinating narra-tologically, does nevertheless have its drawbacks. This can be a problem because the reader, although normally very accepting of semantic reductions, often reacts very poorly to its opposite—that is, excessive jargonization. And the line is extremely fine between what the reader will tolerate (for educative purposes or otherwise) and what will be rejected out of hand as gratuitous affectation on the author's part. In the latter instance, excessive technicisms can temporarily short-circuit the seriousness of the passage, provoking a sense of parody or even of malicious satire. Consider, for example, certain passages from Molière's *Les Précieuses ridicules*, Flaubert's *Bouvard et Pécuchet*, or such passages as Lautré-amont's mocking "Angle the binarity of your patellas towards the ground" (*Chants de Maldoror* 270, IIIA) when exhorting all Positivistic bourgeois persons to kneel in prayer.

Sensitive to this danger, Verne most often assumes a tonge-in-cheek approach when animating such technical postulations—making them intentionally quite humorous. Consider, for example, such "scientific" comparisons and metaphors as the one describing a jovial fellow whose "zygomatic muscles, necessary for the action of laughter, were never in repose" (*City* 21, IA), or that of a crowd whose terrified flight is described in Newtonian fashion as "Their courage was inversely proportional to the square of their velocity . . . in running away" (*Drama* 180, IA). A similar formulaic definition of a woman's amorous penchant for an overweight scientist is described in the following manner: "she felt herself attracted to him in proportion to his mass and inversely to the square of the distance between them. And, accordingly, J.-T. Maston was of sufficient corpulence to exert upon her an irresistible pull" (*Topsy* 46-47, IA). Finally, take the following "chemical" depiction of a number of English tourists who simply refuse to stay together as a group: "'A body of English tourists,' Roger whispered into the ear of his friend, 'is without doubt a mass which has the lowest temperature of fusion. I offer this as an observation of transcendent chemistry.' 'True!' answered Robert with a laugh. 'But I think the process is now completed. The solution must have reached the saturation point'" (*Thompson* 300, IA). In all of these instances, the reader immediately senses the comical incongruity of technical terminology being used to describe perfectly mundane matters, but obligingly "plays along" with the author's stylistic game.

At other times, Verne purposely satirizes excessive jargonization. Note, for example, his use of Ardan as a vox populi critic of Barbicane and Nicholl's algebraic wrangling in *Around the Moon* (213, IA), the pseudo-scientific pedantry of Aristobulus Ursiclos in *The Green Ray* (64, 98, 133, IA), the numerical speech patterns of the statistician Poncin in *The Amazing Adventure of the Barsac Mission* (193-95, 204-5, 294-95, IA), or the animal merchant Mathias Van Guitt's incorrigible use of taxonomic jargon in *The Steam House*:

"But, Monsieur Van Guitt," said Banks, "could you tell me if the benefits of the profession outweigh the risks?"

"Sir," answered the zoo-provider, "they used to be very lucrative. However, for several years now, I am obliged to recognize that the need for wild animals is on the decline. You can judge to what extent by the current prices in the last wholesale catalogue. Our main market is the zoological gardens of Anvers. Winged creatures, ophidians, samples from the simian and saurian families, representatives from the carnivores of two worlds, it's there that I usually expedite my expeditions' . . ."

Captain Hod winced at the latter word.

". . . products, caught during adventurous outings in the forests of the Indian peninsula. But the public's tastes seem to have altered of late. And the sale prices have begun to taper off to below my net costs! . . . As for the proboscideans . . ."

"Proboscideans?" said Captain Hod.

"We use this term to designate those pachyderms that Nature has endowed with a trunk."

"You mean elephants!"

"Yes, elephants. Since the Quaternary Period, the mastodons of the prehistoric era. . . ."

"Thank you," said Captain Hod.

"As for the proboscideans . . . Mathias Van Guitt began again. (311–12, IA)

Such purposely self-conscious technicisms—used here to show derision but nonetheless quite effective pedagogically—can assume yet another form in Verne's texts: humorous neologisms. In this particular variant, Verne might use a technical term to create an entirely new part of speech, or combine two terms into one, or invent a technicism from nontechnical words. Note, for instance, Paganel's mathematical-geographical portmanteau in "this geometrigraphic axiom that states that two islands similar to a third island resemble each other" (*Grant* 324, IA) or Frascolin's "ethno-anthropogeographical studies" (*Propeller* 244, IA). Consider also the very Latin-sounding appellation given to the tulips of the town of Quiquendone, "tulipa quiquendonia" (*Ox* 73, IA) or that given to the dog in *The Boy Captain* who reads lettered blocks and is thereafter dubbed "canis alphabeticus" (58, IA). Or note the following *mot juste* when characterizing the singularly mechanical bent of the American people: "From there came the very 'Americhanical' idea of creating an entire artificial island that would be the last word in modern industrial metallurgy" (*Propeller* 48, IA). The use of such tongue-in-cheek quasi-technical vocabulary serves to augment the playful quality of Verne's texts without sacrificing their fundamentally pedagogical character.

As might be surmised from the above, one of the most effective animators in Verne's pedagogy is humor. And it is one of the most frequent as well. Comparatively rare are those didactic passages in the *Voyages Extraordinaires* that are totally devoid of some form of joke, jest, or jibe. The frequency of humor in these texts is matched only by the heterogeneity of its form, for example, slapstick, situation comedy, witticisms, exaggerations, social satire, understatement, ethnic humor, absurdities, black humor, and so on. Few subject matters are exempt from levity (with the exception of course, of sex and Catholicism), for example, nationalities, race, politics, human foibles, violence, money, social institutions, and so forth. Even science itself, as pointed out, occasionally serves as a springboard to the comic in Verne's narratives, especially if it is the source of hubris, vanity, or pedantic esotericism.

Most didactic slapstick humor in Verne's texts follows the same basic format: the usefulness of the lesson is dramatically underscored by a comical straight man who suffers some slight physical misfortune, such as Conseil's "shocking" encounter with an electric ray in *Twenty Thousand Leagues under the Sea* (543, IA), the "oxygenated" villagers of Quiquendone in *Docteur Ox* (45–77, IA), Passepartout's drubbing by the natives for having worn shoes into an Indian temple in *Around the World in 80 Days* (68, IA), or the scene where Dr. Clawbonny explains to his comrades how he is able to drink scalding coffee:

"But you'll burn up, Doctor!" Altamont warned.

"Never," the Doctor replied.

"Do you have a copper-coated palate?" asked Johnson.

"No, my friends. And I encourage you to follow my example. There are certain people, and I count myself among them, who like to drink their coffee at a temperature of 131 degrees (55 Centigrade)."

"131 degrees!" exclaimed Altamont. "But the hand cannot tolerate such heat!"

"Very true, Altamont, since the hand can endure no more than 122 degrees (50 Centigrade) in water. But the mouth's palate and tongue are less sensitive than the hand and they can withstand such heat."

"You amaze me," said Altamont.

"Well then, I'll show you."

And the Doctor, taking a thermometer from the living quarters, plunged it into his boiling cup of coffee. He waited until it read more than 131 degrees, and then he gulped the liquid down with obvious pleasure.

Bell, bravely wishing to imitate the good Doctor, promptly scorched himself and began to howl.

"Lack of practice," the Doctor noted. (*Hatteras* 312, IA)

The textual succession of a mystery, a pedagogical explanation, and a piece of humor (slapstick or otherwise) to conclude the passage and animate the lesson as a whole is a true Vernian trademark. This particular narrative pattern occurs again and again throughout the *Voyages Extraordinaires*, and, surprisingly often, it is the scientist himself who plays the role of the straight man—especially in those novels that feature involuntarily comical (albeit competent) scientists like Lidenbrock, Paganel, cousin Bénédict, Palyrin Rosette, or Saint-Bérain.

Verne also exhibits a typically Rabelaisian penchant for puns, hyperbolic enumerations, and *carnavalesque* plot reversals—as Bakhtin once described the phenomenon in Rabelais's works (*Rabelais and His World* 34ff., IIIA). For example, certain characters are given names like Doctor Ox and his coworker Ygène, the cook in *The Steam House* whose name was Parazard (*par hasard*, by chance), or one particularly vain protagonist in *The Raton Family* called Kissador (*qui s'adore*, who loves himself). Paganel of *The Children of Captain Grant*, later to be tattooed himself by the natives, quips that "The more one is illustrious, the more one is illustrated in this country of New Zealand" (714, IA). The young industrious hero of *Little-Fellow* promptly became "a capitalist when he arrived at the capital" of his country (291, IA). Note the often tongue-in-cheek hyperbolic enumerations like Paganel's eight-page encyclopedic recall of Australian explorers for the purpose of winning a wager (*Grant* 340-48, IA), Conseil's fish taxonomies (*20,000* 143-53, IA), the exhaustive listing of all the major newspapers of the world in *Topsy Turvy* (145-46, IA), or the stiff-necked British captain named Turner of *Propeller Island* who "in one long, interminable sentence of 307 words, punctuated throughout with commas and without a single period!" brings suit against the owners of Standard Island and, unknowingly, initiates them to the phenomenon of "legalese" (206-7, IA). Finally, observe the

many comic reversals in Verne's texts: for example, the trapper of wild animals
who is trapped by wild animals (*Steam* 311, IA), Conseil's ability to classify but
not to recognize fish and Ned Land's ability to recognize but not to classify
them (*20,000* 152, IA), or the anthropologist who lives among the apes in order
to study human evolution and progressively de-evolves into an ape himself
(*Village* 193, IA).

There are other brands of ostensibly pedagogical humor in these narratives
that are not as innocent as the above—where Verne plays to the seamier side of
his implied reader's tastes in comedy. Consider the anti-Semitic humor in Verne's
straight man portrayal of Isac (sic) Hakhabut as the Jewish miser in *Hector
Servadac* (194-97, IA); or the recurrent racial slurs (equating blacks with apes,
or worse) throughout *Five Weeks in a Balloon* (103, IA), *The Adventures of Captain Hatteras* (506, 519, IA), *Mysterious Island* (406, IA), *Robur the Conqueror*
(41-42, 125-29, IA), *The Village in the Treetops* (8, 12, 34, IA), and *The Amazing Adventure of the Barsac Mission* (90, 444, IA). Note also Verne's rather
mysogynistic antiwomen jibes in *Topsy Turvy* (3-4, IA), *Around the World in
80 Days* (243, IA), and *Claudius Bombarnac* (132, IA), among others. In each of
these instances, the shared cultural-ideological presuppositions of a Jew's avarice,
a black's intellectual inferiority, and a woman's intrinsic frailty are used to provide a kind of *entre nous* humor to the scientific lesson in question.

Finally, there is yet another brand of pedagogical humor in Verne's texts—one
that might be called *humour noir* or sick humor. It might take the form, for
example, of the proudly competitive massacres perpetrated by members of the
Gun Club at the outset of *From the Earth to the Moon*:

> Previously, in the "good old days," a 36 shell, at a distance of 300 feet,
> would mow down 36 horses and 68 men. But that was the mere infancy of
> the art. Since then, much progress has been made. The Rodman cannon,
> which could fire a projectile of a half-ton over seven miles, would have
> easily mown down 150 horses and 300 men. Unfortunately, if the horses
> had consented to try this experiment, there was a shortage of men who
> were willing to do so.
>
> Be that as it may, cannons proved to be very deadly and, with each dis-
> charge, combatants fell like chaffs of wheat cut by a scythe. Of what sig-
> nificance, in the light of these figures, was that famous cannonball fired at
> Coutras in 1587 which put 25 men out of action, or that other at Zorn-
> dorff, in 1758, which killed infantrymen, or the Austrian cannon at
> Kesseldorf which, in 1742, neutralized over 70 soldiers each time it fired?
> . . .
>
> What need to comment on these numbers, so eloquent in themselves?
> Nothing. Nor is there any need to contest the following calculation worked
> out by the statistician Pitcairn. Dividing the total number of cannonball
> victims by the number of Gun-Club members, he found that each of them
> had killed an "average" of two thousand three hundred and seventy-five
> men, plus a fraction.

In considering such a figure, it is obvious that the unique preoccupation of this honorable society was the philanthropic destruction of humanity and the perfectability of weapons of war, the latter viewed as civilizing instruments. (5–7, IA)

Or consider the way in which a given topic—cannibalism, for example, the sometimes horrifyingly realistic details of which were discussed earlier—is now treated humorously, to make a pedagogical point:

"So," said Glenarvan, "in your opinion, Paganel, cannibalism will only disappear when there is an abundance of sheep, cattle, and pigs on the prairies of New Zealand."

"That is so, my dear lord, and years would still pass before the Maoris would lose their taste for New Zealander flesh, which they prize above all others, because the sons will continue to like what their fathers liked. To listen to them, this meat tastes like pork but a bit more spicy. As for white meat, they are less partial to it. White men put salt on their food, which gives them a particularly unappetizing taste to the gourmet palate."

"They are demanding!" said the Major. "But this flesh, white or dark, do they eat it raw or cooked?"

"What's that to you, Monsieur Mac Nabbs?" asked Robert.

"Well now, my son," answered the Major quite seriously, "if I had to finish my days in the teeth of a cannibal, I would prefer to be cooked!"

"Why?"

"So as not to be eaten alive!"

"Fine, Major!" continued Paganel. "But if it's only to be cooked alive?"

"The fact is," answered the Major, "I wouldn't want to have to make the choice!"

"If it makes you feel any better, Mac Nabbs," replied Paganel, "the New Zealand cannibals only eat their meat cooked or smoked. They are well-bred folks and have a highly developed sense of cuisine." (*Grant* 673, IA)

Thus, Verne's repeated use of humor in the *Voyages Extraordinaires* serves to vary the narrative register not only of his fictional episodes but also of the pedagogy in these texts. As an animator of didactic discourse, it is unmatched in its capacity to both lighten the academic tone of such passages and render them truly memorable.

VALORIZORS

The next instructional ancillary device to note in Verne's works is that of the valorizors, those textual elements that ceaselessly emphasize the value of learning. In contrast to reiterators and animators, they are not usually linked to a specific pedagogical lesson in the text, but, rather, function throughout the entire narrative as a ubiquitous motivational backdrop that continually touts the high value of knowledge possession. The term *possession* is doubly significant in this context, dovetailing as it does with the persistent quantitative/materialistic/ ownership themes around which, from an ideological standpoint, the majority of the *Voyages Extraordinaires* are constructed. As previously discussed, in Verne's fictional world, knowledge is portrayed as an object to be possessed—one that confers social status, wealth, and, above all, *power* to the possessor, at the same time morally requiring him to use it for the benefit of humanity. The great heroes of this series—Barbicane and Ardan, Hatteras and Clawbonny, Nemo, Fogg, Robur, Cyrus Smith, Dick Sand, Mathias Sandorf, Little-Fellow, and others—are all possessors of such knowledge. The same can be said for the most memorable of the Vernian villains—Doctor Ox, Herr Schultze, the later Robur, Ker Karraje, Rodolphe de Gortz—but they, of course, choose to use their learning for less than altruistic purposes, and are appropriately punished. Further, the topos of humanity's "quest for knowledge" is itself the thematic heart of the majority of these fictions—intrinsically valorizing education and raising its relevancy to a transindividual philosophical level. And the happy ending motif so common in these novels always involves more than just the winning of a wife, the acquisition of fame and glory, the recovery of a lost family member, or the righting of a wrong. The triumphant protagonists are consistently portrayed as having conquered *more knowledge*—for themselves and for the world.

Thus, the didactic structure of the *Voyages Extraordinaires* as a whole functions as the greatest valorizer of learning in these works. It is also important to note how the virtues of education are repeatedly proselytized within the structure of these texts. This is most often done via two somewhat different modes. On the one hand, the text utilizes the twofold technique of *narrator approbation* (of individuals who are good learners, of specific countries and/or teaching methodologies that are educationally superior) *and narrator condemnation* (of illiteracy, laziness, ignorance, superstition). On the other, the text consistently encourages reader *emulation*—of the narrator, of certain protagonists, or of situational models depicting the educative process itself.

Narrator value judgments—due to his implicit textual authority—can be powerful valorizors of the pedagogical. Consider the manner in which the majority of fictional protagonists in these texts are initially portrayed. Whether primary or secondary to the plot itself, the Vernian protagonist's "worth" is almost always described in terms of his or her personal educational development: older characters in terms of their already acquired knowledge or expertise (or lack thereof), younger ones in terms of their capacity for learning and the rapidity of their intellectual growth. For example, Cyrus Smith is "very learned, very practical" (*Mysterious* 13, IA), Barbicane has a "prodigious . . . intellect" (*Earth/ Moon* 186, IA), Cyprien Méré is a "former student of the Ecole Polytechnique" (*Star* 15, IA). On occasion, the text even outlines in detail the early schooling of these heroes. Fergusson's youth is described in the following manner: "His father, a learned man, did not neglect to cultivate his son's intelligence with serious studies in hydrography, physics, mechanics, a little botany, medicine, and astronomy" (*Five* 5, IA). Mathias Sandorf as a young man, in spite of his immense family wealth, is shown having firmly decided to complete his university education—and becomes a true "man" as a result:

> Mathias Sandorf had received a very serious education. Rather than contenting himself with the leisure activities that his fortune permitted him, he had decided to pursue his interests in the physical sciences and in medical studies. He enrolled successively at the University of Pesth, the Academy of Sciences at Presburg, and the Ecole Normale of Temeswar where he was considered among their most diligent of students. This studious life firmed up and strengthened the natural qualities of his character. They made of him a man, in the broadest sense of this word. (*Mathias* 30, IA)

As regards the younger protagonists, the same palpable link between education and morality constantly makes itself felt in these texts, whether it be in the case of relatively inconsequential characters such as the son of a passenger aboard the *Chancellor* described as "a good son . . . an intelligent and learned young man" (11, IA) or the infinitely more consequential Axel in *Journey to the Center of the Earth* who, in addition to being the first-person narrator of the text, undergoes an intensive "Bildungsroman-initiatory" education through his underground quest—one that completes his growth as a scientist and as an adult.

The Vernian narrator is also very explicit about countries that have better than average educational systems. For example, among its other (sometimes humorously idiosyncratic) qualities, the United States is described as a nation "where everyone knows how to read" (*Earth/Moon* 158, IA). Scotland is "a country where there are very few unlettered people because great efforts have been made to stamp out illiteracy" (*Black* 29, IA). And English boarding schools (although not everyone is allowed to attend them) provide "a very complete education" (*Vacation* 37, IA). In the case of the latter, specific educational methodologies are reviewed and endorsed as highly effective:

> In the English private schools, the education is rather different from the one given in France. The students are permitted more freedom and, as a result, they have a greater sense of initiative when they become older. . . . They grow up to be more courteous, attentive, cleaner dressed, and—something worth noting—much less inclined to lie or dissimulate, even when threatened by a just punishment. It must also be noted that, in these schools, the young men are less often required to follow rules set down for everyone concerning daily life or periods of silence. There is no supervisor to watch over them. The reading of novels and newspapers is allowed, there are frequent holidays, the hours of study are limited, and exercise for the body is included like boxing and games of every sort. But, as a counterweight to this rarely-abused independence, there is corporal punishment by the whip. But, to be whipped is in no way deemed to be dishonorable to these young Anglo-Saxons, and they submit to it without protest so long as they recognize that they deserve it. (*Vacation* 38–39, IA)

Rousseau-like in its practicality and its naturalness, the ideal Vernian educational system balances discipline with freedom, leisure with study, books for the mind with exercise for the body. The practice of corporal punishment is seen not only as an "exemplary punishment" (230, IA) but also as a means to teach bravery: "where a French schoolboy would be ashamed, the English schoolboy would be ashamed only to appear fearful of a beating" (230, IA). And, above all, such instruction must always be useful—in terms of the student's own frame of reference. In the case of children, reading, writing, and arithmetic (the building blocks of learning) should be taught through "hands-on" techniques: "At five years of age one is still a child, and it is perhaps better to teach via practical games rather than theoretical lessons which are necessarily a bit arduous" (*Boy* 48, IA). In the case of young adults, education is emphasized as a prerequisite for upward mobility: "he had worked hard at educating himself . . . the young miner was not long in acquiring the knowledge which enabled him to rise in the hierarchy of the mine" (*Black* 29, IA). And finally, the educational benefits of travel are consistently cited as a sound and valuable method for developing observational skills: "Travel strengthens youth" (*Grant* 98, IA). "To see is a science. There are people who don't know how to see, and who travel with as much intelligence as a shellfish" (*Grant* 71, IA).

As the latter quotation indicates, if the Vernian narrator is quite explicit in his approbation of good educational practices, he is no less unequivocal in his condemnation of those he views as inferior. Such disapproval can be expressed in many different ways in these texts. One means is through contrast and exception, commending a protagonist's accomplishments in spite of his milieu, as in the case of the Corsican Andréa Ferrato and his wife in *Mathias Sandorf*: "Since both of them could read, write, and count, they were relatively educated if compared with the 100,000 illiterates that a modern census has shown to still exist today among the 260,000 inhabitants of the island" (151, IA). Another is through shared moral indignation over poor teaching, as in the narrator's portrayal of an orphanage supervisor named O'Bodkins in *Little-Fellow*:

> As for the instruction, a Mister O'Bodkins was in charge of dispensing it to the orphans of Galway. He was supposed to teach them to read, to write, and to count, but he didn't require it of any of them. And, after two or three years under his directorship, it was difficult to locate ten youngsters who could read a sign. . . . What a terrible shame, and what a total lack of social responsibility, when the natural intelligence of a child, needing only to be cultivated, is left untended. Can we know what is lost to the future by the sterilization of a young mind, a mind that Nature has perhaps planted with important seeds that will never germinate? (26–27, IA)

And even humor can function as an instrument of condemnation, as in the case of young Toliné in *The Children of Captain Grant* (471–75, IA), an Australian boy who won first prize in his (British) school's geography contest by firmly asserting that most countries of the world were English colonies!

But the most frequent textual valorizor of education in the *Voyages Extra-ordinaires* is not the positive or negative comments of the narrator himself but, rather, those situational role models presented for purposes of reader emulation. The analogical intent of these narratives is quite clear: the many teacher-student relationships throughout the *Voyages Extraordinaires* are meant to parallel the reader's *own* relationship to the didacticism contained in these novels. Again and again, learning is shown to be most effectively acquired when done in a manner that is both *utile y dulce*.

At times, such emulation techniques may involve the narrator himself when he speaks as a kind of vox populi pointing out what all educated persons presumably already know:

> As everyone knows, fishes are grouped in the fourth and last class of the phylum of vertebrates. (*20,000* 148, IA)

> It would then produce a flame of remarkable brilliance, a flame whose brightness would rival that of an electric light—which, as everyone knows, is equal to 1160 candles according to the experiments of Casselmann. (*Ox* 24, IA)

> As we know, in effect, between the Russian calendar and the French there is a difference of eleven days. (*Servadac* 432n, IA)

But most often the objects of emulation are the text's fictional protagonists themselves, the majority of whom are cast in the pedagogical role of either teachers or students. Once again, the exact configuration can vary greatly: scientist/common man or woman (for example, Dr. Clawbonny and Hatteras's crew, Professor Aronnax and Ned Land, Cyrus Smith and his castaway companions, Cyprien Méré and Miss Watkins, Harry Ford and Nell), scientist/pupil (Cyrus Smith and Harbert, Paganel and Robert, Lidenbrock and Axel), older pupil/younger pupil (Dick Sand and Jack, Little-Fellow and Bob, Gordon-Doniphan-Briant and the other children of *The Two Year Vacation*), "civilized" man/aborigine (Cyprien Méré and Matakit), or even that of man/animal and animal/man (Nab and the orangutan Jup, Service and the ostrich, or those super-intelligent dogs who frequently "instruct" their masters in novels like *Mysterious Island* or *The Boy Captain*).

Excepting the ostrich—who "refused to make any progress at all" (*Vacation* 219, IA)—such "students" are invariably portrayed as bright, hardworking, and very "desirous of educating themselves" (*Grant* 410, IA). It is no surprise (given the Positivist and capitalistic underpinnings of a great number of the *Voyages Extraordinaires*) that idleness and unproductivity are repeatedly denounced as two major evils that must be totally eliminated through instruction:

> How could they know exactly how long they would spend on this island? If they did eventually manage to leave it, what satisfaction they would have knowing that they had used their time profitably! With the few books

provided by the schooner's library, the older boys could expand their knowledge by instructing the younger ones. An excellent task, which would usefully and agreeably fill the long winter hours! (*Vacation* 203, IA)

With discussion during work and reading during the idle hours, the time flew by with profit for everyone. (*Mysterious* 457, IA)

But, narratologically, it is also interesting to note *where* a great deal of the anti-idleness pedagogy takes place in these texts and how it dovetails with the action-packed plot structures of the *Voyages Extraordinaires*. In general, such moments of didacticism fill the "holes" in the narrative—those moments when the heroes are not actively exploring, fighting for their lives, conducting experiments, or rescuing those in peril. For example, if the narrative format is basically that of a *robinsonnade* (as in *Mysterious Island, The Two Year Vacation,* or *Hector Servadac*), mimesis dictates that during periods of inclement weather the protagonists remain in their cave or some other shelter. It is at these moments, in order to avoid *oisiveté* and ennui, that they (as well as the reader) are educated via shared readings that are morally edifying, or via amusing and informative anecdotes. If the narrative format requires a long ocean cruise (as in *Twenty Thousand Leagues under the Sea, The Children of Captain Grant,* or *The Boy Captain*), mimesis dictates that—at least for those landlubbers aboard—there will be long periods of inactivity. And those moments are dutifully spent with the same "profitable" pursuits. In fact, during any typically Vernian voyage (as in *Around the Moon, Journey to the Center of the Earth,* or *The Adventures of Captain Hatteras*), the same narrative pattern exists—making all moments of rest (for the protagonists and for the reader) pedagogically "useful." As a member of the party searching for Captain Grant once expressed it when forced to a halt because of a threatening storm: "This is not the first time that bad weather has forced us to educate ourselves. Speak to us, Monsieur Paganel" (*Grant* 697, IA). In these words, one almost hears echoes of the opening chapters of Chaucer's *Canterbury Tales* or of Boccaccio's *Decameron*.

Thus, wherever there is a valorization of education in these texts—whether through the narrator or through the reader's identification with the fictional protagonists and their experiences—there is an implicit valorization of the *Voyages Extraordinaires* themselves. Wherever there is a clarification of what constitutes sound pedagogical technique, there is an accompanying fictional narrative that actualizes it. Wherever there is a call in these texts to spend leisure time profitably, there is an implicit call to purchase another novel in this series and be entertained while learning. As didactic discourse, Verne's novels are self-referential in the extreme.

BUFFERS

Throughout Verne's oeuvre there exists a built-in psychological support structure that acts as a reassuring buffer to the reader's encounter with the novum and/or the scientific pedagogy in these texts. As a rule, the new is always embedded in the old, the strange is always anchored in the traditional, and the extraordinary is always firmly rooted in the ordinary. In every Vernian "voyage," all movement is duly measured and all phenomena classified (as in the localization motif discussed earlier). Each narrative begins with a concrete reference to time and place; characterization is stereotypical; overall plot development is predictable; and the status quo is continually maintained, both ideologically throughout the text and narratologically in its conclusion. Good always conquers evil; machines are always anthropomorphized; chronology is always respected; good-natured humor always lightens the seriousness of tone; maps and predecessors always indicate the right path. There are no time warps, space warps, or mind warps. All is mimetic or rendered mimetic in short order. Thus, the structural simplicity and one-dimensionality of this series largely compensate for its intrinsic subject matter of continual "otherness."

But there is one seemingly omnipresent buffer in these texts that is of particular note. It is subliminal in nature but nevertheless quite palpable in the majority of the *Voyages Extraordinaires* and consistently provides a kind of "comforting" emotional security to the voyager/reader. And, as we shall see, it ties in very significantly to the overall ideological character of these works. Roland Barthes was among the first to call attention to it in a 1957 essay in *Mythologies* entitled *"Nautilus* et Bateau Ivre" ("*Nautilus* and the Drunken Boat"):

> Verne put together a kind of self-referential cosmogony which has its own categories, its own time and space, its own richness, and even its own existential principle.
>
> This principle seems to me to be the continual gesture of enclosure. In Verne's works, the imagination of travel corresponds to the exploration of enclosed space, and the connection between Verne and youth does not come from any banal mystique of adventure but, rather, from the common happiness of the finite—the kind one finds in a child's passion for cabins and tents: to close oneself in and make a home. Such is the existential dream both of childhood and of Verne. . . .
>
> Verne was a fanatic of plenitude. He never stopped completing the world and furnishing it, making it full like an egg . . . Verne never tried to expand the world in the manner of the Romantics by escapism or by mystical plans of the infinite. He always tried to constrict it, to people it, to reduce it to an enclosed and familiar space, in which Man could then comfortably reside. . . . (80–81, IIIA)

The construction and/or habitation of enclosed and safe spaces is a constantly recurring theme throughout Verne's works. And it usually offers not only the protagonist/reader with a privileged observational vantage point but also the text with a means to initiate its pedagogy. Such spaces include the many ambulatory homes of the *Voyages Extraordinaires*: the *Nautilus* of *Twenty Thousand Leagues under the Sea*, the *Géant d'acier* of *The Steam House*, the artificial island of *Propeller Island*, and the *Albatros* of *Robur the Conqueror* among others. The

The interior of Barbicane's "space bullet"
(*Earth/Moon*, engraving by H. de Montaut, 1865)

"armchair voyage" character of these novels is quite literally that, as each vehicle doubles as a real home—complete with plush Victorian furniture, artworks, study, and dining room as well as such "necessary" items as devoted servants and nearly inexhaustible provisions for the comfort of the passengers. These mobile mansions epitomize the ultimate bourgeois dream of taking along *all* of one's possessions when away from home—a revealing commentary on the psychic dimension of bourgeois materialism. And, as might be expected, such modes of transportation are repeatedly praised as "Progress's last word in matters of travel!" (*Steam* 28, IA)—the term *progress* being defined, of course, principally in terms of the "property" and "will to accumulate" *epistemes* discussed earlier.

Further, each vehicle invariably features some form of window in order to allow the heroes—"from the comfort of their own home"—to take in the movie-like spectacle of the outside world. Quite often, such windows (like those of the *Nautilus* or of Barbicane's space bullet) also function to safeguard the inhabitants from the dangers of the exterior environment, while providing an excellent "interface" for its firsthand study. In all cases, such windows serve to designate the boundary between the "us" and the "them," between the secure familiarity of the known and the threat posed by the "other" (the elements, indigenous natives, flora and fauna, and such). And they serve also as the tangible point of contact between the reassuringly insular world of "owned" and "filled" space and that exterior "empty" space yet to be possessed by humankind. As one critic has observed, a subliminal fear of the abyss—of the comfortless void—can often be discerned in Verne's texts. In addition to its possible psychoanalytical and ideological (and, one might add, narratological) significance, this phobia might further be viewed as a sociohistorical expression of a growing nineteenth-century crisis of faith, that is, the beginnings of the modern age of alienation, of a universe without God.[3]

Other snugly enclosed Vernian vehicles include the many sea-going vessels of the *Voyages Extraordinaires*. Each ship is a self-contained microcosm of human space floating in the vast expanses of ocean. And the security-oriented relationship between the ship's passengers and their craft is even more pronounced in that of the ship's captain. In the latter, the vessel is (as per tradition) often portrayed as a surrogate wife/mother figure, that is, supporter, protector, and lover, or, as Nemo phrased it: "Yes, Professor," Captain Nemo answered with true emotion, "and I love it like the flesh of my flesh!" (*20,000* 134, IA).

The obviously maternal and womblike nature of these vehicles is also evident in a number of Verne's favorite topographical milieus: caverns and islands. The former, whether they be huge underground caves (*Journey to the Center of the Earth*), ocean grottoes (*The Green Ray*), abandoned mines (*The Black Indies*), or extinct and hollow volcanoes (*For the Flag*), are an omnipresent topos throughout the *Voyages Extraordinaires*. And serving as secure havens from the elements or other dangers, they frequently act as narratological catalysts to long passages of geological pedagogy. "Triply enclosed," for example, would be a scene such as the one from *Mysterious Island* in which the aged Nemo and his

Nautilus rest within an underground cavern located on an island. And it is from this locale that he, quite suggestively, is able to play "God" to the castaways of Lincoln Island.

As for the latter, the island motif is the epitome of (although Verne would have shuddered at the word) *mise-en-abŷme* geography and civilization—to the extent that it is continually used as a pedagogical locale in these texts. In fact, one critic has pointed out that some 42 of the 63 novels in this series contain one or more important island scenes, all of which are extremely rich in terms of their mythic dimension (Hephaestus-Vulcan, Ulysses, Latona-Leto), the psychoanalytic implications (Oedipal and others), and their structural significance (for plot progression, pedagogy, exoticism, and so on).[4]

Conversely, active volcanoes—particularly those located on islands—constitute the reverse side of the same narratological coin. They inspire terror, chaos, and morbid fascination among the various Vernian protagonists[5] and exemplify the violent bursting of enclosed space. As such, they function as a counterpoint to the cavern/island motif and, as one might expect, also figure regularly in these texts (although less as a springboard to pedagogy than to pure melodrama).

Moreover, when viewed from this perspective, the comprehensive educational project of the *Voyages Extraordinaires* is itself a kind of totalizing enclosure of knowledge into one organized and assimilable body. As discussed in an earlier chapter, such knowledge is viewed as concretely finite in nature (albeit evergrowing) and within intellectual reach of those who wish to "possess" it. And the appropriation of such knowledge is always "easy" for those who study and who are willing to work hard. Even the erudite Dr. Clawbonny dismisses his exceptional encyclopedic abilities as follows: "I am only a man who has been blessed with a good memory and who has read a lot" (*Hatteras* 273, IA).

Further, the sometimes quite dense and enumerative didactic passages that continually punctuate these narratives constitute in themselves a kind of circumgraphic model of such enclosed learning—one that is on textual display (in museumlike fashion). And the strong narratological closure of these novels—often using a variety of retrospective "see how far we've come" value judgments—is almost always doubled by a strong emphasis on the enlarged sum of knowledge now owned by the protagonists and their world, as well as (the text implies) by the reader.

Thus, this three-dimensional enclosure buffer provides the reader, on the subliminal level, with a comfortable and totally dealienated vantage point from which to absorb the text's pedagogy. But, adjacent to it, there exists yet another buffer that is two-dimensional: predictable circularity. All Vernian "voyages" invariably return to their original point of departure—geographically, ideologically, and mimetically. The novum disappears or is destroyed. The status quo is re-established. Lost family members are reunited, heritages are retrieved, and newly matured sons take over from their fathers. Good guys triumph, bad guys are punished, and the prenarrative world reassumes its normalcy. With the same assurance as one would have in the fact that the Earth revolves around the Sun or that "what goes up must come down," the reader of the *Voyages Extra-ordinaires* knows that his or her own textual "voyage" through Verne's narratives will never leave one permanently shipwrecked, either geographically, ideologically, or mimetically. The narrative *boucle* will always be *bouclée*. As Michel Serres once expressed it:

> in the 19th century, it is necessary to tie things up and finish all possible encounters. Moreover, to travel is to take a road toward a destination, a line and a point. It's also desire, to feel the attraction of a Pole, of a journey's end. Whether because the Earth is round or because it is always necessary to return to one's home port, as to Ithaca . . . the journey is always a circular one. To be repeated. Points and circles, nothing more than going and returning. (*Jouvences* 83, IIC)

Such continuous and predictable circularity—or, perhaps even better, circulation—is a fundamental trademark of the Vernian text. All is circular motion: the protagonists as they circumnavigate the globe (Phileas Fogg, Nemo), the moon (Barbicane, Ardan, Nicholl), or the solar system (Hector Servadac); the propulsion systems of the Vernian machines themselves (where electrical "circuits" provide the uninterrupted power); the social "return to the fold" of wayward individuals (Ayrton, Nemo, Kin-Fo); the movement of investment capital (*Little-Fellow, The Last Will of an Eccentric*); even knowledge itself (as communicated by the hero-scientists of these fictions, or by the *Voyages Extra-ordinaires* themselves as a whole). All is—as Nemo chose to say—"mobilis in mobili" within clearly circumscribed space.[6]

Similarly, all obstacles to such circulatory motion are portrayed as repressive, counterproductive, or, in moral terms, evil. For example, consider a host of typically Vernian antiheroes such as Silfax of *The Black Indies* who wishes to block the "recycling" of an abandoned mine, Herr Schultze or Harry Killer of *The Begum's Fortune* and *The Amazing Adventure of the Barsac Mission*, respectively, who tyranically forbid the free circulation of their workers in Stahlstadt and Blackland, or even Isac (sic) Hakhabut of *Hector Servadac* who incarnates the stereotype of the greedy miser (who refuses to "circulate" his money—crucial to capitalism). Other short-circuits to circular movement are depicted in the same negative fashion: the mutiny of Hatteras's crew during his voyage to and from the North Pole, the sabotaged ship's compass in *The Boy Captain*, or the internal bickering of the starboard and port populations of *Propeller Island* (which ultimately immobilizes their unique vessel, and then destroys it). Finally, observe Verne's curious treatment of civil matters such as marriage: it permanently removes his heroes from "circulation" and (quite appropriately) occurs only at the end of their initiatory journey, that is, of the text itself. The overall buffered lesson of these novels seems quite clear: Let the circ-ulation not be broken.

Thus, by evoking motifs of enclosure and circ-ulation at all levels of his narration, Verne facilitates and enhances his scientific pedagogy by providing a familiar, predictable, and comfortable setting in which the reader can assimilate it. For the reader, the many lessons contained in the *Voyages Extraordinaires* involve a continual "alien encounter of the third kind," and the learning of them requires not only a physical and intellectual interaction with the text, but an emotional one as well. And it is the role of the Vernian buffers to address this latter need in the de-alienation process.

But they also do more. They constitute an important epistemological focal point for the *Voyages Extraordinaires* as a social artifact. For the nineteenth-century bourgeois reader, such narrative devices evoked a fictional universe that was self-referential and intrinsically relevant. Thus, for the modern reader, they can be viewed as valuable analytical stepping-stones to a more accurate historical understanding of the underlying factors defining such mimesis. For the nineteenth-century reader, the ultimate pedagogical lesson of these texts was the very real but complex interrelationship of science and society. But for the modern reader of the late twentieth century—decoding retrospectively from a world of tomorrow—that lesson now involves not only science and society, but the social function of literature as well.

NOTES

1. V. Philippe Mustière, "Jules Verne et le roman-catastrophe," *Europe* 595–96 (1978), 43–47.

2. V. Andrew Martin, "Chez Jules: Nutrition and Cognition in the Novels of Jules Verne," *French Studies* XXXVII:1 (January 1983), 47–58.

3. Mark Rose, "Filling the Void: Verne, Wells, and Lem," *Science-Fiction Studies* 8 (1981), 121–23.

4. Daniel Compère, *Approche de l'île chez Jules Verne* (Paris: Minard, 1977), pp. 5–165.

5. V. *Five Weeks in a Balloon* (189–90), *The Adventures of Captain Hatteras* (454–56), and *Mysterious Island* (843–58), among others.

6. V. Marc Angenot, "Jules Verne: The Last Happy Utopianist," in *Science Fiction: A Critical Guide*, P. Parrinder, ed. (New York: Longman, 1979), pp. 18–32.

Conclusion: Jules Verne and SF:
The "Adaptivity Effect"

As the preceding pages attempt to demonstrate, Jules Verne's scientific novels are a unique brand of industrial-age epic literature: one that not only portrays modern Man's continual encounter with the unknown "other"—geographical, technological, anthropological—but that also provides the pedagogical means to neutralize the alienation generated by such encounters.

Each novel in the *Voyages Extraordinaires* is a kind of initiatory journey in difference and/or change—often toward what Michel Butor has termed a *point suprême.*[1] Knowledge is consistently valorized as the most effective tool for the painless "domestication" of difference and change as well as one's ultimate reward for having confronted them. Learning to cope with change and difference is shown to be the prerequisite for growth—in the world at large (scientific, industrial, economic) and in the individual's own life (psychological, moral, intellectual). And broadened horizons—in all senses of the term—are the tangible fruits of such growth.

One need not, however, physically travel the globe in order to have access to such experiences, or spend long years among dusty library shelves accumulating facts and figures in order to have access to such knowledge. Both are immediately available—within the comfort of one's own home—through reading. Therein lies the implicit (and purposely self-referential) message of this series of didactic novels.

That is to say, Verne's *roman scientifique* functioned during the nineteenth century not as only an *utile y dulce* pedagogical instrument for the popularization of scientific knowledge, but also as an emulative model of social adaptation. As such, it closely resembles (in its time) what Lewis Mumford has called cultural "shock absorbers," that is, certain institutional developments that "decreased the tensions that the machine produced" in those Western societies struggling to cope with the effects of the Industrial Revolution (*Technics and Civilization* 311, IIIA).

In this regard, uncanny parallels also seem to exist with our modern late-twentieth-century world. In 1970, for example, Alvin Toffler pointed out the severe lack in contemporary society of what he termed "change regulators"—mechanisms that would develop "creative strategies for shaping . . . change selectively . . . to increase adaptivity" (*Future Shock* 373, IIIA). In 1982 a best-seller by John Naisbitt described society's critical need for more "high tech/high touch" approaches in industry in order to better balance "the material wonders of technology with the spiritual demands of our human nature" (*Megatrends* 36, IIIA). Clearly, the complex problems associated with accelerated social change due to scientific and technological growth (and the various forms of alienation resulting from it) was not unique to Jules Verne's era. It is very much a part of contemporary daily living.[2]

Earlier in this book, I pointed out what I see as the vast differences separating the scientific fictions of Jules Verne from most modern science fiction: how his portrayed universe is highly mimetic and in close alignment with the ideological mandates of his times, how the hermeneutic structure of his texts is patterned on various time-honored literary topoi and very traditional modes of referentiality (as opposed to that of absent paradigms), and how his overtly explicit and nonconjectural didacticism would seem to preclude his being labeled the "father of SF."

But the time has now come to qualify somewhat that critical stance. Although substantially different in their chosen themes, extrapolative qualities, ideology, and signifying structures, Verne's *Voyages Extraordinaires* and modern SF nevertheless do have something important in common—most particularly if one considers them in the context of their own historical periods and the "adaptivity" effect they appear to have had on their respective readers.

The exact rationale for such a rapprochement is twofold. First, modern SF might also quite justifiably be considered a twentieth-century variant of epic literature[3]—defined principally as an heroic coming to grips with an alien "other." Second, the spectacular rise in popularity of all forms of SF—novels, films, art, and others—since the 1960s might likewise be viewed as part of this same social phenomenon of cultural shock absorbers that contributed to the huge commercial success of Verne's texts during his lifetime.

A number of literary critics and writers have pointed out this implicit didactic dimension of SF narratives, that is, how such fictions tend to "broaden the horizons" of their readers by postulating radically new perspectives on technological growth, social problems, human behavior, and the nature of reality as a whole. One critic, for example, has stated that "SF has the noteworthy mission to prepare us, with empathy and imagination, for the innovations that science has in store for us" (Plank 76, IIIB). Another affirms that SF "teaches adaptability and elasticity of mind in the face of change" (Ketterer, *New Worlds for Old* 25, IIIA). And Maurice Blanchot as early as 1959 described the capacity of SF to alter the habitual thinking patterns of its readers, forcing them to question their most basic assumptions about the nature of the universe:

> As G. Bachelard once said, in the past 20 years the physician has been obliged to reconstruct, two or three times over, his entire way of reasoning and, intellectually speaking, redo his whole life. It's essentially that, this change of reasoning, which has created science fiction and which the latter represents with a remarkable virulence. The world has not only drastically altered, but has also become a plurality of structures, to such an extent that we suddenly have at our disposal much more than the immense universe, we have an immensity of universes . . . That's the role played, more or less successfully, by this new form of writing. It is an essentially intellectual exercise where what is desired is always a total reconsideration of our basic premises. ("Le Bon usage de la science-fiction" 95–96, IIIB)

Other critics have noted the capacity of the SF narrative to promote "scientific" thinking and more rational cognition in the reader (as mentioned earlier in Verne's case):

> What is important in the definition of science fiction is not the appurtenances of ray guns and lab coats, but the "scientific" habits of mind: the idea that paradigms do control our view of all phenomena, that within these paradigms all normal problems can be solved, and that abnormal occurrences must either be explained or initiate the search for a better (usually more inclusive) paradigm. In science fiction, these habits of mind and their associated bodies of knowledge determine the outcome of events. . . . (Rabkin, "Genre Criticism" 92)

> If the *novum* is the necessary condition of SF (differentiating it from "naturalistic" fiction), the validation of the novelty by scientifically methodological cognition into which the reader is inexorably led is the *sufficient* condition for SF. . . . The presence of scientific cognition . . . differentiates thus SF from the "supernatural" genres or fantasy in the wider sense, which includes fairy tales, mythical tales, moral allegories, etc. over and above horror or heroic "fantasy" in the narrower sense. (Suvin, "The State of the Art in SF Theory" 37, IIIB)

And some have even commented on the recent upsurge of SF popularity and its relation to the rapidly changing social patterns of our contemporary postindustrial society: "Perhaps science fiction is one symptom of a change in sensibility (and culture) as profound as that of the Renaissance. . . . It is as if literary and dramatic art were being asked to perform tasks of analysis and teaching as a means of dealing with some drastic change in the conditions of human life" (Russ 117, IIIB).

In the light of such comments, it is no wonder that Toffler selected SF as required reading for all of today's students—seeing in this particular fictional genre the necessary "mind-stretching" attributes that would better equip them to deal with what he terms "future shock":

> what is needed is a concentrated focus on the social and personal implica-
> tions of the future, not merely on its technological characteristics.
>   We do not have a literature *of* the future for use in these courses, but
> we do have a literature *about* the future, consisting not only of the great
> utopias but also of contemporary science fiction.... science fiction has
> immense value as a mind-stretching force for the creation of the habit of
> anticipation. Our children should be studying Arthur C. Clarke, William
> Tenn, Robert Heinlein, Ray Bradbury and Robert Sheckley, not because
> these writers can tell them more about rocket ships and time machines but,
> more important, because they can lead young minds through an imagina-
> tive exploration of the jungle of political, social, psychological, and ethical
> issues that will confront these children as adults. (*Future Shock* 424–25,
> IIIA)

In Toffler's exhortation to read more SF in today's schools, one can almost hear echoes of Verne's publisher, P.-J. Hetzel, as he ceaselessly promoted the *Voyages Extraordinaires* in much the same fashion.

Thus, the social function of a great deal of modern SF seems to closely resemble the role played by Verne's scientific novels within the society of his time. Much like the latter's series of pedagogical adventure stories, SF has the effect of mitigating the negative effects of the impact of technological and social change by "stretching the mind" of the reader/viewer well beyond the world of his or her own technological present (which by comparison appears rather tame), by depicting advanced societies fully acclimated to such change and by portray-ing basic human values as essentially unaltered in spite of it.

In this study of Jules Verne and his scientific novel, I have touched upon a wide variety of biographical, sociohistorical, ideological, and narratological aspects of this very prolific author. For purposes of concision and breadth, I chose Verne's didacticism as the focus for my investigations—a topic that has heretofore (and quite curiously) been left unexplored by modern Vernian crit-icism. Throughout its completion, I have been acutely aware of the parallels between Verne's expressed educational project (the dealienation of science) and my own endeavors, that is, the dealienation of Jules Verne himself. Given his known-yet-unknown status within the American public, this study has truly been, for me at least, a *Voyage dans les mondes connus et inconnus*.

But, repeating the words of Dr. Olivier Dumas, president of the Société Jules Verne, "until now, we have only scratched the surface of this subject matter. There remains so much to discover and to make known."[4] Such in my view is (or should be) the true spirit of all literary criticism: an "extraordinary voyage" through the text, one that is filled with adventure and learning, but one that seeks also to communicate to others, in a manner that is both *utile y dulce*, the myriad wonders of the human imagination.

NOTES

1. Michel Butor, "Le Point suprême et l'âge d'or à travers quelques oeuvres de Jules Verne," *Arts et Lettres* 15 (1949), 3–31, reprinted in *Répertoire* 1 (Paris: Ed. de Minuit, 1960), pp. 130–62.

2. V. William Serrin, "Worry Grows Over Upheaval as Technology Reshapes Jobs," *New York Times* (July 4, 1982), pp. 1, 29; John Culhane, "Special Effects are Revolutionizing Film," *New York Times* (July 4, 1982), sect. 2, pp. 1, 13; Isadore Barmash, "Retailing Changes under Technological Impact," *New York Times* (March 27, 1983), sect. 27, pp. 55–60; Edward B. Fiske, "New Priority: Technological Literacy," *New York Times* (April 14, 1983), sect. 12, pp. 1, 43, 68; Judith Kelman, "Feeling Low About High Technology," *New York Times* (April 24, 1983), sec. 12, p. 79; Katherine G. DaCosta, "Anticomputerism," *New York Times* (August 27, 1984), p. A19, among hundreds of other articles, books, and television programs outlining the continuing impact of the electronic and computer revolution on contemporary society.

3. V. Patrick Parrinder, "Science Fiction as Truncated Epic." In Slusser, Guffey, and Rose, eds., *Bridges to Science Fiction* (Edwardsville, IL: So. Illinois University Press, 1980), pp. 91–106; also, Boris Vian's comment that SF is "the resurrection of epic poetry" in his early article with Stéphane Spriel entitled "Un nouveau genre littéraire: la science-fiction," *Les Temps modernes* (1951), 626.

4. Conversation of June 9, 1985 after we participated in a colloquium at Amiens sponsored by the Université de Picardie and entitled (quite appropriately) *Modernité de Jules Verne*.

Bibliography

I. PRIMARY SOURCES

Many of Verne's fictional works first appeared in *feuilleton* format or as short stories in the following periodical publications: *Le Magasin d'Education et de Récréation* (Paris: 1864–1909), *Le Journal des Débats* (Paris: 1865–86), *Le Musée des Familles* (Paris: 1851–72), *Le Temps* (Paris: 1872–87), *Le Journal d'Amiens* (Amiens: 1873), *Mémoires de l'Académie de sciences, des lettres et des arts d'Amiens* (Amiens: 1873), *Le Figaro illustré* (Paris: 1884, 1891, 1893), *The Forum* (London: 1889), *Le Soleil* (Paris: 1892), *Les Annales politiques et littéraires* (Paris: 1893), *The Strand Magazine* (London: 1892, 1895), *Le Journal* (Paris: 1908–10), *La Revue de Paris* (Paris: 1910), *Le Matin* (Paris: 1914). These editions of Verne's works are most commonly referred to as the "preoriginal" versions.

IA. Original Verne Publications and Reprints

1. *Géographie de la France et de ses colonies.* Paris: Bibliothèque d'Education et de Récréation, 1868.
2. *Histoire des grands voyages et des grands voyageurs.* 3 vols. Paris: Bibliothèque d'Education et de Recréation, 1870–80.
3. *The Works of Jules Verne.* Claire Boss, ed. New York: Crown, 1983.
4. *Voyages Extraordinaires.* Paris: Editions Hetzel, 1863–1914.

    The *Voyages Extraordinaires* series includes the titles listed below, which were normally first published in an "in-18" format with no illustrations, and then in a deluxe "grand in-8" illustrated version. The titles are first listed in their French form chronologically by date of publication. An asterisk preceding the title indicates posthumous publication. Second, to facilitate referencing from the parenthetical citations in the text, the titles are listed alphabetically by their English abbreviations, indicating for each title its full English equivalent (which may or may not correspond to the one chosen for the published translations) and the French title. The third list contains the modern French reprint used for quoting purposes (where applicable).

Voyages Extraordinaires Titles by Date of Publication

1863 *Cinq Semaines en ballon*
1864 *Voyage au centre de la Terre*
1865 *De la Terre à la Lune*
1866 *Voyages et adventures du capitaine Hatteras*
1867 *Les Enfants du capitaine Grant*
1870 *Vingt mille lieues sous les mers*
     Autour de la Lune
1871 *Une Ville flottante*, suivi de *Les Forceurs du blocus*
1872 *Aventures de trois Russes et de trois Anglais*
1873 *Le Pays des fourrures*
     Le Tour du monde en 80 jours
1874 *Le Docteur Ox*, receuil de nouvelles comprenant: *Une Fantaisie du docteur Ox, Maître Zacharius, Un Hivernage dans les glaces, Un Drame dans les airs*
     L'Ile mystérieuse
1875 *Le Chancellor*, suivi de: *Martin Paz*
1876 *Michel Strogoff*, suivi de: *Un Drame au Mexique*
1877 *Hector Servadac*
     Les Indes Noires
1878 *Un Capitaine de quinze ans*
1879 *Les Cinq cents millions de la Bégum*, suivi de: *Les Révoltés de la Bounty*
     Les Tribulations d'un Chinois in Chine
1880 *La Maison à vapeur*
1881 *La Jangada*
1882 *Le Rayon vert*, suivi de: *Deux heures de chasse*
     L'Ecole des Robinsons
1883 *Kéraban-le-Têtu*
1884 *L'Archipel en feu*
     L'Etoile du Sud

1885 *Mathias Sandorf*
     L'Epave du Cynthia
1886 *Robur-le-Conquérant*
     Un Billet de loterie, suivi de: *Frritt-Flacc*
1887 *Chemin de France*, suivi de: *Gil Braltar*
     Nord contre Sud
1888 *Deux ans de vacances*
1889 *Sans dessus dessous*
     Famille-sans-nom
1890 *César Cascabel*
1891 *Mistress Branican*
1892 *Le Château des Carpathes*
     Claudius Bombarnac
1893 *P'tit-Bonhomme*
1894 *Les Mirifiques aventures de maître Antifer*
1895 *L'Ile à hélice*
1896 *Face au drapeau*
     Clovis Dardentor
1897 *Le Sphinx des glaces*
1898 *Le Superbe Orénoque*
1899 *Le Testament d'un excentrique*
1900 *Seconde Patrie*
1901 *Le Village aérien*
     Les Histoires de Jean-Marie Cabidoulin
1902 *Les Frères Kip*
1903 *Bourses de voyage*
1904 *Maître du monde*
     Un Drame en Livonie
1905 *L'Invasion de la mer*
     Le Phare du bout du monde
1906 *Le Volcan d'or*
1907 *L'Agence Thompson and Co.*
1908 *La Chasse au météore*
     Le Pilote au Danube
1909 *Les Naufragés du "Jonathan"*
1910 *Le Secret de Wilhelm Storitz*
     Hier et demain, recueil de

nouvelles comprenant: La   Au XXIXème siècle, Journée
Famille Raton, Monsieur   d'un journaliste américain
Ré-Dièze et Mademoiselle   en 2889, et L'Eternel Adam
Mi-bémol, La Destinée de   1919 *L'Etonnante aventure de la
Jean Morénas, Le Humbug,   mission Barsac

English Abbreviations of *Voyages Extraordinaires* Titles

Adam—see *Yesterday.*

Antifer—"The Adventures of Captain Antifer"; *Les Mirifiques aventures de maître Antifer.* Lausanne: Ed. Rencontre, 1971.

Archipelago—"The Archipelago on Fire"; *L'Archipel en feu.* Lausanne: Ed. Rencontre, 1969.

Barsac—"The Amazing Adventure of the Barsac Mission"; *L'Etonnante aventure de la mission Barsac.* Paris: Les Humanoides associés, 1977.

Begum—"The Begum's Fortune"; *Les Cinq cents millions de la Bégum.* Paris: Livre de poche, 1966.

Black—"The Black Indies"; *Les Indes Noires.* Paris: Livre de poche, 1968.

Bombarnac—"Claudius Bombarnac"; *Claudius Bombarnac.* Lausanne: Ed. de l'Agora, 1981.

Bounty—"Mutiny on the Bounty"; *Les Révoltés de la Bounty.*

Boy—"The Boy Captain"; *Un Capitaine de quinze ans.* Paris: Hachette, "Intégrales Jules Verne," 1978.

Branican—"Mistress Branican"; *Mistress Branican.* Paris: Livre de poche, 1970.

Cabidoulin—"The Tales of Jean-Marie Cabidoulin"; *Les Histoires de Jean-Marie Cabidoulin.* Paris: Les Humanoides associés, 1978.

Castle—"The Carpathian Castle"; *Le Château des Carpathes.* Paris: Livre de poche, 1966.

César—"César Cascabel"; *César Cascabel.*

Chancellor—"The Chancellor"; *Le Chancellor.* Paris: Livre de poche, 1968.

City—"A Floating City"; *Une Ville flottante.* Paris: Livre de poche, 1970.

Clovis—"Clovis Dardentor"; *Clovis Dardentor.* Paris: Ed. 10/18, 1978.

Cynthia—"The Wreck of the Cynthia"; *L'Epave du Cynthia.* Paris: Les Humanoides associés, 1977.

Danube—"The Danube Pilot"; *Le Pilote au Danube.* Paris: Ed. 10/18, 1978.

Drama—see *Ox.*

Earth/Moon—"From the Earth to the Moon"; *De la Terre à la Lune.* Paris: Livre de poche, 1966.

80—"Around the World in 80 Days"; *Le Tour du monde en 80 jours.* Paris: Livre de poche, 1966.

Family—"Family Without a Name"; *Famille-sans-nom.* Paris: Ed. 10/18, 1978.

Five—"Five Weeks in a Balloon"; *Cinq semaines en ballon.* Paris: Livre de poche, 1966.

Flag—"For the Flag"; *Face au drapeau.* Paris: Livre de poche, 1967.

Flight—"Flight to France"; *Chemin de France.*

Frritt—"Frritt-Flacc"; *Frritt-Flacc.*

Fur—"The Fur Country"; *Le Pays des fourrures.* Paris: Livre de poche, 1966.

Gil Braltar—"Gil Braltar"; *Gil Braltar.*

Grant—"The Children of Captain Grant"; *Les Enfants du capitaine Grant*. Paris: Livre de poche, 1967.

Hatteras—"The Adventures of Captain Hatteras"; *Voyages et aventures du capitaine Hatteras*. Paris: Hachette, "Intégrales Jules Verne," 1978.

Humbug—see *Yesterday*.

Hunting—"Ten Hours of Hunting"; *Dix heures de chasse*.

Invasion—"Invasion of the Sea"; *L'Invasion de la mer*. Lausanne: Ed. Rencontre, 1970.

Jonathan—"The Survivors of the 'Jonathan'"; *Les Naufragés du "Jonathan."* Paris: Hachette, "Intégrales Jules Verne," 1979.

Journey—"Journey to the Center of the Earth"; *Voyage au centre de la Terre*. Paris: Livre de poche, 1966.

Kéraban—"Kéraban the Obstinate"; *Kéraban-le-Têtu*. Paris: Livre de poche, 1969.

Kip—"The Brothers Kip"; *Les Frères Kip*.

Lighthouse—"The Lighthouse at the Edge of the World"; *Le Phare du bout du monde*. Lausanne: Ed. Recontre, 1971.

Little—"Little-Fellow"; *P'tit-Bonhomme*. Lausanne: Ed. Rencontre, 1970.

Livonia—"A Drama in Livonia"; *Un Drame en Livonie*.

Lottery—"A Lottery Ticket"; *Un Billet de loterie*.

Master—"Master of the World"; *Maître du monde*. Lausanne: Ed. Rencontre, 1968.

Mathias—"Mathias Sandorf"; *Mathias Sandorf*. Paris: Livre de poche, 1967.

Meteor—"The Hunt for the Meteor"; *La Chasse au météore*. Lausanne: Ed. Rencontre, 1970.

Mexico—"A Drama in Mexico"; *Un Drame au Mexique*.

Moon—"Around the Moon"; *Autour de la Lune*. Paris: Livre de poche, 1966.

Morenas—see *Yesterday*.

Mysterious—"The Mysterious Island"; *L'Ile mystérieuse*. Paris: Livre de poche, 1966.

North—"North Against South"; *Nord contre Sud*. Paris: Livre de poche, 1969.

Orénoque—"The Orénoque River"; *Le Superbe Orénoque*. Lausanne: Ed. Rencontre, 1972.

Ox—"Doctor Ox," a collection of short stories including "A Fantasy of Doctor Ox" (*Ox*), "Master Zacharius" (*Zacharius*), "Wintering in the Ice" (*Wintering*), and "A Drama in the Air" (*Drama*); *Le Docteur Ox*, receuil de nouvelles comprenant: *Une Fantaisie du docteur Ox, Maître Zacharius, Un Hivernage dans les glaces, Un Drame dans les airs*. Paris: Livre de poche, 1966.

Paz—"Martin Paz"; *Martin Paz*.

Propeller—"Propeller Island"; *L'Ile à hélice*. Paris: 10/18, 1978.

Raft—"The Jangada Raft"; *La Jangada*. Paris: Hachette, "Intégrales Jules Verne," 1978.

Raton—see *Yesterday*.

Ray—"The Green Ray"; *Le Rayon vert*. Paris: Livre de poche, 1968.

Ray Sharp—see *Yesterday*.

Robur—"Robur the Conqueror"; *Robur-le-Conquérant*. Lausanne: Ed. Rencontre, 1968.

Runners—"The Blockade Runners"; *Les Forceurs du blocus.* Paris: Ed. Glénat, 1978.

Scholarships—"Travel Scholarships"; *Bourses de voyage.* Lausanne: Ed. Rencontre, 1970.

School—"The School for Crusoes"; *L'Ecole des Robinsons.* Paris: Livre de poche, 1968.

Second—"A Second Homeland"; *Seconde Patrie.*

Servadac—"Hector Servadac"; *Hector Servadac.* Paris: Livre de poche, 1967.

Sphinx—"The Ice Sphinx"; *Le Sphinx des glaces.* Paris: Livre de poche, 1970.

Star—"The Southern Star"; *L'Etoile du Sud.* Paris: Livre de poche, 1967.

Steam—"The Steam House"; *La Maison à vapeur.* Paris: Livre de poche, 1967.

Storitz—"The Secret of Wilhelm Storitz"; *Le Secret de Wilhelm Storitz.* Paris: Les Humanoides associés, 1977.

Strogoff—"Michel Strogoff"; *Michel Strogoff.* Paris: Livre de poche, 1967.

Thompson—"The Thompson Travel Agency"; *L'Agence Thompson and Co.* Paris: Hachette, "Intégrales Jules Verne," 1982.

Three—"The Adventures of Three Russians and Three Englishmen"; *Aventures de trois Russes et de trois Anglais.* Lausanne: Ed. Rencontre, 1970.

Topsy—"Topsy Turvy"; *Sans dessus dessous.* Paris: Ed. Glénat, 1976.

Tribulations—"The Tribulations of a Chinaman"; *Les Tribulations d'un Chinois in Chine.* Paris: Livre de poche, 1968.

2889—see *Yesterday*.

20,000—"Twenty Thousand Leagues under the Sea"; *Vingt mille lieues sous les mers.* Paris: Livre de poche, 1966.

Vacation—"The Two Year Vacation"; *Deux ans de vacances.* Paris: Livre de poche, 1967.

Village—"The Village in the Treetops"; *Le Village aérien.* Paris: Les Humanoides associés, 1977.

Volcano—"The Golden Volcano"; *Le Volcan d'or.* Lausanne: Ed. Rencontre, 1970.

Will—"The Last Will of an Eccentric"; *Le Testament d'un excentrique.* Paris: Hachette, "Intégrales Jules Verne," 1979.

Wintering—see *Ox.*

Yesterday—"Yesterday and Tomorrow" collection of short stories including: "The Raton Family" (*Raton*), "Mr. Ray Sharp and Miss Me Flat" (*Ray Sharp*), "The Fate of Jean Morenas" (*Morenas*), "The Humbug" (*Humbug*), "In the Twenty-ninth Century: The Day of an American Journalist in 2889" (*2889*), "Eternal Adam" (*Adam*); *Hier et demain*, recueil de nouvelles comprenant: *La Famille Raton, Monsieur Ré-Dièze et Mademoiselle Mi-bémol, La Destinée de Jean Morénas, Le Humbug, Au XXIXème siècle, Journée d'un journaliste américain en 2889, L'Eternel Adam.* Paris: Livre de poche, 1967.

Zacharius—see *Ox.*

Modern French Reprints .

Due to the large number of editions and formats, the following modern French reprints of Verne's *Voyages Extraordinaires* are listed more or less chronologically. Each is followed by a brief description of its features as regards overall presentation, integrity of text, and completeness of collection.

Voyages Extraordinaires. Paris: Hachette "Collection Hetzel," 1914–34. Hardcover, facsimile reproduction of "grand in-8" Hetzel publications plus posthumous works, unabridged texts, original illustrations.

Voyages Extraordinaires. Paris: Hachette "Bibliothèque Verte," 1924 to present. Hardcover and paperback, heavily abridged texts, destined for children, modern illustrations, incomplete collection of approx. 33 titles.

Voyages Extraordinaires. Paris: Lidis-Grund, 1957–68. Hardcover, unabridged texts, modern illustrations, incomplete collection of approx. 14 titles.

Voyages Extraordinaires. Paris: Gonon, 1961–67. Hardcover, unabridged texts, modern illustrations, incomplete collection of approx. 14 titles.

Voyages Extraordinaires. Paris: Livre de Poche, 1966–68. Paperback, unabridged texts, original illustrations, incomplete collection of approx. 40 titles.

Oeuvres romancées complètes de Jules Verne. Lausanne: Editions Rencontre, 1966–71. Hardcover, unabridged texts, original illustrations, large but incomplete collection of approx. 45 titles.

Voyages Extraordinaires. Paris: Glénat "Marginalia," 1976–78. Paperback, unabridged texts, no illustrations, incomplete collection of 2 titles only.

Voyages Extraordinaires. Michel de l'Ormeraie, 1976–84. Hardcover, facsimile reproduction of original Hetzel editions, unabridged texts, original illustrations, complete collection.

Voyages Extraordinaires. Paris: Gallimard "Folio Junior," 1977 to present. Paperback, some abridged and some unabridged texts, modern illustrations, destined for children, incomplete collection of approx. 8 titles.

Voyages Extraordinaires. Paris: Hachette, "Les Intégrales Jules Verne," 1977 to present. Hardcover, unabridged texts, original illustrations, incomplete collection to date—approx. 55 titles—but continuing.

Voyages Extraordinaires. Paris: Les Humanoïdes Associés "Bibliothèque aérienne," 1977–78. Paperback, unabridged texts, no illustrations, incomplete collection of approx. 7 titles.

Voyages Extraordinaires. Lausanne: Ed. de l'Agora, 1978–82. Hardcover, facsimile reproduction of "grand in-8" Hetzel publications, unabridged texts, original illustrations, incomplete collection of approx. 30 titles.

Voyages Extraordinaires. Paris: UGE "10/18," 1978 to present. Paperback, unabridged texts, no illustrations, incomplete collection of approx. 15 titles.

IB. Modern English Translations of Verne's Works

These selected titles by Jules Verne are listed alphabetically.

The Adventures of Captain Hatteras, trans. I. O. Evans; 2 vols.: *At the North Pole* and *The Wilderness of Ice*. London: Arco Publications, 1961.

An Antarctic Mystery (Le Sphinx des glaces), intro. David G. Hartwell. Boston: Gregg Press, 1975.

The Annotated Jules Verne: From the Earth to the Moon, ed., trans. Walter James Miller. New York: T. Y. Crowell, 1978.

The Annotated Jules Verne: Twenty Thousand Leagues under the Sea, trans. Walter James Miller. New York: T. Y. Crowell, 1978.

Around the World in Eighty Days, trans. Jacqueline and Robert Baldick. New York: E. P. Dutton, 1968.

Around the World in Eighty Days, intro. Anthony Boucher. New York: Dodd, Mead, 1956.

Around the World in Eighty Days, trans. I. O. Evans. London: Arco Publications, 1967.

Around the World in Eighty Days, trans. Lewis Mercier. New York: Collier Books, 1962.

The Barsac Mission, trans. I. O. Evans; 2 vols.: *Into the Niger Bend* and *The City in the Sahara*. Westport, CT: Associated Booksellers, 1960.

The Begum's Fortune, trans. I. O. Evans. London: Bernard Hanison, 1958.

Black Diamonds (Les Indes Noires), trans. I. O. Evans. London: Arco Publications, 1961.

Captain Grant's Children, trans. I. O. Evans. London: Arco Publications, 1964.

Carpathian Castle, trans. I. O. Evans. London: Arco Publications, 1963.

César Cascabel, trans. I. O. Evans; 2 vols.: *The Travelling Circus* and *The Show on Ice*. London: Arco Publications, 1966.

The Chancellor, trans. I. O. Evans. London: Arco Publications, 1965.

The Clipper of the Clouds (Robur-le-conquérant), trans. I. O. Evans. London: Arco Publications, 1962.

The Danube Pilot, trans. I. O. Evans. London: Arco Publications, 1967.

Doctor Ox and Other Stories, trans. I. O. Evans. London: Arco Publications, 1964.

A Drama in Livonia, trans. I. O. Evans. London: Arco Publications, 1967.

A Family Without a Name, trans. I. O. Evans; 2 vols.: *Leader of the Resistance* and *Into the Abyss*. London: Arco Publications, 1963.

Five Weeks in a Balloon, trans. I. O. Evans. London: Bernard Hanison, 1958.

Flight to France, trans. I. O. Evans. London: Arco Publications, 1966.

For the Flag, trans. I. O. Evans, London: Arco Publications, 1961.

From the Earth to the Moon, ed. Willy Ley. New York: Fawcett, 1958.

From the Earth to the Moon and Around the Moon, intro. Jean Jules-Verne. New York: Limited Editions Club, 1970.

From the Earth to the Moon and Round the Moon, intro. Arthur C. Clarke. New York: Dodd, Mead, 1962.

The Giant Raft (La Jangada), trans. I. O. Evans; 2 vols.: *Down the Amazon* and *The Cryptogram*. London: Arco Publications, 1967.

The Golden Volcano, trans. I. O. Evans; 2 vols.: *The Claim on the Forty Mile Creek* and *Flood and Famine*. London: Arco Publications, 1962.

The Green Ray, trans. I. O Evans. London: Arco Publications, 1965.

Hector Servadac, trans. I. O. Evans. London: Arco Publications, 1965.

The Hunt for the Meteor, trans. I. O. Evans. London: Arco Publications, 1965.

Journey to the Center of the Earth, trans. Robert Baldick. New York: Penguin Books, 1965.

Journey to the Center of the Earth, trans. Willis T. Bradley. New York: Ace Books, 1956.

Journey to the Center of the Earth, intro. Arthur C. Clarke. New York: Dodd, Mead, 1959.

Journey to the Center of the Earth, trans. I. O. Evans. London: Arco Publications, 1961.

Journey to the Center of the Earth, ed. Robert A. W. Lowndes. New York: Airmont, 1965.

A Long Vacation, trans. Olga Marx. New York: Holt, Rinehart and Winston, 1967.

Master of the World, ed. Robert A. W. Lowndes. New York: Airmont, 1965.

The Master of the World, trans. I. O. Evans. London: Arco Publications, 1962.

Michel Strogoff, trans. I. O. Evans. Westport, CT: Associated Booksellers, 1959.

The Mysterious Island, trans. Lowell Bair. New York: Bantam Books, 1970.

The Mysterious Island, intro. Anthony Boucher. New York: Dodd, Mead, 1958.

The Mysterious Island, intro. Ray Bradbury. Baltimore: Limited Edition Club, 1959.

The Mysterious Island, trans. I. O. Evans. London: Bernard Hanison, 1959.

The Mystery of Arthur Gordon Pym by Edgar Allan Poe and Jules Verne, trans. I. O. Evans, ed. Basil Ashmore. London: Arco Publications, 1961.

The Narrative of Arthur Gordon Pym and Le Sphinx des glaces, ed. Harold Beaver. Harmondsworth, England: Penguin Books, 1975.

North Against South, trans. I. O. Evans; 2 vols.: *Burbank the Northerner* and *Texar the Southerner*. London: Arco Publications, 1963.

Propeller Island, trans. I. O. Evans. London: Arco Publications, 1961.

The Purchase of the North Pole (Sans Dessus Dessous), trans. I. O. Evans. London: Arco Publications, 1966.

Round the Moon, ed. Robert A. W. Lowndes. New York: Airmont, 1965.

Salvage from the Cynthia, trans. I. O. Evans. London: Arco Publications, 1964.

The School for Crusoes, trans. I. O. Evans. London: Arco Publications, 1966.

The Sea Serpent: The Yarns of Jean Marie Cabidoulin, trans. I. O. Evans. London: Arco Publications, 1967.

The Secret of Wilhelm Storitz, trans. I. O. Evans. Westport, CT: Associated Booksellers, 1963.

The Southern Star Mystery, trans. I. O. Evans. London: Arco Publications, 1966.

The Steam House, trans. I. O. Evans; 2 vols.: *The Demon of Cawnpore* and *Tigers and Traitors*. Westport, CT: Associated Booksellers, 1959.

The Survivors of the Jonathan, trans. I. O. Evans; 2 vols.: *The Masterless Man* and *The Unwilling Dictator*. London: Arco Publications, 1962.

The Thompson Travel Agency, trans. I. O. Evans; 2 vols.: *Package Holiday* and *End of the Journey*. London: Arco Publications, 1965.

The Tribulations of a Chinese Gentleman, trans. I. O. Evans. London: Arco Publications, 1963.

Twenty Thousand Leagues under the Sea, trans. Anthony Bonner and intro. Ray Bradbury. New York: Bantam Books, 1962.

Twenty Thousand Leagues under the Sea, trans. I. O. Evans. London: Arco Publications, 1960.

Twenty Thousand Leagues under the Sea, trans. Walter James Miller. New York: Washington Square Press, 1965.

Two Years' Holiday, trans. I. O. Evans; 2 vols.: *Adrift in the Pacific* and *Second Year Ashore*. London: Arco Publications, 1964.

The Village in the Treetops, trans. I. O. Evans. London: Arco Publications, 1964.
The Works of Jules Verne, ed. Claire Boss. New York: Crown Publishers, 1983.
Yesterday and Tomorrow, trans. I. O. Evans. London: Arco Publications, 1965.

IC. Correspondence

Bottin, André. "Lettres inédites de Jules Verne au lieutenant colonel Henne-bert." *Bulletin de la Société Jules Verne* 18 (1971), 36–44.
De Balzac à Jules Verne—un grand éditeur du XIXème siècle, P.-J. Hetzel. Catalogue de la Bibliothèque Nationale. Paris, 1966.
Fonds Hetzel (lettres: Verne/Hetzel), premier série, vols. 73–80. Bibliothèque Nationale.
Martin, Charles-Noël. *La Vie et l'oeuvre de Jules Verne.* Paris: Michel de l'Ormeraie, 1978.
Parménie, A. et C. Bonnier de la Chapelle. *Histoire d'un éditeur et de ses auteurs, P.-J. Hetzel (Stahl).* Paris: Albin Michel, 1953.
Parménie, A. "Huit lettres de Jules Verne à son éditeur P.-J. Hetzel." *Arts et Lettres* (1949), 102–7.
Verne, Jules. "Correspondance avec Fernando Ricci." *Europe* 613 (1980), 137–38.
———. "Correspondance avec Mario Turiello." *Europe* 613 (1980), 108–35.
———. "Lettres diverses." *Europe* 613 (1980), 143–51.
———. "Jules Verne: 63 lettres." *Bulletin de la Société Jules Verne* 11–13 (1938), 47–129.
———. "Souvenirs d'Enfance et de Jeunesse." Reprinted in *Cahiers de l'Herne* 25 (1974), 57–62.
———. "Trente-six lettres inédites." *Bulletin de la Société Jules Verne* 68 (1983), 4–50.
———. "Vingt-deux lettres de Jules Verne à son frère Paul." *Bulletin de la Société Jules Verne* 69 (1984), 3–25.

II. SECONDARY SOURCES

IIA. Bibliographies and References

Angenot, Marc. "Jules Verne and French Literary Criticism (I)." *Science-Fiction Studies* 1:1 (1973), 33–37.
———. "Jules Verne and French Literary Criticism (II)." *Science-Fiction Studies* 3:1 (1976), 46–49.
Gallagher, Edward J., Judith A. Mistichelli, and John A. Van Eerde. *Jules Verne: A Primary and Secondary Bibliography.* Boston: G. K. Hall, 1980.
Gondolo della Riva, Piero. *Bibliographie analytique de toutes les oeuvres de Jules Verne*, vol. 1. Paris: Société Jules Verne, 1977.
Hillegas, Mark R. "A Bibliography of Secondary Materials on Jules Verne." *Extrapolation* 2 (December 1960), 5–16.
Margot, Jean-Michel. *Bibliographie documentaire sur Jules Verne.* Ostermundigen, Suisse: Margot, 1978; vol. II, 1982.
Raymond, François et Daniel Compère. *Le Développement des études sur Jules Verne.* Paris: Minard, Archives des Lettres Modernes, 1976.

IIB. Biographies

Allott, Kenneth. *Jules Verne*. London: Crescent Press, 1940.

Allotte de la Fuÿe, Marguerite. *Jules Verne*, trans. Erik de Mauny. London: Staples Press Limited, 1954.

——. *Jules Verne, sa vie, son oeuvre*. Paris: Simon Kra, 1928; reprint Paris: Hachette, 1953, 1966.

Jules-Verne, Jean. *Jules Verne*. Paris: Hachette, 1973.

——. *Jules Verne: A Biography*, trans. Roger Greaves. New York: Taplinger, 1976.

Lemire, Charles. *Jules Verne*. Paris: Berger-Levrault, 1908.

Soriano, Mark. *Jules Verne*. Paris: Julliard, 1978.

IIC. Critical Studies—Books

L'Arc 29 (1966).

Born, Franz. *The Man Who Invented the Future: Jules Verne*. New York: Prentice-Hall, 1963; reprint New York: Scholastic Books, 1967.

Bridenne, Jean-Jacques. *La Littérature française d'imagination scientifique*. Lausanne: Dassonville, 1950.

Brisson, Adolphe. *Portraits intimes*. Paris: Armand Colin, 1899.

Cahiers de l'Herne 25 (1974).

Cambiare, C. P. *The Influence of Edgar Allan Poe in France*. New York: G. E. Stechert, 1927; reprint New York: Haskell House, 1970.

Chesneaux, Jean. *Une Lecture politique de Jules Verne*. Paris: Maspero, 1971.

——. *The Political and Social Ideas of Jules Verne*. London: Thames and Hudson, 1972.

Chotard, Robert. *Comment Julies Verne vient de tracer dans l'espace et le temps le destin de l'homme avec Apollo 8 et les Soyouz 4 et 5 (1968-1969)*. Paris: Chotard, 1969.

Clarétie, J. *Jules Verne*. Paris: A. Quantin "Collection Célébrités contemporains," 1883.

Compère, Daniel. *Approche de l'île chez Jules Verne*. Paris: Lettres Modernes, 1977.

——. *Un Voyage imaginaire de Jules Verne: Voyage au centre de la Terre*. Paris: Archives des Lettres Modernes, 1977.

Compère, François. *Jules Verne humoriste*. Amiens: Office Culturel Municipal, 1977.

Costello, Peter. *Jules Verne: Inventor of Science Fiction*. London: Hodder and Stroughton, 1978.

Courville, Luce. *Catalogue Exposition Jules Verne*. Nantes: Bibliothèque Municipale, 1966.

Diesbach, Ghislain de. *Le Tour de Jules Verne en quatre-vingts livres*. Paris: Julliard, 1969.

Escaich, René. *Voyage au monde de Jules Verne*. Paris: Editions Plantin, 1955.

Evans, I. O. *Jules Verne and His Works*. London: Arco, 1965.

——. *Jules Verne: Master of Science Fiction*. London: Sidgwick and Jackson, 1956.

Europe 33:112–13 (1955).

Europe 595–96 (1978).

Exposition Jules Verne (25–30 avril, 1966). Paris: Livre de Poche, 1966.

Frank, Bernard. *Jules Verne et ses voyages.* Paris: Flammarion, 1941.

Goupil, Armand. *Jules Verne.* Paris: Larousse, 1975.

Grand Album Jules Verne. Paris: Hachette "Les Intégrales Jules Verne," 1982.

Haining, Peter. *The Jules Verne Companion.* Norwich, England: Souvenir Press, 1978.

Huet, Marie-Hélène. *L'Histoire des Voyages Extraordinaires.* Paris: Minard, 1973.

Jules Verne et les sciences humaines. Centre Culturel de Cerisy-la-Salle. Paris: UGE 10/18, 1979.

Jules Verne—filiations, rencontres, influences. Colloque d'Amiens (II). Paris: Minard, 1980.

Lahy-Hellebec, M. *Les Charmeurs d'enfants.* Paris: Baudinière, n.d.

Lacassin, François. *Passagers clandestins.* Paris: UGE 10/18, 1979.

Latzarus, Marie-Thérèse. *La Littérature enfantine en France dans la seconde moitié du XIXème siècle.* Paris: PUF, 1924.

Lemire, Charles. *Jules Verne.* Paris: Berger-Levrault, 1908.

Livres de France 5 (1955).

Marcucci, Edmondo. *Les Illustrations des Voyages Extraordinaires de Jules Verne.* Bordeaux: Ed. de la Société Jules Verne, 1956.

Martin, Andrew. *The Knowledge of Ignorance from Cervantes to Jules Verne.* Cambridge: Cambridge University Press, 1985.

Martin, Charles-Noël. *La Vie et l'oeuvre de Jules Verne.* Paris: Michel de l'Ormeraie, 1978.

Miller, Walter J. *The Annotated Jules Verne: From the Earth to the Moon.* New York: Thomas Crowell, 1978.

——. *The Annotated Jules Verne: Twenty Thousand Leagues under the Sea.* New York: Thomas Crowell, 1976.

Moré, Marcel. *Nouvelles explorations de Jules Verne.* Paris: NRF, 1963.

——. *Le Très Curieux Jules Verne.* Paris: NRF, 1960.

Nicolson, Marjorie. *Voyages to the Moon.* New York: Macmillan, 1948.

Noiray, Jacques. *Le Romancier et la machine: l'image de la machine dans le roman français (1850–1900),* tome 2. Paris: José Corti, 1982.

Nouvelles recherches sur Jules Verne et le voyage. Colloque d'Amiens (II). Paris: Minard, 1978.

Parménie, A. et C. Bonnier de la Chapelle. *Histoire d'un éditeur et de ses auteurs, P.-J. Hetzel (Stahl).* Paris: Albin Michel, 1953.

Pividal, Rafael. *Le Capitaine Nemo et la science.* Paris: Grasset, 1972.

Raymond, Francois, ed. *Jules Verne I: Le Tour du monde.* Paris: Minard, 1976.

——. *Jules Verne II:L'Ecriture vernienne.* Paris: Minard, 1978.

——. *Jules Verne III: Machines et imaginaire.* Paris: Minard, 1980.

——. *Jules Verne IV: Texte, image, spectacle.* Paris: Minard, 1983.

Robin, Christian. *Un Monde connu et inconnue.* Nantes: Centre universitaire de recherches verniennes, 1978.

Serres, Michel. *Jouvences sur Jules Verne.* Paris: Editions de Minuit, 1974.

Topin, Marius. *Romanciers contemporains.* Paris: Charpentier, 1876.

Vierne, Simone. *L'Ile mystérieuse de Jules Verne.* Paris: Hachette, 1973.

——. *Jules Verne.* Paris: Ed. Ballard, 1986.

——. *Jules Verne et le roman initiatique.* Paris: Ed. de Sirac, 1973.

Voyage au centre de la Terre. Dossier et Program, Théatfe des Amandiers (12 Nov.-2 Dec. 1975). Centre dramatique de Nanterre.

IID. Critical Studies—Articles

Abraham, Pierre. "Jules Verne?" *Europe* 112-13 (1955), 3-10.

"The Absolute Utmost." *Nation* 183 (December 1, 1956), 470.

Andreev, Cyrille. "Préface aux Oeuvres Complètes en URSS." *Europe* 112-13 (1955), 22-48.

Angenot, Marc. "Albert Robida's Twentieth Century." *Science-Fiction Studies* 10 (1983), 237-40.

——. "Jules Verne and French Literary Criticism I." *Science-Fiction Studies* 1 (1973), 33-37.

——. "Jules Verne and French Literary Criticism II." *Science-Fiction Studies* 3 (1976), 46-49.

——. "Jules Verne: The Last Happy Utopianist." *Science Fiction: A Critical Guide*, ed. Patrick Parrinder. New York: Longman, 1979, pp. 18-32.

——. "Science Fiction in France before Verne." *Science-Fiction Studies* 5:1 (1978), 58-66.

Asimov, Issac. "Introduction." In Jules Verne's *Journey to the Center of the Earth.* New York: Heritage Press, 1966, pp. ix-x.

Badou, Jacques. "Jules Verne et la cryptographie." *Cahiers de l'Herne* 25 (1974), 324-29.

Barthes, Roland. "Nautilus et Bateau Ivre." In *Mythologies.* Paris: Seuil, 1957, pp. 90-92.

——. "Par où commencer?" *Poétique* 1 (1970), 3-9.

Bastard, Georges. "Célébrité contemporaine: Jules Verne en 1883." *Gazette illustrée* (8 Sept. 1883). Reprinted in *Cahiers de l'Herne* 25 (1974), 11-15.

Bellemin-Noël, Jean. "Analectures de Jules Verne." *Critique* 26 (1970), 692-704.

Belloc, Marie A. "Jules Verne at Home." *Strand Magazine* 9 (February 1895), 207-13.

Bellour, Raymond. "Le Mosaïque." *L'Arc* 29 (1966), 1-4.

Bennett, Maurice S. "Edgar Allan Poe and the Literary Tradition of Lunar Speculation." *Science-Fiction Studies* 10 (1983), 137-47.

Berri, Kenneth. "Les *Cinq Cents Millions de la Bégum* ou la technologie de la fable." *Stanford French Review* 3 (1979), 29-40.

Bessière, Jean. "*Voyage au centre de la Terre* ou l'ordre du quotidien." In *Nouvelles recherches sur Jules Verne et le voyage.* Colloque d'Amiens (I). Paris: Minard, 1978, pp. 37-56.

Blum, Léon. "Jules Verne." *L'Humanité* (3 avril 1903). Reprinted as Préface to Jules Verne's *L'Invasion de la mer.* Paris: UGE 10/18, 1978, pp. 7-8.

Boia, L. "La Conquête imaginaire de l'espace: Jules Verne et Camille Flammarion." *Bulletin de la Société Jules Verne* 67 (1983), 91-95.

Bombard, Alain. "Jules Verne: Seer of the Space Age." *UNESCO Courier* 31 (March 1978), 31-36.

Bond, F.-F. "Jules Verne, Master of the Improbable." *New York Times* (January 4, 1925), sect. 3, p. 21.

Bonnefis, Philippe. "A voir et à manger." In *Jules Verne IV: texte, image, spectacle*, ed. François Raymond. Paris: Minard, 1980, pp. 37–54.

———. "La Mécanique des chutes." In *Jules Verne III: Machines et imaginaire*, ed. François Raymond. Paris: Minard, 1980, pp. 63–90.

Borderie, Roger. "Une Leçon d'abîme." *Cahiers de l'Herne* 25 (1974), 172–79.

Borgeaud, Georges. "Les Illustrateurs de Jules Verne." *Arts et Lettres* 15 (1949), 71–72.

———. "Jules Verne et ses illustrateurs." *L'Arc* 29 (1966), 43–45.

Boudet, Jacques. "Jules Verne et les mondes du XIXème siècle." *Arts et Lettres* 15 (1949), 78–99.

Bradbury, Ray. "The Ardent Blasphemers." In Jules Verne's *Twenty Thousand Leagues under the Sea*, trans. Anthony Bonner. New York: Bantam Books, 1962, pp. 1–12.

———. "La Révolution invisible." In *Jules Verne et les sciences humaines.* Centre Culturel International de Cerisy-la-Salle, colloque 1978. Paris: UGE 10/18, 1979, pp. 358–81.

Bridenne, J.-J. "Jules Verne, père de la science-fiction? (I)" *Fiction* 6 (1954), 112–15.

———. "Jules Verne, père de la science-fiction? (II)" *Fiction* 7 (1954), 108–12.

———. "Jules Verne, père de la science-fiction? (III)" *Fiction* 8 (1954), 113–17.

———. "Les Thèmes scientifiques chez Jules Verne. (I)" *Fiction* 20 (1955), 107–12.

———. "Les Thèmes scientifiques chez Jules Verne. (II)" *Fiction* 21 (1955), 110–16.

Brion, Marcel. "Le Voyage initiatique." *L'Arc* 29 (1966), 26–32.

Brosse, Monique. "Jules Verne et le roman maritime." In *Nouvelles recherches sur Jules Verne et le voyage*. Colloque d'Amiens. Paris: Minard, 1978, pp. 57–66.

Buisine, Alain. "Un Cas-limite de la description: l'énumération. L'Exemple de *Vingt mille lieues sous les mers*." In *La Description*. Univ. de Lille III. Paris: Ed. universitaires, 1974, pp. 81–102.

———. "Circulations en tous genres." *Europe* 595–96 (1978), 48–56.

———. "Machines et énergétique." In *Jules Verne III: Machines et imaginaire*, ed. François Raymond. Paris: Minard, 1980, pp. 25–52.

———. "Repères, marques, gisements: à propos de la robinsonnade vernienne." In *Jules Verne II: L'Ecriture vernienne*, ed. François Raymond. Paris: Minard, 1978, pp. 113–41.

———. "Verne appellation d'origine." In *Jules Verne et les sciences humaines.* Centre Culturel International de Cerisy-la-Salle, colloque 1978. Paris: UGE 10/18, 1979, pp. 101–34.

Butcher, William. "Crevettes de l'air et baleines volantes." *La Nouvelle Revue Maritime* 386–87 (mai-juin 1984), 35–40.

———. "Graphes et graphie: Circuits et voyages extraordinaires dans l'oeuvre de Jules Verne." *Regards sur la théorie des graphes*, Actes du Colloque de Cerisy (12–18 juin 1980), 177–82.

———. "Les Dates de l'action dans *Les Voyages Extraordinaires*: Une mise au point." *Bulletin de la Société Jules Verne* 67 (1983), 101–3.

——. "Le Sens de *L'Eternel Adam.*" *Bulletin de la Société Jules Verne* 58 (1981), 73–81.

——. "Le Verbe et la chair, ou l'emploi du temps." In *Jules Verne IV: texte, image, spectacle*, ed. François Raymond. Paris: Minard, 1983, pp. 125–48.

Butor, Michel. "Homage to Jules Verne," trans. John Coleman. *New Statesman* 72 (July 15, 1966), 94.

——. "Lectures de l'enfance." *L'Arc* 29 (1966), 43–45.

——. "Le Point suprême et l'age d'or à travers quelques oeuvres de Jules Verne." *Arts et Lettres* 15 (1949), 3–31. Reprinted in *Repertoire* I. Paris: Ed. de Minuit, 1960, pp. 130–62.

Carrouges, Michel. "Le Mythe de Vulcain chez Jules Verne." *Arts et Lettres* 15 (1949), 32–58.

Chambers, Ross. "Cultural and Ideological Determinations in Narrative: A Note on Jules Verne's *Les Cinq cents millions de la Bégum.*" *L'Esprit Créateur* XXI:3 (Fall 1981), pp. 69–78.

Chesneaux, Jean. "Les Illustrations des romans de Jules Verne." *Bulletin de la Société Jules Verne* 37–38 (1976), 114–15.

——. "L'Invention linguistique chez Jules Verne." In *Langues et techniques, Nature et Société I*, eds. J. M. C. Thomas et Lucien Bernot. Paris: Klincksieck, 1972, pp. 345–51.

Chevrel, Yves. "Questions de méthodes et d'idéologies chez Verne et Zola." In *Jules Verne II: L'Ecriture vernienne*, ed. François Raymond. Paris: Minard, 1978, pp. 69–90.

Citron, Pierre. "Sur quelques voyages au centre de la Terre." In *Nouvelles recherches sur Jules Verne et le voyage*. Colloque d'Amiens. Paris: Minard, 1978, pp. 67–80.

Cluny, Claude-Michel. "Des Machines pour rêver." *Magazine littéraire* 119 (1976), 9–11.

Cluzel, Etienne. "Curiosités dans l'oeuvre de Jules Verne (I)." *Bulletin de la Société Jules Verne* 2 (1937), 2–10.

——. "Curiosités dans l'oeuvre de Jules Verne (II)." *Bulletin de la Société Jules Verne* 3 (1937), 2–10.

Compère, Cécile. "Jules Verne et la misogynie." In *Grand Album Jules Verne*. Paris: Hachette, 1982, pp. 252–64.

——. "Monsieur Verne, président et présidé." *Bulletin de la Société Jules Verne* 69 (1984), 26–32.

Compère, Daniel. "L'Attentat du 9 mars 1886." In *Grand Album Jules Verne*. Paris: Hachette, 1982, pp. 252–55.

——. "Le Bas des pages." *Bulletin de la Société Jules Verne* 68 (1983), 147–53.

——. "Une Figure du récit vernien: la doublure." In *Jules Verne et les sciences humaines*, Centre Culturel International de Cerisy-la-Salle: colloque, 1978. Paris: UGE 10/18, 1979, pp. 241–63.

——. "Fenêtres latérales." In *Jules Verne IV: texte, image, spectacle*, ed. François Raymond. Paris: Minard, 1983, pp. 55–72.

——. "Filmographie des oeuvres de Jules Verne." *Bulletin de la Société Jules Verne* 12 (1969), 82–84. Additions and updates in *BSJV* 11 (1970), 137 and *BSJV* 21 (1972), 123.

——. "Les Indes Noires sur blanc." *Bulletin de la Société Jules Verne* 42 (1977), 60–63.

——. "Jules Verne à la radio et à la télévision." *Bulletin de la Société Jules Verne* 31–32 (1974), 189–90. Additions and updates in *BSJV* 33–34 (1975), 48; *BSJV* 35–36 (1975), 95–96; *BSJV* 39–40 (1976), 190; *BSJV* 41 (1977), 32.

——. "Jules Verne et la modernité." *Europe* 595–96 (1978), 27–36.

——. "Les Machines à écrire." In *Jules Verne III: Machines et imaginaire*, ed. François Raymond. Paris: Minard, 1980, pp. 91–102.

——. "Le Monde des études verniennes." *Magazine Littéraire* 119 (1976), 27–29.

——. "M. Jules Verne, conseilleur municipal." *Cahiers de l'Herne* 25 (1974), 127–41.

——. "Poétique de la carte." *Bulletin de la Société Jules Verne* 50 (1979), 69–74.

——. "Les Suites dans les *Voyages Extraordinaires*." *Bulletin de la Société Jules Verne* 14 (1970), 122–28.

——. "Trois Russes, Trois Anglais, et quelques autres." *Magazine Littéraire* 119 (1976), 18–19.

——. "Voyage dans les lieux communs." In *Jules Verne IV: texte, image, spectacle*, ed. François Raymond. Paris: Minard, 1983, pp. 189–94.

Compère, E. et V. Dehs. "Tashinar and Co.—Introduction à une étude des mots inventés dans l'oeuvre de Jules Verne." *Bulletin de la Société Jules Verne* 67 (1983), 107–11.

Coste, Dider. "Où Jules Verne montre son jeu: *Le Chateau des Carpathes* comme allégorie de la communication narrative." In *Jules Verne IV: texte, image, spectacle*, ed. François Raymond. Paris: Minard, 1983, pp. 161–78.

Coutrix-Gouaux, Mireille. "A Propos de matière et énergie chez Jules Verne." *Europe* 595–96 (1978), 3–9.

——. "Mythologie vernienne." *Europe* 595–96 (1978), 10–18.

Davy, Jacques. "A Propos de l'antropophagie chez Jules Verne." *Cahiers du Centre d'études verniennes et du Musée Jules Verne* 1 (1981), 15–23.

De Amicis, Demondo. "A Visit to Jules Verne and Victorien Sardou." *The Chautauquan* 24 (1897), 702–7.

Delabroy, Jean. "La Machine à démonter le temps." In *Jules Verne III: Machines et imaginaire*, ed. François Raymond. Paris: Minard, 1980, pp. 5–14.

Destombes, Marcel. "Le Manuscrit *Vingt mille lieues sous les mers* de la Société de Géographie de Paris." *Bulletin de la Société Jules Verne* 35–36 (1975), 56–69.

Devaux, Pierre. "Jules Verne est-il encore un prophète?" *Arts et Lettres* 15 (1949), 73–77.

Duhamel, Georges. "Le Souvenir de Jules Verne." *Livres de France* 5 (1955), 3.

Dumas (fils), Alexandre. "A Propos de Jules Verne." *Livres de France* 5 (1955), 11.

Dumas, Olivier. "A Propos d'*Un Express de l'avenir*." *Bulletin de la Société Jules Verne* 67 (1983), 115.

——. "*Les Aventures de Trois Russes et de Trois Anglais*, revues et corrigées." *Bulletin de la Société Jules Verne* 67 (1983), 104–5.

———. "Les Deux versions de *Dix Heures de Chasse*." In *Grand Album Jules Verne*. Paris: Hachette, 1982, pp. 158–63.

———. "*Hector Servadac* à 100 ans. Une lecture comparée." *Bulletin de la Société Jules Verne* 42 (1977), 55–59.

———. "Jules Verne et Benett." In *Jules Verne IV: texte, image, spectacle*, ed. François Raymond. Paris: Minard, 1983, pp. 181–88.

———. "Quand Jules Verne voyageait dans *La Maison à vapeur*." *Bulletin de la Société Jules Verne* 54 (1980), 215–19.

———. "Quand Marguerite se contredit." *Bulletin de la Société Jules Verne* 64 (1982), 312.

———. "Le Sécret du *Village aérien*." In *Grand Album Jules Verne*. Paris: Hachette, 1982, pp. 188–96.

———. "Les Versions de *Fritt-Flacc* ou la liberté retrouvée." *Bulletin de la Société Jules Verne* 59 (1981), 98–100.

Dumas, Olivier et al. "Bibliographie des oeuvres de Jules Verne." *Bulletin de la Société Jules Verne* 1 (1967), 7–12. Additions and updates: *BSJV* 2 (1967), 11–15, *BSJV* 3 (1967), 13, *BSJV* 4 (1967), 15–16.

Dumonceaux, Pierre. "Cuisine et dépaysement." *Europe* 595–96 (1978), 127–37.

Durand-Dessert, M. et René Guise. "Le Voyage dans la Lune en France au début du XIXe siècle—l'orginalité de Jules Verne." In *Nouvelles recherches sur Jules Verne et le voyage*. Colloque d'Amiens. Paris: Minard, 1978, 17–36.

Eggleston, G. C. "Jules Verne and his Work." *American Homes* 8 (1875), 34–35.

Escaich, R. "A Propos des *Aventures du Capitaine Hatteras*." *Bulletin de la Société Jules Verne* 28 (1973), 87–89.

Evans, Arthur B. "L'Etrange cas de la planète disparue—*Hector Servadac*." *Bulletin de la Société Jules Verne* 75 (1985), 233.

———. "Science Fiction vs. Scientific Fiction in France: From Jules Verne to J.-H. Rosny Aîné." *Science-Fiction Studies* XV:1 (1988), 1–11.

Evans, I. O. "Jules Verne et le lecteur anglais." *Bulletin de la Société Jules Verne* 6 (1937), 3–6.

Faivre, Jean-Paul. "Le Romancier des sept mers." *Cahiers de l'Herne* 25 (1974), 264–83.

Foucault, Michel. "L'Arrière-fable." *L'Arc* 29 (1966), 5–13.

Foucrier, Chantal. "Jules Verne et l'Atlantide." In *Nouvelles recherches sur Jules Verne et le voyage*. Colloque d'Amiens. Paris: Minard, 1978, 97–111.

Fournier, Georges. "Le Capitaine Nemo est toujours vivant." *Arts et Lettres* 15 (1949), 111–13.

Frank, Bernard. "Comment naquirent les *Voyages Extraordinaires*." *Livres de France* 5 (1955), 4–8.

Fuye, Roger de la. "Le Paysage dans l'oeuvre de Jules Verne." *Arts et Lettres* 15 (1949), 64–68.

Gaillard, Françoise. "*L'Eternel Adam* ou l'évolutionnisme à l'heure de la thermodynamique." In *Jules Verne et les sciences humaines*. Centre Culturel International de Cerisy-la-Salle: colloque, 1978. Paris: UGE 10/18, 1979, pp. 293–325.

Gasmarra, Pierre. "Jules Verne ou le printemps." *Arts et Lettres* 15 (1949), 49–54.

Gauthier, Théophile. "Les Voyages imaginaires de M. Jules Verne." *Moniteur Universel* 197 (1866). Reprinted in *Histoire des Oeuvres de Théophile Gauthier*, tome II, p. 321, and in *Cahiers de l'Herne* 25 (1974), 85–87.

Gehu, Edmond. "La Géographie polaire dans l'oeuvre de Jules Verne." *Bulletin de la Société Jules Verne* 11–13 (1938), 176–78.

Golding, William. "Astronaut by Gaslight." *Spectator* 206 (June 9, 1961), 841–42.

Gondolo Della Riva, Piero. "A Propos des oeuvres posthumes de Jules Verne." *Europe* 595–96 (1978), 73–82.

——. "A Propos d'une nouvelle." *Cahiers de l'Herne* 25 (1974), 284–85.

——. "Jules Verne et l'Académie Française." In *Grand Album Jules Verne*. Paris: Hachette, 1982, pp. 174–79.

——. "Jules Verne et l'Italie." In *Grand Album Jules Verne*. Paris: Hachette, 1982, pp. 105–8.

——. "La Troisième série du *Magasin d'Education et de Récréation*." *Bulletin de la Société Jules Verne* 13 (1970), 98–99.

Goracci, Serge. "Jules Verne: un romancier populaire?" *Bulletin de la Société Jules Verne* 42 (1977), 38–42.

——. "Quelques rapports entre les romans verniens et le roman populaire." *Bulletin de la Société Jules Verne* 50 (1979), 60–67.

Guider, Charles. "Jules Verne, plus jeune que jamais." *Lectures pour tous* 150 (1966), 10–16.

Guiges, Louis-Paul. "Baroquisme de Jules Verne." *Arts et Lettres* 15 (1949), 63–70.

Guillaud, Laurie. "Du *Voyage au centre de la Terre* au monde perdu." *Cahiers du Centre d'études verniennes et du Musée Jules Verne* II (1982), 1–7.

Hazeltine, M. W. "Jules Verne's Didactic Fiction." In his *Chats About Books, Poets and Novelists*. New York: Charles Scribner's, 1883, pp. 337–46.

Helling, Cornelius. "Les Illustrateurs des *Voyages Extraordinaires*." *Bulletin de la Société Jules Verne* 11–13 (1938), 140–46.

——. "Le Roman le plus Poe-esque de Jules Verne." *Bulletin de la Société Jules Verne* 3 (1937), 8.

Hetzel, P.-J. "A Nos Lecteurs." In *Magasin d'Education et de Récréation* 10 (1869), 376–77.

Heuvelmans, Bernard. "Le Père contesté." *Cahiers de l'Herne* 25 (1974), 121–26.

Horne, Charles F. "Jules Verne." In *Works of Jules Verne*, ed. Charles F. Horne. New York: Vincent Parke, 1911, pp. vii–xviii.

Huet, Marie-Hélène. "L'Ecrivain tératologue." In *Jules Verne III: Machines et imaginaire*, ed François Raymond. Paris: Minard, 1980, pp. 53–56.

——. "Exploration du jeu." In *Jules Verne I: Le Tour du Monde*, ed. François Raymond. Paris: Minard, 1976, pp. 95–108.

——. "L'Itinénaire du texte." In *Jules Verne et les sciences humaines*. Centre Culturel International de Cerisy-la-Salle: colloque, 1978. Paris: UGE 10/18, 1979, pp. 9–35. Reprinted in *Stanford French Review* 3 (1979), 17–28.

Jan, Isabelle. "Children's literature and bourgeois society in France since 1860." *Yale French Studies* 43 (1969), 57–72.

——. "Le *Voyage au centre de la Terre* est-il un livre pour les enfants?" In *Nouvelles recherches sur Jules Verne et le voyage*. Colloque d'Amiens. Paris: Minard, 1978, pp. 81–88.

Jones, Gordon. "Jules Verne at Home." *Temple Bar* 129 (1904), 664–70.

"Jules Verne." *Book Buyer* 7 (1890), 281–82.

"Jules Verne: A True Friend to Every Boy." *Current Literature* 38 (1905), 395–96.

"Jules Verne, 1828–1905." *France Education*. Bulletin des Services Culturels de l'Ambassade de France aux Etats-Unis, #13 (1978), 1–6.

"Jules Verne's *From the Earth to the Moon*." *Book Buyer* 7 (1873), 33.

Kanipe, Esther. "Hetzel and the *Bibliothèque d'Education et de Recréation*." *Yale French Studies* 43 (1969), 72–83.

Kanters, Robert. "Situation de Jules Verne." *Le Figaro Littéraire* (21 avril 1966), 5.

Ketterer, David. "Fathoming 20,000 Leagues under the Sea." *The Stellar Gauge: Essays on Science Fiction Writers*. Carlton, Australia: Nostrillia Press, 1981, pp. 7–24.

Klein, Gérard. "Pour lire Verne (I)." *Fiction* 197 (1970), 137–43.

———. "Pour lire Verne (II)." *Fiction* 198 (1970), 143–52.

Knight, Damon. "Afterword." In Jules Verne's *Twenty Thousand Leagues under the Sea*. New York: Washington Square Press, pp. 383–86.

L. M. "Bibliographie." *Revue des Deux Mondes* 43 (1863), 769.

Lacassin, Francis. "Le Communard qui écrivit 3 romans de Jules Verne." *Europe* 595–96 (1978), 94–105.

———. "Du Pavillion noir au Québec libre." *Magazine Littéraire* 119 (1976), 22–26.

———. "Les Naufragés de la terre." *L'Arc* 29 (1966), 66–68.

Lacaze, Dominique. "Lectures croisées de Jules Verne et de Robida." In *Jules Verne et les sciences humaines*. Centre Culturel International de Cerisy-la-Salle: colloque, 1978. Paris: UGE 10/18, 1979, pp. 76–100.

Lagarde, L. "Jules Verne et le movement de la géographie." *Bulletin de la Société Jules Verne* 60 (1981), 154–59.

Lebois, André. "Poétique secrète du *Tour du Monde*." In *Jules Verne I: Le Tour du Monde*, ed. François Raymond. Paris: Minard, 1976, 21–30.

Lecomte, Marcel. "Le Thème du Grand Nord." *L'Arc* 29 (1966), 66–68.

Leiris, Michel. "Une Lettre de Raymond Roussel." *Arts et Lettres* 15 (1949), 100–1.

Lowndes, Robert A. W. "Introduction." In Jules Verne, *Journey to the Center of the Earth*. New York: Airmont, 1965, p. 3.

———. "Introduction." In Jules Verne, *Round the Moon*. New York: Airmont, 1969, pp. 5–6.

Macherey, Pierre. "Jules Verne ou le récit en défaut." In his *Pour une théorie de la production littéraire*. Paris: Maspero, 1966, pp. 183–266. Reprinted in English in *A Theory of Literary Production*, trans. Geoffrey Wall. London: Routledge and Kegan Paul, 1978, pp. 159–240.

MacKensie, Norman. "Four Million Words Without a Ghost." *New Statesman* 52 (1956), 320–21.

Martin, Andrew. "Chez Jules: Nutrition and Cognition in the Novels of Jules Verne." *French Studies* XXXVII:1 (January 1983), 47–58.

———. "The Entropy of Balzacian Tropes in the Scientific Fictions of Jules Verne." *Modern Language Review* 77:1 (1982), 51–62.

Martin, Charles-Noël. "La Guerre de la baleine et de l'éléphant." *Bulletin de la Société Jules Verne* 67 (1983), 112–13.

Martucci, Vittorio. "Jules Verne et l'origine de l'homme: *Le Village aérien.*" *Bulletin de la Société Jules Verne* 53 (1980), 186–89.

Merchot, D. "Le Seigneur Pittonaccio—ange déchu du bizarre?" *Bulletin de la Société Jules Verne* 48 (1978), 266–67.

Miannay, Régis. "L'Humour dans *Voyage au centre de la Terre.*" In *Jules Verne II: L'Ecriture vernienne*, ed. François Raymond. Paris: Minard, 1978, pp. 97–112.

Micha, Réné. "Les Légendes sous les images." *L'Arc* 29 (1966), 50–55.

Miller, Walter James. "Jules Verne in America: A Translator's Preface." In Jules Verne, *Twenty Thousand Leagues under the Sea.* New York: Washington Square Press, 1965, pp. vii–xxii.

Moré, Marcel. "Un Révolutionnaire souterrain." *L'Arc* 29 (1966), 33–42.

Mustière, Philippe. "Le Chiffre et la lettre: la forclusion de nom du père dans le récit vernien." In *Jules Verne IV: texte, image, spectacle*, ed. François Raymond. Paris: Minard, 1983, pp. 95–104.

———. "Jules Verne et le roman-catastrophe." *Europe* 595–96 (1978), 43–47.

Neefs, Jacques. "*Le Château des Carpathes* et la question de la representation." In *Jules Verne et les sciences humaines.* Centre Culturel International de Cerisy-la-Salle: colloque, 1978. Paris: UGE 10/18, 1979, pp. 382–409.

"The New Pictures: *A Journey to the Center of the Earth.*" *Time* 85 (February 15, 1960), 85.

Noel, Xavier. "Pachal Grousset." *Cahiers du Centre d'études verniennes et du Musée Jules Verne* 3 (1983), 48–50.

Oliver-Martin, Yves. "Dans le sillage de Jules Verne." *Bulletin de la Société Jules Verne* 31–32 (1974), 180–83.

———. "Jules Verne et le roman populaire." *Cahiers de l'Herne* 25 (1974), 289–304.

———. "Jules Verne et sa postérité." *Bulletin de la Société Jules Verne* 18 (1971), 45–52.

Ozanne, Henriette. "De quelques sources verniennes." In *Nouvelles recherches sur Jules Verne et le voyage.* Colloque d'Amiens. Paris: Minard, 1978, pp. 7–16.

Pavolini, A. "Les Chiens dans l'oeuvre de Jules Verne." In *Grand Album Jules Verne.* Paris: Hachette, 1982, pp. 22–29.

Picard, Michel. "Le Trésor de Nemo: *L'Ile mysérieuse* et l'idéologie." *Littérature* 16 (1974), 88–95.

Picot, Jean-Pierre. "Hublots, miroirs, projecteurs, spectacles de la mort." In *Jules Verne IV: texte, image, spectacle*, ed. François Raymond. Paris: Minard, 1983, pp. 15–36.

———. "Véhicules, nature, artifices." In *Jules Verne III: Machines et imaginaire*, ed. François Raymond. Paris: Minard, 1980, pp. 103–26.

Pillorget, René. "Optimisme ou pessimisme de Jules Verne." *Europe* 595–96 (1978), 19–26.

Poncey, J.-P. "Misère de Jules Verne ou l'échec d'un projet." In *Jules Verne I: Le Tour du monde*, ed. François Raymond. Paris: Minard, 1976, pp. 53–66.

Pourvoyeur, Robert. "De l'invention des mots chez Jules Verne." *Bulletin de la Société Jules Verne* 25 (1973), 19–24.

———. "Jules Verne économiste." In *Jules Verne et les sciences humaines.* Centre Culturel International de Cerisy-la-Salle, colloque, 1978. Paris: UGE 10/18, 1979, pp. 264–92.

———. "Jules Verne et le futurisme." *Bulletin de la Société Jules Verne* 67 (1983), 96–97.

———. "Réflexions sur l'esprit scientifique de Jules Verne." *Bulletin de la Société Jules Verne* 35–36 (1975), 83–91.

———. "Quelle langue parlait Hans Bjelke?" *Bulletin de la Société Jules Verne* 31 (1974), 176–77.

———. "Théâtre et musique chez Jules Verne." In *Grand Album Jules Verne.* Paris: Hachette, 1982, pp. 85–101.

Psichari, Henriette. "Que pensent les jeunes lecteurs?" *Arts et Lettres* 15 (1949), 55–59.

Raymond, Charles. "Jules Verne." *Musée des Familles* 42 (1875).

Raymond, François. "Confrontation." In *Jules Verne II: L'Ecriture vernienne,* ed. François Raymond. Paris: Minard, 1978, pp. 5–10.

———. "Le Héros épinglé." In *Jules Verne III: Machines et imaginaire,* ed. François Raymond. Paris: Minard, 1980, pp. 157–75.

———. "L'Homme et l'horloge." *Cahiers de l'Herne* 25 (1974), 141–51.

———. "Littérature et anticipation chez Jules Verne." *Bulletin de la Société Jules Verne* 67 (1983), 86–89.

———. "L'Odyssée du naufragé vernien." In *Jules Verne et les sciences humaines.* Centre Culturel International de Cerisy-la-Salle: colloque, 1978. Paris: UGE 10/18, 1979, pp. 36–75.

———. "Postface." In Jules Verne's *Sans dessus dessous.* Grenoble: Marginalia, 1976, pp. 181–90.

———. "Pour une connaissance appliquée." In *Jules Verne III: Machines et imaginaire,* ed. François Raymond. Paris: Minard, 1980, pp. 5–14.

———. "Pour une espace de l'exploration." In *Jules Verne I: Le Tour du monde,* ed. François Raymond. Paris: Minard, 1976, pp. 5–11.

———. "Procédés verniens, prodédés rousseliens." In *Jules Verne I: Le Tour du monde,* ed. François Raymond. Paris: Minard, 1976, pp. 67–68.

———. "Le Recours à la science dans les *Voyages Extraordinaires.*" *Bulletin de la Société Jules Verne* 68 (1983), 125–26.

———. "Le Voyage à travers l'impossible." In *Grand Album Jules Verne.* Paris: Hachette, 1982, pp. 127–38.

———. "*Voyage à travers l'impossible* et *Voyages Extraordinaires.*" In *Jules Verne IV: texte, image, spectacle,* ed. François Raymond. Paris: Minard, 1983, pp. 105–24.

Regrain, Raymond. "Voyages dans un fauteuil en France et au centre de la Terre." In *Nouvelles recherches sur Jules Verne et le voyage.* Colloque d'Amiens. Paris: Minard, 1978, pp. 89–96.

"Review of *Journey to the Center of the Earth.*" *Illustrated Review* (December 16, 1872), 373–74.

Richer, Jean. "Note sur la constellation du marin." *Cahiers de l'Herne* 25 (1974), 71–73.

Riegert, Guy. "Voyages au centre des noms—ou les combinaisons verniennes." In *Jules Verne IV: texte, image, spectacle*, ed. François Raymond. Paris: Minard, 1983, pp. 73–94.

Rivière, François. "Jules Verne s'avance masqué." In *Grand Album Jules Verne*. Paris: Hachette, 1982, pp. 238–42.

———. "Littérature pour la Génèse." In *Jules Verne et les sciences humaines*. Centre Culturel International de Cerisy-la-Salle, colloque, 1978. Paris: UGE 10/18, pp. 135–46.

———. "L'un commerce, l'autre continue." *Europe* 595–96 (1978), 37–42.

———. "Préface" to Jules Verne's *Le Secret de Wilhelm Storitz*. Paris: Les Humanoïdes Associés, 1977, pp. 7–12.

Robin, Christian. "Le Jeu dans *Robur-le-Conquérant*." *Europe* 595–96 (1978), 106–16.

———. "Jules Verne à l'université." In *Jules Verne II: L'Ecriture vernienne*, ed. François Raymond. Paris: Minard, 1978, pp. 11–18.

———. "Livre et musée: sources et fins de l'éducation encyclopédique proposée aux jeunes lecteurs de Jules Verne." *97eme Congrès national des société savantes*. Nantes, 1972, tome II, pp. 473–86.

———. "Le Récit sauvé des eaux: du *Voyage au centre de la Terre* au *Sphinx des glaces*—réflexions su le narrateur vernien." In *Jules Verne II: L'Ecriture vernienne*, ed. François Raymond. Paris: Minard, 1978, pp. 35–50.

Rosa, Guy. "Jules Verne et l'idéologie: le grand instituteur du sujet jeune." In *Jules Verne et les sciences humaines*. Centre Culturel International de Cerisy-la-Salle: colloque, 1978. Paris: UGE 10/18, 1979, pp. 147–71.

Rose, Marilyn. "Two Mysogynist Novels: A Feminist Reading of Villiers and Verne." *19th Century French Studies* VII: 1–2 (1980–81), 119–23.

Rose, Mark. "Filling the Void: Verne, Wells and Lem." *Science-Fiction Studies* 8 (1981), 121–42.

Roth, Edward. "Preface." In Jules Verne, *The Baltimore Gun Club*. Philadelphia: King and Baird, 1874, pp. 3–6.

"Science in Romance." *The Saturday Review* 99 (April 1, 1905), 414–15.

Serres, Michel. "Géodésiques de la Terre et du Ciel." *L'Arc* 29 (1966), 14–20.

———. "India (The Black and the Archipelago) on Fire." *Sub-stance* 8 (1974), 49–60.

Sherard, R. H. "Jules Verne at Home." *McClure's Magazine* II:2 (1894), 115–24.

———. "Jules Verne revisited." *T.P.'s Weekly* (1903), p. 589.

Sichel, Pierre. "Les Illustrateurs de Jules Verne." *Europe* 112–13 (1955), 90–98.

Slonim, Marc. "Revival of Jules Verne." *New York Times Book Review* (May 22, 1966), 42.

Soriano, Marc. "Adapter Jules Verne." *L'Arc* 29 (1966), 86–91.

———. "Vernir/Devenir?" *Europe* 595–96 (1978), 3–9.

Sonday, Paul. "A Rush of Anniversaries in Paris." *New York Times Book Review* (March 4, 1928), p. 311.

Steinmetz, Jean-Luc. "La Plus dangereuse figure de rhétorique." In *Jules Verne et les sciences humaines*. Centre Culturel International de Cerisy-la-Salle: colloque, 1978. Paris: UGE 10/18, 1979, pp. 172–211.

Stevenson, K. "Jules Verne in Victoria." *Southerly* 19:1 (1958), 23–25.

Suvin, D. "Communication in Quantified Space: the Utopian Liberalism of Jules Verne's Science Fiction." *Clio* 4 (University of Wisconsin, 1974), 51–

71. Reprinted in his *Metamorphoses of Science Fiction*. New Haven: Yale University Press, 1979, pp. 147–63.

———. "The Rise of Alternative History." *Science-Fiction Studies* 10 (1983), 148–69.

Taussat, R. "L'Anarchisme divin: de l'île Lincoln à l'île Hoste." *Cahiers de l'Herne* 25 (1974), 242–55.

Taylor, Charles H. "A Journey to the Moon." *American Homes* (February 1874), 181.

Terrasse, P. "Un Centenaire: *La Maison à vapeur* ou quelques coïncidences." *Bulletin de la Société Jules Verne* 54 (1980), 221–24.

———. "Jules Verne et les chemins de fer." In *Grand Album Jules Verne*. Paris: Hachette, 1982, pp. 30–44.

———. "Jules Verne et les grandes écoles scientifiques." *Bulletin de la Société Jules Verne* 12 (1969), 72–78.

Thines, Raymond. "En compagnie de Jules Hetzel." *Bulletin de la Société Jules Verne* 11–13 (1938), 130–39.

Thomas, Theodore. "The Watery Wonders of Captain Nemo." *Galaxy* 20 (1961), 168–77.

Touttain, Pierre-André. "Un Certain Jules Verne." *Cahiers de l'Herne* 25 (1974), 11–15.

———. "Une Cruelle fantaisie: *Le Docteur Ox*." In *Jules Verne II: L'Ecriture vernienne*, ed. François Raymond. Paris: Minard, 1978, pp. 155–64.

———. "Vingt mille ronds de fumée." In *Grand Album Jules Verne*. Paris: Hachette, 1982, pp. 45–84.

Van Herp, Jacques. "Alexandre Dumas et le *Voyage au centre de la Terre*." *Cahiers de l'Herne* 25 (1974), 222–24.

———. "La Survie des héros de Jules Verne." *Cahiers de l'Herne* 25 (1974), 305–7.

Versins, Pierre. "Le Sentiment de l'artifice." *L'Arc* 29 (1966), 56–65.

Vierne, Simone. "L'Authenticité de quelques oeuvres de Jules Verne." In *Grand Album Jules Verne*. Paris: Hachette, 1982, pp. 197–204.

———. "Critiques et lecteurs de Jules Verne en France." In *Grand Album Jules Verne*. Paris: Hachette, 1982, pp. 164–73.

———. "Hetzel et Jules Verne, ou l'invention d'un auteur." In *Europe* 619–20 (1980), 53–63.

———. "Kaléidoscope de *L'Ile mystérieuse*." In *Jules Verne II: L'Ecriture vernienne*, ed. François Raymond. Paris: Minard, 1978, pp. 19–32.

———. "Paroles gelées, paroles de feu." *Europe* 595–96 (1978), 57–66.

———. "Le Poète autour du monde." In *Jules Verne I: Le Tour du monde*, ed. François Raymond. Paris: Minard, 1976, pp. 89–94.

———. "Puissance de l'imaginaire." *Cahiers de l'Herne* 25 (1974), 152–71.

———. "Trompe l'oeil et clin d'oeil dans l'oeuvre de Jules Verne." In *Jules Verne et les sciences humaines*. Centre Culturel de Cerisy-la-Salle: colloque, 1978. Paris: UGE 10/18, 1979, pp. 410–40.

Vivien Saint-Martin, Louis. "Les Anglais au Pôle Nord, histoire du Capitaine Hatteras." *L'Année géographique* I (1864), 270.

Wagner, Nicolas. "Le Soliloque utopiste des *500 Millions de la Bégum*." *Europe* 595–96 (1978), 117–26.

Winandy, André. "The Twilight Zone: image and reality in Jules Verne's *Strange Journeys*." *Yale French Studies* 43 (1969), 101–10.

IIE. Critical Studies—Dissertations and Theses

Butcher, William. "A Study of Time in Jules Verne's *Voyages Extraordinaires*." Ph.D. diss. Queen Mary College, London, 1983.

Choffel, Dominique. "Recherches sur les illustrations des *Voyages Extraordinaires* de Jules Verne." Mémoire de maîtrise, Université de Paris X (Nanterre), 1982.

Clough, Raymond J. "The Metal Gods: A Study of the Historic and Mythic Aspects of the Machine Image in French Prose 1750–1940." Ph.D. diss. SUNY (Buffalo), 1973.

Delabroy, Jean. "Jules Verne et l'imaginaire, ses representations principales dans la période de formation de l'oeuvre romanesque." Thèse de Doctorat d'Etat, Université de Paris III (Sorbonne), 1980.

Evans, Arthur B. "Jules Verne and the Scientific Novel." Ph.D. diss. Columbia University, 1985.

Froidenfond, Alain. "L'Etude de Maître Zacharius." Mémoire de maîtrise, Université de Paris VII (Jussieu), 1980.

Luce, Stanford L. Jr. "Jules Verne: Moralist, Writer, Scientist." Ph.D. diss. Yale University, 1953.

Martin, Andrew. "The Knowledge of Ignorance: Science, Nescience, and Omniscience in Some French Writers of the Eighteenth and Nineteenth Centuries." Ph.D. diss. University of Cambridge, 1982.

Martin, Charles-Noël. "Recherches sur la nature, l'origine, et le traîtement de la science dans l'oeuvre de Jules Verne." Thèse de Doctorat d'Etat, Université de Paris VII (Jussieu), 1980.

III. OTHER CITED WORKS

IIIA. Books

Anderson, R. D. *Education in France 1848–1870*. Oxford: Clarendon Press, 1975.

Bakhtin, M. M. *The Dialogic Imagination*, ed. and trans. Michael Holquist. Austin: University of Texas Press, 1981.

———. *Rabelais and his World*, trans. H. Iwolsky. Cambridge: MIT Press, 1968.

Balibar, Renée. *Les Français fictifs*. Paris: Hachette, 1974.

Barthes, Roland. *Leçon*. Paris: Seuil, 1978.

———. *Mythologies*. Paris: Seuil, 1957.

———. *Le Plaisir du texte*. Paris: Seuil, 1973.

———. *S/Z*, trans. Richard Miller. New York: Hill and Wang, 1974.

Benjamin, Walter. *Illuminations*, ed. Hannah Arendt, trans. H. Zohn. New York: Harcourt, Brace, Jovanovich, 1968.

Chevallier, P., et al. *L'Enseignement français de la Révolution à nos jours*. Paris: Mouton, 1968.

Culler, Jonathan. *Structuralist Poetics*. Ithaca, NY: Cornell University Press, 1975.

Durkheim, Emile. *L'Evolution pédagogique en France*. Paris: PUF, 1969.

Foucault, Michel. *The Archeology of Knowledge* and *The Discourse on Language*, trans. A. M. Sheridan Smith. New York: Pantheon Books, 1972.

————. *Les Mots et les choses*. Paris: Gallimard, 1966.

Genette, Gérard. *Figures I*. Paris: Seuil, 1966.

————. *Figures II*. Paris: Seuil, 1969.

————. *Figures III*. Paris: Seuil, 1972.

Gillispie, Charles C. *The Edge of Objectivity*. Princeton, NJ: Princeton University Press, 1960.

Harari, Josué V., ed. *Textual Strategies: Perspectives in Post-Structuralist Criticism*. Ithaca, NY: Cornell University Press, 1979.

Hetzel, Pierre-Jules et al. *Magasin d'Education et de Recréation*. Paris: Hetzel, 1864–1915.

Huxley, Aldous. *Literature and Science*. New Haven, CT: Leete's Island Books, 1963.

Jameson, Fredrick. *Marxism and Form*. Princeton, NJ: Princeton University Press, 1971.

Ketterer, David. *New Worlds for Old*. Bloomington: Indiana University Press, 1974.

Lukács, Georg. *Marxism and Human Liberation*. New York: Dell, 1973.

————. *The Theory of the Novel*, trans. Anne Bostock. Cambridge: MIT Press, 1971.

Macherey, Pierre. *Pour une théorie de la production littéraire*. Paris: Maspero, 1966.

Mumford, Lewis. *Technics and Civilization*. New York: Harcourt, Brace and World, 1934.

Naisbitt, John. *Megatrends*. New York: Warner Books, 1982.

Parrinder, Patrick, ed. *Science Fiction: A Critical Guide*. New York: Longman, 1979.

Prost, Antoine. *Histoire de l'enseignement en France 1800–1967*. Paris: Armand Colin, 1968.

Rastier, François. *Essais de sémiotique discursive*. Paris: Mame, 1973.

Rose, Mark, ed. *Science Fiction: A Collection of Critical Essays*. Englewood Cliffs, NJ: Prentice Hall, 1976.

Saint-Simon, C.-Henri de. *Oeuvres choisies*. Bruxelles: Van Meenen, 1859.

————. *Oeuvres complètes de Saint-Simon et Enfantin*. Paris: Librairie de la Société des Gens de Lettres, 1865–76.

————. *Social Organization, the Science of Man, and other Writings*, trans. Felix Markham. New York: Harper, 1964.

Slusser, Guffey, and Rose, eds. *Bridges to Science Fiction*. Edwardsville, IL: Southern Illinois University Press, 1980.

Suvin, Darko. *Metamorphoses of Science Fiction*. New Haven, CT: Yale University Press, 1979.

Todorov, Tzvetan, ed. *Théorie de la littérature*. Paris: Seuil, 1965.

Toffler, Alvin. *Future Shock*. New York: Random House, 1970. Reprint Bantam Books, 1971.

————. *The Third Wave*. New York: Morrow, 1980. Reprint Bantam Books, 1981.

Tompkins, Jane P., ed. *Reader-Response Criticism*. Baltimore: Johns Hopkins
    University Press, 1980.
Willett, John, ed. *Brecht on Theatre*. New York: Hill and Wang, 1979.

IIIB. Articles

Angenot, Marc. "The Absent Paradigm: An Introduction to the Semiotics of
    Science Fiction." *Science-Fiction Studies* VI:17 (1979), 9–19.
———. "Le Paradigm absent: éléments d'une sémiotique de la science-fiction."
    Poétique 33 (1978), 74–89.
Barthes, Roland. "L'Effet de réel." *Communications* 11 (1968), 84–89.
Benjamin, Walter. "The Work of Art in the Age of Mechanical Reproduction."
    Illuminations, ed. Hannah Arendt, trans. H. Zohn. New York: Harcourt,
    Brace, Jovanovich, 1968, 217–51.
Benstock, Shari. "At the Margins of Discourse: Footnotes in the Fictional Text."
    PMLA XCVIII:2 (March 1983), 204–23.
Blanchot, Maurice. "Le Bon usage de la science-fiction." *La Nouvelle Revue
    Française* (janv. 1959), 91–100.
Hamon, Philippe. "Un Discours contraint." *Poétique* 16 (1973), 411–45.
———. "Qu'est-ce qu'une description?" *Poétique* 12 (1972), 465–85.
Jan, Isabelle. "Children's Literature and Bourgeois Society in France Since 1860."
    Yale French Studies 43 (1969), 60–71.
Kanipe, Esther. "Hetzel and the *Bibliothèque d'Education et de Recréation*."
    Yale French Studies 43 (1969), 72–83.
Parrinder, Patrick. "Science Fiction as Truncated Epic." In *Bridges of Science
    Fiction*, eds. Slusser, Guffey, and Rose. Edwardsville, IL: Southern
    Illinois University Press, 1980, pp. 91–106.
Plank, Robert. "Quixote's Mills: The Man-machine Encounter in SF." *Science-
    Fiction Studies* I:2 (1973), 68–78.
Poulet, Georges. "Criticism and the Experience of Interiority." In *Reader-
    Response Criticism*, ed. Jane P. Tompkins. Baltimore: Johns Hopkins
    University Press, 1980, pp. 56–72.
Russ, Joanna. "Toward an Aesthetic of Science Fiction." *Science-Fiction Studies*
    I:4 (1974), 255–69.
Sainte-Beuve, C.-A. "De la littérature industrielle." *La Revue des Deux Mondes*
    (1 Sept. 1839), 675–91.
Sebeok, Thomas A. and Harriet Margolis. "Captain Nemo's Windows: Semiotics
    of Windows in Sherlock Holmes." *Poetics Today* III:1 (1982), 110–39.
Spriel, Stéphan and Boris Vian. "Un Nouveau genre littéraire: la science-fiction."
    Les Temps modernes (1951), 618–27.
Suvin, Darko. "The State of the Art in Science Fiction Theory: Determining and
    Delimiting the Genre." *Science-Fiction Studies* VI:1 (1979), 32–45.

Index

Aborigines, 43–44

Adventures of Captain Hatteras, The: Captain Hatteras, 54–56, 68; censorship by Hetzel of, 27–28; diary journal, 47, 127; *en passant* pedagogy, 113–14; exoticism, 64–65, 68; footnotes, 139–40; intertext of, 57 n.3, 116; location of pedagogy in, 152; museum motifs, 40; nature motifs, 59, 64–65; Providence in, 88; racial slurs in, 146; realia and illustrations in, 117–19; scientific methodology, 50, 52; scientists, 40, 44, 82, 156; slapstick humor, 144–45

Alienation: definition of, 9–10; religious, 155; to the "other," 159; to science and technology (nineteenth century), 9–12; to science and technology (twentieth century), 160

Amazing Adventure of the Barsac Mission, The: criticism of jargon in, 143; diary journal, 47; first-person narrator, 126; "incompetent" scientist, 83; "mad" scientist, 90–93, 157; racial slurs, 146; repression of emotions, 55

Animators, pedagogical (narrative devices): 109, 134, 141–47; defi-

[Animators] nition of, 141; exotic flora and fauna, 141; foreign customs, 141; humor, 144–47; pedagogical medium, 141–42; "scientific" tropes, 142–43; unusual foods, 141

Anthropomorphisms: of electricity, 73–74; of machines and technology, 65–69; of science, 77–78; and scientific discourse, 126

Arago, François, 20, 30

Arago, Jacques, 20

Around the Moon: characterizations, 53, 77–79; competition and contest, 57 n.5; illustrations in, 118; intertext of, 57 n.3, 116; location of pedagogy, 152; satire of scientific jargon, 76–79, 143; scientists, 44, 52, 76–79; as a serial novel, 48, 57 n.4; theoretical debates, 135

Around the World in Eighty Days: absence of science, 31 n.2; antiwomen slurs, 146; characterization, 53; competition and contest, 57 n.6; narrator, 122–23; railways, 95; repetition of pedagogy, 139; slapstick humor, 144; speed, 49

Astronomy, 78, 111

Atlantis, 59–61, 98

Authority, textual: first-person narrator, 126–27; intertexts of own
novels, 47–48; narrator's interventions, 122–24; pedagogy via footnotes, 115–16; scientists and journal-
ists, 126–27

Babinet, Jacques, 20, 21 n.2
Bacon, Francis, 11, 49, 56
Bakhtin, Mikhail, 106–7, 145
Balloon Trip, A, 18
Balzac, Honoré, 107
Barthes, Roland, 105, 117, 128,
137 n.15, 153
Begum's Fortune, The: "mad" scien-
tist, 83–85; scientific methodology,
52; technology, 49
*Bibliothèque d'Education et de
Récréation,* 24
Bibliothèque Nationale, Verne's
research in the, 18
Black Indies, The: antihero, 157; censorship by Hetzel, 27; education in
Scotland, 149–50; electricity in, 71;
enclosed spaces, 155; environment,
93; labor force as beehive, 53; narrator intervention, 123; technology,
49
Blanchot, Maurice, 160–61
Boy Captain, The: characterization, 54;
dictionaries, 142; educational theories, 150; instinct, 96–97; location
of pedagogy, 152; museum motifs,
40; neologisms, 144; Providence, 88;
"short-circuits," 157; teacher-
student relationships, 151
Brothers Kip, The, 119
Buffers, pedagogical, narrative devices:
circular motifs as, 156–57; definition
of, 104, 110, 152–53; enclosed spaces
as, 153–56; function of, 152–53
Butor, Michel, 159

Cannibalism: censorship by Hetzel,
43–44; exoticism, 141; ideological
function, 44; portrayal of, 43–44;
"sick" humor, 147

Carpathian Castle, The: electricity,
71; "irresponsible" scientist, 88–
89; narrator, 123; technology, 49
Chancellor, The: characterization, 56;
diary journal, 47; education as character determinant, 149; "incompetent" scientist, 83; narrator, 129
Children of Captain Grant, The: cannibals, 43, 147; censorship by Hetzel,
31 n.3; characterization, 53; educational benefits of travel, 150; exotic
flora and fauna, 64; footnotes, 114;
localization motifs, 38; museum
motifs, 40; narrator, 123, 128;
neologisms, 144; pedagogy, 139,
152; realia and illustrations, 117,
119; search for father, 61; as serial
novel, 48, 57 n.4; "scientific"
tropes, 142; scientist, 40, 45, 83;
students, 151; wordplay, 145
Circularity motifs, 156–57
Claudius Bombarnac: antiwomen slurs,
146; intertext of own works, 57 n.3;
railways, 95; repetition of pedagogy,
139
Clovis Dardentor, 31 n.3
"Common Man." *See* Vox populi
Competition and contests, 55–56,
57 n.4, 134–36
Comte, Auguste, 11–12
"Coralie," myth of, 21 n.2
Criticism, Vernian (English and
French): contemporary develop-
ments, 1, 3–5; doctoral studies,
5 n.7
Cryptograms, 39, 50
Culler, Jonathan, 106

Darwinism, social, 84
"Dealienation" techniques: animators,
141–47; buffers, 153–58; maps, 118;
narrative devices, 4, 34, 37–38, 56,
66–74, 103–4, 108, 159–62; narrator,
136; repetition, 138–40; valorizors,
148–52
Deductive reasoning. *See* Object-ive
rationalism

Diary journals: as "anchoring" narrative device, 38; historical document, 99–100; narrator credibility, 127–28; pedagogical medium, 141; as verisimilitude builder, 42, 47, 129

Didacticism, general: animators, 141–47; buffers, 152–58; effects on narrative structure, 53–56; first-person narration, 126–37; knowledge as power, 148; location of, 152; moral, 3–4, 29–35, 44–45, 88–90; realia and illustrations, 116–21; reduced presence of, 81; repetition, 138–40; scientific, 3–4, 14–15, 29–35, 37–38; semiotic function, 107–8; valorizors, 147–48

Direct exposition (pedagogy without fictional narrator): definition of, 110; *en bloc* type, 110–13; *en passant* type, 113–14; extratextual type, 114–17; nonlinguistic types, 217–21

Doctor Ox, 47, 144–45, 151

Drama in the Air, A, 143

"Dream machines": definition and function of, 68–69; secret construction of, 70

Dumas, Alexandre, père, 17–19, 30

Duruy, Victor, 12–13

Dystopias, 83–85, 90–93

Education, French public: Falloux Law, 13; politics of, 12–13; reforms under the Third Republic, 14; scientific instruction, 12–14; Second Empire, 4, 12–14

Educational project of the *Voyages Extraordinaires*: as defined by Hetzel and Verne, 14–15, 29–34, 37, 56–57, 124; as "enclosure" of knowledge, 156; parallels with this study, 162

Educational theory, 149–51

Effet de réel (reality effect), 63, 114, 119, 129

Egalitarianism, 74–79

Electricity: circuit motifs, 157; industrial uses, 69–71, 91; narrative function of, 70–71; in Nature, 71–74

Emulation, reader: scientists as moral role models, 44–45; student-teacher, 151–52

En bloc pedagogy: definition of, 110; examples of, 111–13, 136–37 n.2; function of, 111

Encyclopedias, 40–41

Energy (as character determinant), 56, 57 n.7, 91

En passant pedagogy: definition and function of, 113; examples of, 113

Environmental concerns, 81, 88–89, 93–96

Estrangement (*ostranenie*), 104

Eternal Adam, 97–101

Evolution: cosmic, 62–63, 111; human, 61, 98–100; social, 84–85; versus creationism, 62

Exoticism: customs, 63–64; definition, 63; destruction of by industrialization, 94–96; didactic integration, 104; flora and fauna, 64–65; footnotes, 114; illustrations, 118–19; languages, 64; locales, 63; machines, 69; narrative function, 63–64; in selection of pedagogy, 141

Family Without a Name, 31 n.4

Ferry, Jules, 81

Figuier, Louis, 12

First Ships of the Mexican Navy, 18

Five Weeks in a Balloon: cannibals, 43; disappearance of technology at end, 69; education of hero, 148–49; footnotes, 114; "heroic" scientist, 82; Hetzel and, 23, 27, 29; illustrations, 119; inspiration and sources, 19–20; Providence, 88; racial slurs, 146; religious misgivings, 88

Flammarion, Camile, 142

Flaubert, Gustave, 13, 107, 142

Floating City, A: "incompetent" scientist, 83; narrator, 129; scientific jargon, 143

Footnotes, 5, 114–16, 124, 137 n.5

For the Flag: enclosed spaces in, 155; labor force as beehive, 53; "mad" scientist, 52, 90

Foucault, Michel, 105, 121
Franco-Prussian War, 34
Freud, Sigmund, 10
Fritt-Flacc, 29, 31 n.5
From the Earth to the Moon: American
  education, 149; characterizations,
  53–54, 76–79; competition and context, 57 n.5; education of hero, 148;
  en bloc pedagogy, 111; footnotes,
  115; Hetzel and, 29; illustrations,
  119; intertext of, 57 n.3, 116; mathematicians, 83; myth-ification motifs,
  65–66; narrator interventions, 123–
  24; object-ive rationalism, 52; origins
  of universe, 61–63; repetition of
  pedagogy, 139–40; scientific and
  literary sources, 20; scientists, 45,
  54; as serial novel, 48, 57 n.4;
  "sick" humor, 146–47; theoretical
  debates, 135
"Future shock," 10, 159–62

Garcet, Henri, 20
Green Ray, The: enclosed spaces, 155;
  "incompetent" scientist, 83; satire of
  jargon, 143; "scientific" tropes, 142

Hector Servadac: antisemitic humor,
  146; competition and contest, 57 n.5;
  "eccentric" scientist, 83; education,
  151; illustrations, 119; intertext of,
  57 n.3, 116; logic, 52; narrator,
  122–23; as *robinsonnade* narrative,
  152; "short-circuits," 157; social
  stereotypes, 42
Hegel, Friedrich, 10
Helmholtz, Hermann von, 49
Heterogeneity, 37–38, 103–4
Hetzel, Pierre-Jule: 2, 4, 14, 18, 20,
  23–30; as censor, 26–29, 31 nn.2–5;
  correspondence, 24–25, 27–28, 81;
  early publishing career, 23; first
  encounter with Verne, 20; *Magasin
  d'Education et de Récréation*, 24–
  25, 34; pedagogical goals, 23–27;
  political beliefs, 23–25; predecessors,
  25–26; as promoter, 162; role in
  Voyages Extraordinaires, 23–31, 34,

[Hetzel] 58, 101; as "spiritual father"
  to Verne, 26; views on education,
  24–25; views on morality, 24, 28–30,
  33–34
Hierarchies, social: 41–49; as determined by merit, 41; as determined
  by scientific knowledge, 41
Hugo, Victor, 129
Humor: "black," 89; butts of, 145; to
  condemn poor educational practices,
  150–51; hyperbolic enumerations,
  145; pejorative, 146; satire of science
  and scientists, 76–79, 104; "scientific" tropes, 142–44; scientists'
  sense of, 44; "sick," 146–47; slapstick, 144–45; turnabouts, 135–36;
  types of, 144; wordplay, 124, 145;
  vox populi, 104
Huxley, Aldous, 105

Ice Sphinx, The: danger to whales, 93–
  94; electricity, 69; "fictional" footnotes, 115–16; first-person narrator,
  126, 129, 131; instinct, 97
Ideology: bourgeois, 43–44, 148;
  cyclical nature of Verne's, 100–101;
  general, 33–37; imperialist, 82, 85;
  materialist, 148, 155; mixture of
  Positivist and Romantic, 37–38, 58,
  79–81; Positivist, 37–58, 156; of
  power, 148; Romantic, 58–101;
  scientific discourse, 105–6; selection
  of narrators, 126–27; status quo,
  153, 156
Illustrations: frequency of, 117;
  scholarship on, 137 n.7; types and
  function of, 117–18
*In the Twenty-Ninth Century: The
  Day of an American Journalist in
  2889*, 49, 71
Indirect exposition (pedagogy via protagonists): 125–37; choice of narrators, 126–27; definition of, 125;
  diary journal, 127–28; "doubting
  Thomas" strategy, 131–32; effectiveness of, 132; enhancing credibility of first-person narrator, 126–37;
  nonfictional sources quoted, 125;

[Indirect exposition] normalcy of
   narrators, 126–29; "vaccination"
   strategy, 131–32, 137 n.15; via
   dialogue, 133–36
Industrial Revolution: description of,
   4, 9–15; impact on social structures,
   9–10, 159–60
Instinct, valorization of in Verne's
   protagonists, 96–97
Intertexts, 47–48, 57 n.3
Inventories, 110–11, 136 n.1
Island and cavern motifs, 155–56

James, Henry, 126
Jargonization, dangers of, 142–43
Journey to the Center of the Earth:
   competition and contest, 57 n.6;
   credibility of narrator, 128–29;
   diary journals, 47, 127; education,
   149; electricity, 71–74; enclosed
   spaces, 155; errors, 74, 97; footnotes, 115; location of pedagogy,
   152; prehistory and evolution, 61–
   63; Positivism, 2; realia, 121; scholarship on, 3; science portrayals, 29,
   31 n.2, 39, 52; scientists, 45, 47, 54,
   83, 135–36; servant, 128; social
   stereotypes, 42; taxonomic methodology, 50; technicisms, 140

Knowledge, scientific: abuses, 84–93,
   148; constructive uses, 34, 148,
   159; as an "enclosed" entity, 156;
   goals, 41; heroes and villains, 148;
   limitations, 100, 102 n.17; as a metaphysical model, 38–40, 148, 156;
   moral obligations, 45

Last Will of an Eccentric, The: air pollution, 94; circulation motifs, 157;
   en bloc pedagogy, 113; letters, 141;
   realia, 121; speed, 49
Lavoisier, scientific principles of, 49
Linnaean taxonomies, 49
Little-Fellow: circulation of capital,
   157; localization motifs, 38; narrator,
   122–23; poor teaching practices, 150;
   premonitions, 97; social criticism,

[*Little-Fellow*] 31 n.4; wordplay,
   145
Localization motifs: ideological significance, 38–39, 41–42; maps, 117–18;
   pedagogical strategy, 48–49, 111,
   152; scientific variants, 49–53; spiritual and esthetic variants, 59;
   "transparent" locations, 128
Locomotives and railroads, 94–95
Logic, portrayals of. *See* Object-ive
   rationalism

Macé, Jean, 12–13
Magic, treatment of science and technology as, 69–74
Maps: ideology of, 39–40; narrative
   function of, 117–18, 121; scholarship on, 137 n.7
Martin Paz, 18
Marx, Karl, 10
Magasin d'Education et de Récréation:
   creation of by Hetzel, 13–14, 23–24;
   goals, 24–25; moral stance, 28–31;
   predecessors, 25; Verne's role in, 26;
   writers contributing to, 26
Master of the World: competition and
   contest, 57 n.5; illustrations, 119;
   "mad" scientist, 85–87; as serial
   novel, 48, 57 n.4; technology, 69
Master Zacharius, 18, 100
Mathias Sandorf: characterizations,
   53, 55–56; education of hero, 149;
   electricity, 69, 71; energy, 56; *en
   passant* pedagogy, 114; illustrations
   and realia, 118–19; poor educational
   systems, 150; science portrayal, 56
Maupassant, Guy de, 126
Michel Strogoff: censorship by Hetzel,
   28; intertext of own works, 57 n.3
Mistress Branican: cannibalism, 43;
   diary journal, 47; women's intuition,
   97
Molière (Jean-Baptiste Poquelin), 142
Mumford, Lewis, 9, 159
Musée des Familles, 18–19
Museums, 40–41
Mysterious Island: class structures, 42;
   diary journal, 127; disappearance of

[*Mysterious Island*] technology, 69; education of hero, 148; egalitarianism, 74; enclosed spaces, 155–56; localization motifs, 38; logic of problem solving, 51–52; precognition, 128; Providence, 88; racial slurs, 146; realia, 117; repetition of pedagogy, 138–39; repression of emotions, 55; as *robinsonnade* narrative, 42; role of Hetzel, 27–28; science portrayals, 31 n.2, 52; scientists, 40–41, 45, 54–56, 74, 82, 148; as serial novel, 48, 57 n.4; taxonomic methodology, 50; teacher-student relationships, 151; technicisms, 140
Myths: Atlantis, 59–61; heroic, 15; island/cavern, 155–56; of machines, 33, 68–71; narrative function of, 61; Pygmalion, 68; of Progress, 65–66; Prometheus, 65

Nadar (Félix Tournachon), 20
Naisbitt, John, 160
Narrative exposition: definition and types, 109–10; direct, 110–21; indirect, 125–36; semidirect, 121–24
Narrators: for approbation and condemnation, 148–51; intervention into text, 123–24; lack of fixity, 122; meta-narrator in semidirect pedagogy, 121–24; to praise scientists, 52; presence of in narrative structure, 109–37; relation to reader, 122; scientists-engineers and reporters-journalists as preferred, 126; strategies for enhancing credibility of first-person, 125–26, 131–32
Nature: class structures as an extension of, 43; conquest of via technology, 48–49, 66; as explainable via science, 39–41, 50–52; the individual and, 11, 55–56, 58–59, 66, 84; narrative function of, 58–59, 66; Positivism and, 11, 39; Romanticism and, 11
Neologisms, 144
Newtonian physics, 49
Nietzsche, Friedrich, 84, 98, 101 n.15

Nonlinguistic narrative devices: definition of, 116–17; function of, 117–21; illustrations, 116, 118–19; maps, 117–18; realia, 121

Object-ive rationalism: 49–57; in characterizations, 53–56; energy, 56; errors in, 52; narrative recipes using, 50; negative aspects of, 84–90, 96–97; object-ification strategies, 52–53; optimistic vs. pessimistic texts, 52; as pathway to knowledge, 49; in praise of logic, 52; for problem solving, 51–52; social and human phenomena, 53–56; usefulness of, 136
Onze-Sans-Femme, 16, 19
Optimism, Verne's: effects of technology, 48–49; loss of, 58
Origins, search for one's, 61–63

Paleontology, 61–63
Pessimism, Verne's: 79–101; causes of, 79–82; increased presence of in works, 58
Phrenology, 53–54
Pitre-Chevalier. See *Musée des Familles*
Ponton d'Amécourt, 20, 21 n.2
Positivism, Positivists: 10–15, 37–57; decline in popularity of, 81; French, 11–12; hierarchies, 41–49; as ideology, 4, 12, 37; as proselytizers of science, 10–14; as reaction to Industrial Revolution, 11; taxonomies, 38–41; versus anti-Positivism, 2; views toward Catholic Church, 12. *See also* Object-ive rationalism
Problem solving. *See* Object-ive rationalism
Progress: definitions of, 39–40, 52; futility of, 100; ideology of, 10; impact on the environment, 93–96; social implications, 43; technological, 48; in travel, 155
Propeller Island: competition and contest, 57 n.5; destruction of pristine cultures, 45–46; disappearance of technology, 69; electricity, 69, 71;

[*Propeller Island*] humorous neologisms, 144; narrator intervention, 123; reference books, 141–42; "short-circuits," 157; Standard Island as an "ambulatory home," 153; technology, 49; word play, 145

Providence, intervention of, 85, 87–90

Rabelais, François, 145

Races, in Verne's novels, 42, 57 n.5, 84–85, 146

Raton Family, The, 145

Reason, use of. *See* Object-ive rationalism

Reading public, Verne's, 2–3, 5 n.4, 24, 30

Realia. *See* Nonlinguistic narrative devices

Reclus, Elisée, 142

Reflection, textual (self-referentiality): of author's own life, 78–79, 129–31; didacticism used as, 152; footnotes as, 116; intertexts of own novels, 57 n.3; localization motifs as example of, 39; scientists' publications as, 47–48; self-conscious humor, 142–43

Reiterators, pedagogical (narrative devices), 109, 138–40

Religion: heroes' concerns about, 87–88, 102 n.17; moral lesson portrayed, 90; Positivism as, 11. *See also* Providence

Renan, Ernest, 11

Repetition of: pedagogy, 138–40; protagonists, 42, 47–48, 57 n.4, 88. *See also* Reiterators

Reputation, Verne's literary: Academe's role in, 4, 5 n.7; basis of, 14–15; in Europe vs. USA, 1–3, 5

Robinsonnade narratives: class structure of, 42; egalitarianism in, 74; as microcosms of civilization, 42, 74; pedagogy in, 151–52

Robur the Conqueror: Albatros as "ambulatory home," 153; anti-Positivism, 2; characterization, 54, 85; competition and contest,

[*Robur the Conqueror*] 57 nn. 5–6; disappearance of technology, 69; electricity, 69–70; illustrations, 119; racial slurs, 146; repetition of pedagogy, 139; scientific methodology, 52; as serial novel, 48; sources, 20, 21 n.2; technology, 49

Roman de la Science, 4, 19–20, 23, 29. *See also* Scientific novel

Romanticism: characteristics of, 10–11; heroes, 74–79; negative aspects of, 82; for personalized scientific discourse, 126; as reaction to Industrial Revolution, 10–11; as social ideology, 4; in the *Voyages Extraordinaires,* 58–102

Rousseau, Jean-Jacques, 150

Saint-Simon, Henri de, 11, 47, 94, 98

School for Crusoes, The: censorship by Hetzel of, 28; use as intertext, 116

Science: alienation to, 9–10; dangers of, 82–93; and esthetic appreciation, 63, 68; and exoticism, 63–65; and history, 61; instruction of, in French public schools, 11–13; and knowledge, 39, 49–50; and literary discourse, 104–9, 126, 142–44; as metaphysical model, 39; Romantic treatment of, 65–79; satire of, 143–44

Science fiction: as antidote to "future shock," 161–62; and didacticism, 160–61; as epic literature, 160, 163 n.3; *novum* definition, 161; popularity, 160–61; semiotic characteristics, 104–8; social function and "adaptivity effect," 160–62; versus scientific fiction, 2, 4, 104, 159–63

Scientific methodology: in characterization, 53–56; classifying, 37–41, 49–50; in describing human relations, 55; experimental logic, 49–50; presuppositions of, 52–53; valorization of, 52

Scientific novel: birth of, 14, 16–21, 29–30, 159; as cultural shock absorber, 159; as historical artifact, 158;

[Scientific novel] as literary genre, 4, 30, 35, 126; narrative structures, 53–56; as pedagogical tool, 14, 30; social function, 159

Scientists: as admirers of technology, 69; as authors and educators, 45–48, 109; as contemplative poets, 59–60; "eccentric" type, 83; egalitarianism of, 74; as encyclopedias, 40, 141; energy of, 56; "incompetent" type, 83; intervention of, to destroy own creations, 92–93; "mad" type, 52, 83–93; as moral models, 44–45, 54–56; as "natural" leaders, 43–44, 54, 82–83; relationship to apprentices and coworkers, 54; repetition of, 42; repression of emotions in, 54–55; responsibility to public of, 92–93; social status of, 42; as "straight man," 145; world fame of, 47

Second Empire, education during, 4, 12–13, 34–35

Second Homeland, A, 119

Secret of Wilhelm Storitz, The: first-person narrator, 131; "mad" scientist, 90; premonitions, 97

Semidirect exposition (pedagogy via narrator), 121–24

Serial novels in the *Voyages Extraordinaires*, 48, 57 n.4

Serres, Michel, 157

Simon, Jules, 12

Southern Star, The: education of hero, 148; morality of scientist, 45; scientific methodology, 52

Speed, portrayal of, in Verne's novels, 48–49, 112

Stahl, P.-J. *See* Hetzel, Pierre-Jules

Steam House, The: "ambulatory homes," 155; comic reversals, 145–46; electricity, 71; *en bloc* pedagogy, 111; *en passant* pedagogy, 113; human-ification of machines, 66–68; illustrations, 118–19; optimism, 48; repetition of pedagogy, 139; satire of scientific jargon, 143–44; scientist, 55; social stereotypes, 42; wordplay, 145

Stereotypes: in characterizations, 42, 153; of the exotic, 63–64; races, 146; social and class, 42; women, 146

Students as protagonists, 50, 54, 151–52

Survivors of the Jonathan, The, 31 n.4

Taine, Hippolyte, 11

Taxonomies, 38–41, 50, 54, 114. *See also* Localization motifs

Technicisms, 65, 142–44

Technology, scientific: abuse of, 81; and contemporary society, 163 n.2; dangers, 82–93; esthetic criticism, 94–95; of Industrial Revolution, 9–10; narrative function, 68–69; and progress, 48–49; Romantic portrayal, 65–74; as secret, 70; social implications, 92–96, 159–60

Theatre, adaptations of *Voyages Extraordinaires* for, 2

Théâtre Lyrique, 17, 19

Third Republic: education during, 14, 34–35

Thompson Travel Agency, The: criticism of progress, 96; localization motifs, 38; premonitions, 97; "scientific" tropes, 143; speed, 49

Toffler, Alvin, 160–62

Topsy Turvy: antiwomen slurs, 146; dangers to environment, 88–90, 93; "irresponsible" scientists, 88–90; scientific error, 52, 89, 97; "scientific" tropes, 143; as a serial novel, 48, 57 n.4; titles from *Voyages Extraordinaires* cited in, 57 n.3, 116; wordplay, 145

Tournachon, Félix. *See* Nadar

Tribulations of a Chinaman, The: absence of science in, 31 n.2; *en passant* pedagogy, 113; narrator intervention, 123; technology, 49

Tropes, use of: dangers of, 142–43; function of, 142–43; humor with, 143–44; puns and wordplay, 146; "scientific" comparisons and metaphors, 142–44

Twenty Thousand Leagues under the Sea: artificial languages, 64; cannibals, 43; Captain Nemo, 54, 68, 70–71, 75–76; censorship by Hetzel, 28–29, 31 n.2, 31 n.5; comic reversals, 146; competition and contest, 57 n.6; contemplation of Nature, 59–60; diary journal, 127–28; disappearance of technology, 69; electricity, 71; illustrations, 119–20; location of pedagogy, 152; museum motifs, 40–41; narrator, 126, 128–35, 151; *Nautilus* as "ambulatory home," 153; *Nautilus* as surrogate wife/mother, 155; nonfictional sources quoted, 125; oceanography, 61; repetition of pedagogy, 139; secret of *Nautilus'* construction, 70–71; as a serial novel, 57 n.4; slapstick humor, 144; social stereotypes, 42; taxonomic methodology, 50; technology, 49, 69; wordplay, 146

Two Year Vacation, The: characterization, 54, egalitarianism, 74; English educational practices, 149–50; narrator, 123; realia, 117; repetition of pedagogy, 139–40; as a *robinsonnade* narrative, 151–52; teacher-student relationships, 151–52

Uncle Robinson. See *Mysterious Island*
Utopias, 69, 74, 83–84

Valorizors, as pedagogical narrative devices: definition, 109–10, 147; didactic structure of *Voyages Extraordinaires* as, 148; function, 147–49; location of pedagogy in narratives, 152; narrator approbation and condemnation, 148–49; reader emulation techniques, 151–52

Verisimilitude in the *Voyages Extraordinaires*: diary journal, 42, 47; electricity, 70–71; *en bloc* pedagogy, 110–11; footnotes, 115–16; illustrations, 118–21; intertexts of own novels, 48; location of pedagogy, 152; strategies for increasing narrator's, 126–37; technological, 66, 69

Verne, Jules: as aspiring playwright in Paris, 16–20; biographies on, 21 n.2; correspondence with family, 16–17; early writing career, 16–21; educational project, 14, 162; erudition, 19–20; law study, 17; literary reputation, 1–2, 4, 5 n.7, 162; marriage, 19; myths concerning, 1–2, 16, 21 n.2; as practical joker and lover of puns, 78; relationship with Hetzel, 26–31; scholarship on, 3, 5, 5 n.6, 31 n.5, 162; scientific and literary sources, 19–20; and SF, 1–2, 104, 159–63; as stock broker, 19–21; views on education, 16, 149–51; views on literature, 17; work habits, 17–20; youth, 16

Verne, Michel (son), 81, 98
Verne, Pierre (father), 17
Village in the Treetops: artificial languages, 64; comic reversals, 146; danger to elephants, 94; portrayal of natural instincts, 97
Villiers de l'Isle-Adam, 107
Vox populi: didactic function of, 50, 76–77, 109; narrator as, 151; for personalizing scientific discourse, 126, 133; for praising technology, 69; for valorizing scientists, 52; as vehicles for satire, 77–79, 104, 143
Voyages Extraordinaires: censorship of, 23–30, 31 nn.2–5; educational goals of, 13–14, 29–30; Hetzel's preface to, 29–30; literary reputation of, 1–2, 4, 5 n.7, 29–30; serial novels in, 47–48, 57 n.4
Voyages in Known and Unknown Worlds (subtitle of *Voyages Extraordinaires*), 30, 162
Voyage Through the Air. See *Five Weeks in a Balloon*

Wells, H. G., 2
Windows, importance of, in Verne's novels, 128, 155
Wintering in the Ice, 18
Women, portrayal of, 42, 146

Zola, Emile, 68, 107

About the Author

ARTHUR B. EVANS is Assistant Professor of Romance Languages at DePauw University. His previous books include *Jean Cocteau and His Films of Orphic Identity*.

**Recent Titles in
Contributions to the Study of World Literature
Series Adviser: Leif Sjoberg**

Guido Gezelle: Flemish Poet-Priest
Hermine J. van Nuis

Voices of the Storyteller: Cuba's Lino Novás Calvo
Lorraine Elena Roses

Lessing and the Enlightenment
Alexej Ugrinsky, editor

Dostoevski and the Human Condition After a Century
Alexej Ugrinsky, Frank S. Lambasa, and Valija K. Ozolins, editors

Russian Romantic Criticism: An Anthology
Lauren Gray Leighton, editor and translator

The Literary Heritage of Childhood: An Appraisal of Children's Classics
in the Western Tradition
Charles Frey and John Griffith

Goethe in the Twentieth Century
Alexej Ugrinsky, editor

The Stendhal Bicentennial Papers
Avriel Goldberger, editor

The Writer Written: The Artist and Creation in the New Literatures
Jean-Pierre Durix

Becoming True to Ourselves: Cultural Decolonization and National Identity
in the Literature of the Portuguese-Speaking World
Maria Luisa Nunes

George Orwell
Courtney T. Wemyss and Alexej Ugrinsky, editors

The Cast of Consciousness: Concepts of the Mind in British and
American Romanticism
Beverly Taylor and Robert Bain, editors